SLACK
The Fun of Climbing
(Volume 2)

Dennis Gray

Pete Scott and Chris Radcliffe had been pioneering hard routes and achieving great feats - the latter two were the first Britons to complete the classic six north faces of the Alps. Mike Mortimer, President of the University Club at that time, was rock climbing to the highest standards of the day and has gone on to be a good servant of the climbing world by writing guidebooks and is a recent President of the Climbers' Club. It is surprising where the sport's current establishment originate from .

As I said, I was too busy studying, writing and climbing to get involved, but in autumn 1968 – although not a member of the club – I became aware of a stirring in the ranks and a new intake of climbers comprising some outstanding personalities such as Bernard Newman, John Porter, Roger Baxter-Jones and John Syrett. They arrived together, and this gave a signal which drew in many other keen activists to the city and its soon to be famous climbing wall. Over the next few years the names of those who studied at Leeds, either as under- or post-graduates, reads like an entry from the pages of a climber's 'Who's Who': Brian Hall, Alex MacIntyre, Ken Wood, Mike Hammill, Chris Hamper, Graham Desroy, Martin Berzins, Jill Lawrence, Pete Livesey, Pete Gomersall, Tony Mitchell, Andy Perkins and Rob Gawthorpe are just some who were involved, to say nothing of those attracted from outside the university such as Allan Austin, Al Manson and Steve Bancroft.

I am getting ahead of myself, however, as in 1968 this was not a development one might readily have forecast, other than to recognise that the decade of the sixties had brought about a social revolution. Rock and roll was here to stay, and youth culture was in the ascendancy. No longer were working class groups like the Rock and Ice reshaping the sport, instead it was the student climber from areas such as Sheffield, Manchester, Bristol and Edinburgh. The advent of improved rock climbing equipment, with the acceptance and development of nut protection, kernmantel ropes and the many innovations in specialist rock boots, was an encouragement to these student leaders to break existing barriers. In the seventies the development of new ice climbing techniques and equipment were to have a similar effect on greater mountaineering.

My first real inkling that something special was stirring occurred in 1969, when the activities of the University Climbing Club became the topic of conversation around the campus. They were branded a bunch of lunatics when for the second year running during rag week a group of their members (including John Syrett, Brian Hall and Gordon Stainforth's twin brother, John) were apprehended after climbing up the front of the Civic Hall and unfurling a banner of protest about the apartheid regime in South Africa. This impressed me. It was no mean feat as the city's main centre of administration is guarded like Fort Knox and is as difficult to ascend as a major crag. They made headlines in the press and on TV. The impression of a strong group coalescing was reinforced at the climbing wall where I met Bernard Newman and John Syrett, and at the Pack Horse pub, the club's historic meeting place in Woodhouse Lane, where I met John Porter and Roger Baxter-Jones.

A second event occurring shortly after that further enhanced the club's status as a group of mad-cap adventurers in the eyes of the rest of the student body. After pub closing hours members had started climbing and traversing on the newly erected university buildings such as the Roger Stevens complex, prompting several incidents of daredevilry. One night Bernard Newman and Valerie Humphries were up on the roofs, traversing a new lecture block with a glass ceiling. Inadvertently Valerie trod on a panel which shattered and she fell through, cutting and badly injuring herself. This was no laughing matter, but fortunately the university authorities judged her fall to be punishment enough. Happily Valerie recovered and was eventually able to rejoin the ranks of the mountaineering club. Climbing on the faculty buildings then lost its popularity until a new generation of students revived the activity in the next decade.

John Syrett and R B-J

It was at Leeds in 1969 that the modern climbing-wall movement began in this country; and the person responsible for this development - more than anyone else I know - was John Syrett. Although the Leeds Wall had existed since 1964, prior to his involvement nobody had thought of using it as an aid to develop their fitness and technique for outdoor climbing.

My first visit to the wall had been to witness Pete Scott and Chris Radcliffe in full Alpine attire of boots, breeches and helmets, roped-up and wearing rucksacks, traversing along the wall a few feet off the ground. I remember thinking 'What a couple of berks!'. They were soon to have the last laugh with successful ascents of routes like the Eigerwand, the Walker Spur of the Grandes Jorasses and the North Face of the Matterhorn. However, the prevailing attitude until Syrett

Ken Wood and Al Manson watch John Syrett make the first ascent of 'Big Greeny', Almscliff.
Photo: John Harwood

changed our perception was, as Bernard Newman observes, 'We used to go to play around on the wall climbing in desert boots or even Hush Puppies. To use EB's was considered cheating'.

John Syrett was one of the most gifted rock climbers of his or any other generation. When young he appeared to be so blessed with ability that a glittering future awaited him in whatever field he chose, which makes his subsequent demise all the more tragic. He arrived at Leeds almost as a beginner in climbing terms. However, during 1969 he trained assiduously on the wall to emerge as an outstanding performer out on the crags. Over the next few years his name was writ large across many hard new routes on the gritstone outcrops and limestone cliffs of Yorkshire.

I first met John at the climbing wall and he immediately changed my perception of what could be achieved from practice on this facility. To see him do his traverse up in the roof above the doorway, from which a fall would surely mean serious injury, was pretty awe-inspiring. I liked him from the start, noting his great joy in climbing and life in general, and arranged to go out to Ilkley with him a short while later.

I had recently married, and when John arrived at my father's house in Cookridge, Leeds where my wife, Leni, and I were staying she immediately remarked on John's good looks. This was the reaction of most women meeting him for the first time: with his curly black hair, athletic build and classical features he was, I suppose, the answer to any woman's prayer. I was more struck by his attire which was flared jeans, desert boots, and an impeccably ironed open-necked white shirt, whilst in either hand he carried a rock boot. That is all; no coat, no jersey as he had run uphill the five kilometres from his lodgings. This was all the more memorable as it was February and snow lay around in abundance.

Nevertheless we drove to Ilkley to the Cow and Calf Rocks - that gritstone outcrop of myth and legend where, despite the cold and snowy conditions, John spent many hours trying to climb the overhanging face of the Calf. A problem which I could not even contemplate solving. He progressed to a point that I never saw anyone else reach in many years of climbing there, until fifteen years later when another Leeds star - Rob Gawthorpe - finally completed the route. It remains one of the hardest problems in the area.

Witnessing this illustration of John's ability to bend and to stretch, coupled with his sheer athleticism and a willingness to go for it - jumping back down again and again quite fearlessly from considerable heights - he reminded me of a youthful Peter Greenwood. What remains in my memory most was the competitive urge which kept him trying when most others would have called it a day. This was allied with an extraordinary ability to withstand the cold, which is extreme on Ilkley's famous moor in winter. After a short exposure to the elements, my wife and I were cowering over a brew in the back of our Dormobile, awaiting the prodigal's return.

Spring was late in 1969, but one sunny day several weeks later I was at Almscliff Crag, which has many historical associations with Leeds University climbers. After several attempts I'd managed to solo Pulpit Corner, a problem first climbed by Frankland in 1927. It lies on a pinnacle that abuts the outcrop's North-West Face. This is the site of many of the crag's most famous routes such as Great Western, The Wall of Horrors and the Big Greeny. Sitting relaxed on top of the Pulpit feeling pleased with my efforts, I was a little miffed when Roger Baxter-Jones arrived and proceeded to join me wearing boots and an alpine helmet, easily ascending the route up which I had just struggled. I had met him before in the pub, but never out climbing. As he was from south of Sheffield, and spoke with a plummy southern accent, I was still somewhat wary of him. In fact, even at that early date, he was being tipped by other Leeds climbers as a successor to either Chris Bonington or David Dimbleby in the role of communicator. He bore more than a passing resemblance to the latter!

Roger Baxter-Jones leading (John Syrett belayed), The Great Wall on Clogwyn Du'r Arddu 1970.   Photo Angela Soper

But it was hard not to warm to R B-J (the Leeds climbers had a saying 'It's all the way with R B-J ') with his powerful frame, infectious enthusiasm and huge grin. It would have been churlish not to fall in with his immediate plan to climb up the second pitch of Pulpit Route. A climb which at that time was shrouded in mystery and I had never seen climbed despite my own attendance at Almscliff over the years. In fact I was unsure of the exact line, but tying myself directly on to the end of Roger's rope, I belayed to the chockstone which is jammed in the crack between the Pulpit and the main face. This was before modern harnesses and belay devices, and I simply held the rope around my waist, playing it out to R B-J as he moved upwards - something I did with great care and trepidation, for two years previously I had burnt my hands severely in holding a fall, and it had left me with badly scarred fingers.

Roger pulled himself off the pinnacle and was away up the steep wall behind, moving first left then back delicately right, climbing neatly and so quickly I could hardly keep pace in letting the rope out. It was soon obvious that, like John Syrett, here was another outstanding performer. However fate decreed otherwise. After suffering a severe accident on the Piz Badile, a few months after our Almscliff climb, it would be several more years before R B-J really achieved what we all felt was his true potential. In his maturity other notable climbers as diverse as Doug Scott, Al Rouse and Paul Braithwaite were to testify that he was one of

Dave Cook, climber and political activist.   Photo Ken Wilson

'Good evening comrade', 'Good evening comrade', came the reply. Communists, it seemed, did not have names, but I noted with satisfaction that all the men sported flat caps, fitting my notion of a socialist.

Shortly after Dave and I went to Ilkley in my van. Dave was tall and powerfully built with a ready smile and a mop of black hair sporting a Teddy boy quiff. Throughout the drive he enthused about gritstone climbing, its history and the characters it bred; the fact that I knew Brown and Whillans distinctly impressed him. He had his mind set on climbing Botterill's Crack, climbed in the early 1900's by Botterill. I cannot accept the latest guide's verdict, casting doubts about the veracity of this ascent. When I started climbing at Ilkley in 1947 there were still several prewar activists about. They knew old climbers who had known climbers from that period and who had never doubted that Fred had climbed this route. But it is a bloody hard and awkward climb.

At the Cow and Calf rocks we walked up into the Hanginstone's Quarry. Botterill's lies on the right wall as you enter. It starts with an awkward layback, then expands into an off-width which is climbed by body jamming and arm bars. Dave decided to give it a try and after changing into his EB's, wearing the then de rigueur jeans and a woolly pullover, he tied direct onto my hawser-laid, overweight nylon rope and set off. He made short work of the layback, then managed to make a kind of mantelshelf onto the ledge inside the crack at approximately half height. He then proceeded to wedge himself into the crack, but instead of facing towards the quarry entrance - as is usual on Botterill's - he had somehow managed to get himself jammed in the other way around.

'Dave, I've never seen anyone climb it facing that way, can you turn round?'
'Bugger off! It's too tight.'

From where 'Cooky' was jammed the left wall of the crack curves away, whilst the right is vertical. You make progress up the fissure by pushing your feet against the vertical wall whilst squirming your back up the curving crack aided by pulling up on arm bars. Somehow Dave managed to get moving upwards by a kind of breast-stroke action. I noted with alarm that he was sinking deeper and deeper inside the fissure. Soon he was so far inside that I could only see an arm and leg.

'Are you OK?' I shouted up. 'No... I'm bloody stuck! ' came a gurgled reply.

Fortunately some other climbers were just arriving and I asked them to go up and rescue 'Cooky'. They rigged a top rope and let it down but he couldn't reach out to grab it, stuck as he was so deep in the gloom. I set off up the layback and, hanging on grimly by one hand, my feet splayed against the edge of the crack, I grabbed the rope and began flicking it up and into where Dave was stuck. To my relief he managed to grab it, but he couldn't tie it round him. 'Take it tight ... tighter...tighter', and then he pulled himself hand over hand out of his tomb with complete faith in his belayers until he could reach the easy finish of the climb.

Undeterred by this contretemps, on our drive back Dave enthused about Fred Botterrill and what a climber he must have been, and how young climbers of our day had no conception of what conditions must have been like for those early climbers, with their nailed boots and hemp ropes.

Subsequently I have read some old documents preserved in the library at Leeds University, about the Botterill brothers. When they started climbing they used to cycle to Ilkley from Leeds 6, out from the city along what is now the Kirkstall Road. This way avoids the lower reaches of Wharfedale and they did not know for quite some time that other nearby outcrops such as Almscliff existed. They made themselves an ice- axe/alpenstock, which they used to garden with and jam in cracks. Fred was carrying this when he climbed his famous slab on Scafell, and I can imagine him using it to clean out his climb at Ilkley. In view of the standard of his other first ascents I have no doubt he climbed it: like Warren Harding, who made the first ascent of the Nose of El Capitan, I prefer to believe all the legends, and so it seemed did Dave Cook.

Dave left Leeds in the 1970s to work in London as a full-time official of the Communist Party organising squats and demonstrations on such issues as 'the right to work', 'the right to decent housing', and green causes like the creation of dedicated cycle lanes in our cities. Later he organised a mass trespass of climbers at Range West in Pembroke which undoubtedly forced the Ministry of Defence, who were barring access, to open the area to climbing, albeit on a limited basis.

Following the break up of the British Communist Party, Dave taught in Wandsworth, in special education with difficult kids. At 50, feeling the onset of midlife crisis, he took off and cycled his way to Australia from London, climbing at every opportunity en route, from which experience he culled a classic adventure tale 'Breaking Loose'. I kept in touch with him, and often met him at the Mile End climbing wall whenever I was in London and enjoyed some memorable evenings in the nearby Palm Tree pub. Dave was a bitter beer connoisseur and it was heartening that he rated Yorkshire brews the best. He never lost his regard for the county's grit climbing either and wrote some classic articles about 'God's own rock'. The one I liked the best was the 'Sombre face of Yorkshire climbing' which appeared in Mountain. This emphasised the stereotype of 'it's grim up north', of hard climbs and even harder climbers. Of course we locals loved it.

Dave's death in 1993 on another cycling/climbing trip, when he was knocked off his bike by a lorry in Turkey, was a great shock. Like Eric Beard before him, another of my friends who died in a road accident, he spent his life trying to make things a little better for others. Dave was no saint and his personal life was often in a turmoil. You cannot easily raise a family and preserve high ideals unless you have money, which Dave never had. But he was one of those people you would go out of your way to meet and he was always interested in what you had been doing and your plans for future trips. He never pushed his politics down anyone's throat and remained to the end an optimistic and witty person. In addition to his boundless enthusiasm for climbing, which he communicated so well both in person and in print, and to his effective role as an access activist, he wrote with great clarity about the ethics of our sport. Thus his untimely death was a great tragedy for British climbing.

The Golden Age of the Wall

The 1970s were the golden era of the Leeds climbing scene, as it was with its soccer team. The university club attracted more talent into its ranks, such as Chris Hamper, Terry Sullivan and Tim Jepson, and its leaders were to make their mark in both greater mountaineering and rock climbing over the next few years. Influential new routes were climbed on the local grit outcrops and on Yorkshire limestone as well as in other areas of the UK and in the Alps.

Perhaps the most outstanding climb in the Alps was the first ascent by Alex MacIntyre and Nick Colton in June 1976 of their route on the North Face of the Grandes Jorasses which they called Rollerwand, but which now is simply referred to as the Colton/MacIntyre route.

Alex arrived at Leeds from his home city of Hull in the academic year '70 -'71 to read law, and initially he was hopeless. I remember being with him at the climbing wall and he had real difficulty in climbing the easiest of problems. He looked like Shirley Temple, with a mass of curly hair and an angelic face which as he aged began to harden a little until he became a doppelganger for Marc Bolan of T Rex. He used to shuffle around the campus in winter dressed in a large overcoat which he never seemed to take off. Sometime in his early days at Leeds he took on a bet that he would not change his clothes for the rest of the term. This led to him earning the nickname of 'Dirty Alex' which stayed with him for the rest of his life. But he had an inner fire which soon began to show by his hitching to Scotland for winter weekends, often on his own. It was on these forays that he began to develop his later phenomenal ice-climbing skills. Due to the initiative of climbers like Hamish MacInnes, Yvon Chouinard and Johnny Cunningham curved pick-ice tools were coming in at this time and, together with front crampon pointing, replaced the laborious step-cutting techniques which had been developed into an art form by the great Scottish climbers of the preceding generation - the likes of Robin Smith, Jimmy Marshall and Tom Patey. The old ways were suddenly found to be unnecessary and with contemporaries such as Mick Geddes, Al Rouse, Gordon Smith and Terry King, Alex quickly embraced these incredibly efficient new methods. These were soon to revolutionise the whole future of mountaineering.

The Leeds Wall was the focus of the climbing scene of those days, and by the end of the 1970s it had become a national institution. Conceived in 1964 by PE lecturer Don Robinson in a corridor of his departmental building, it was 21 metres in length, 5 metres high with three right-angled corners and a doorway on which you could do everything from bridging to hanging by your feet from a large hole on its lip. With the most excruciating brick edges in the country, and where the moves are sensuous, explosive, satisfying, some delicate and always finger knackering, it was unique. It is hard to imagine now with the proliferation of dedicated indoor climbing centres, but then climbers such as Steve Bancroft from other areas of the country were drawn to live in Leeds because of this facility. There was no other such climbing wall then in existence, that is one that had been built with training for high-standard rock climbing in mind.

It was not until the end of the 1960s that this aim began to be appreciated and it was really John Syrett's example that led the way. Not only did he use the wall to improve his strength and fitness, but he did not see any ethical problem in thinking of all his climbing activities within the same field. Thus going to the climbing wall was going climbing!

Al Manson the 'Guru' in action at the Leeds University Wall during its heyday.
Photo Dennis Gray

By this date a team used to meet at the wall every Wednesday night, with Allan Austin, Ken Wood and Al Manson in the van. Austin was the first intense climber of my acquaintance and was a phenomenon in the mid fifties when he first started climbing. He talked incessantly about climbing and did not seem interested in the finer things of life such as rock and roll, motor bikes or sex. I dubbed him 'Tubby' because he appeared to be carrying an enormous gut. In those days our wall strip was jeans (with the crotch exceedingly tight), a sweater and EB's. One night the 'Tubby' myth was exploded when something had gone wrong with the heating and it was like the Sahara. We had to strip off to be able to do even the easy problems and to our surprise we found that Austin was wearing layer upon layer of sweaters. By the time he had peeled off his sixth jumper, explaining that 'he felt the cold more than the rest of us', we observed he was just as skinny as we were, the only difference being he had enormous biceps.

Manson was the star though, and oh how he used to love to destroy visiting opposition. I recall Chris Hamper arriving as a fresh-faced youth and turning up at one of these hothouse sessions. Quizzing Al Manson the guru he demanded; 'How long does it take to get fit on the wall?' Al considered this for some time then answered tongue in cheek, 'I don't know, I've never been unfit!'

My fondest memory of those days is an outrageous one. In 1972 the BMC held the last of its (dangerous) 'Safety Conferences' at Leeds University and Chris Brasher, the Olympic athlete, sometime mountaineer and an outstanding journalist was sent by the Observer to cover the event. In briefings I explained to him about the extraordinary developments now emanating from the wall. I instanced the John Syrett story and he asked for evidence of this miracle. In those days the Physical Education block was open six days a week and although it was a Saturday I was able to take him down to see the wall.

Bernard Newman was there and though he later became a famous photojournalist, editor and an outstanding boulderer, he was in those days a ten-foot wall tiger. I introduced him something like the following, 'This is Bernard Newman. He can tell you how much climbing has now changed from your day. He shares a room with John Syrett and they sleep together!'

To Bernard's eternal credit he neither blinked nor changed expression but merely picked up the story and made it run. 'Yes', he replied deadpan in his nasal Brummie accent, 'but he's bloody inconsiderate!'

'Why?' stammered Chris, unable to believe his ears.

'Well he's a junkie and though he'll share his dope with anybody, he keeps his heroin to himself!'

'Bloody Hell', gasped Brasher ever more wide-eyed. Bernard, warming to his task, carried on.

'When he is on the stuff he becomes incontinent and urinates over me some nights. I can tell you it's putting a real strain on our relationship! I just cannot get out to climb these days, I spend most of my bloody time washing our soiled bed sheets.'

'If that's what modern rock climbing is about, you can keep it!' Brasher snapped as we walked back up to the conference in the Riley Smith Hall. Later that same afternoon Bernard and I met up at the Donald Duff Safety Exhibition which was an adjunct to the conference and enjoyed a laugh at how we had carried off such a joke.

The reader may feel it was in bad taste but it typified our irreverence in those days. We both admired John Syrett enormously, but were not above poking fun at him, at ourselves or anyone else for that matter. The climbing media of today are rarely scurrilous and on occasion it makes me cringe how sycophantic they can be. Tom Patey must be turning in his grave.

As the the '70s got underway jeans gave way to shorts, chalk came in and Genesis were overtaken by the Clash as scene music. Peter Livesey burst into our lives, although he was never a Leeds Wall ace. He favoured the recently-built Rothwell wall and at the time he was helping to change the face of British rock climbing, I used to go there with him and Jill Lawrence to 'train'.

Occasionally we would switch venues and go to the Leeds Wall. Terrifying games of 'Rollerwall' were then organised with two teams trying to traverse the wall starting from opposite ends. When you met you had to try to pull, push or kick your opposite number off the wall. The first to complete the traverse was the winner.

We used to admire Livesey's footwork on the wall, for even in knackered boots he was able to stand on the smallest of the brick edges. One night I found out what his secret was, for being a former canoeist he was familiar with fibreglass! From this material he made a pair of thick insoles. These were secretly slipped into his EB's out of sight around the corner whilst he changed. We used to think he undressed away from the rest of us because he was shy. 'Peter Pan' as we knew him had other tricks up his sleeve, like being super fit, but when it came to tactics he was nearly always one jump ahead of the field.

Why was the Leeds Wall so ahead of its time? Its designer Don Robinson will of course claim it was all planned. Others believe it was an accident and that ignorant brickies pointed the wall upside down! Despite the passage of years and many threats to pull it down for redevelopment, the wall is still going strong. Amazingly with the ever-upward rise in standards new problems are

Bernard Newman when a student.
Photo Dennis Gray

still being pioneered. There are now hundreds of such challenges but my own favourite used to be the first arete by its classic incuts.

Not everyone welcomed these developments and I still recall my disappointment one night when I took Don Whillans to the wall for a session. As he came away he remarked, 'No bloody adventure on climbing walls, no bloody adventure at all!' He might have changed his mind if he had been with me the night I opened the door of the climbing wall just as Tweedledum (half of the wall stars duo Tweedledum and Tweedledee) came hurtling off the top to land at my feet. Crack! I heard his wrist go as he hit the linoleum-covered corridor floor.

'Is it broken? Please look', he whimpered, white with pain. We both nearly fainted at the sight as I examined his injury, it was so obviously fractured. 'It's the Leeds Infirmary for you!' I advised him. Proof that if you solo to the top of the wall and fall off you get plenty in the way of adventure.

Reminiscing about the wall, it is the characters I met there and the stories associated with them that stick in my mind. For instance the memorable night in the '70s when a dancer from the Royal Ballet, then performing at the Leeds Grand, burnt off the cream of the teams. He arrived wearing eye shadow, lipstick, rouge and tights - long before their short vogue on the '80s climbing scene. How the regulars eyed him with suspicion before he began to climb. But he cruised everything they pointed him at and he minced away leaving behind a lot of new ballet fans. Livesey went off and actually started taking lessons!

Chris Hamper, Terry Hirst and Steve Bancroft were all 'made' by the Leeds Wall, with Terry being the star of stars both indoors and outdoors. He kept his abilities to himself, never seeking any publicity. Unfortunately, one night in a moment of euphoria after a particular successful session on the wall, I allowed myself to tell these three plus Al Manson about my activities in the Zamba bar in Panama City - then the most famous bordello in South America. The story concerns eleven able-bodied seamen, one cabin boy and a very good-looking lady from the Argentine, known as the White Virgin (who remains, along with a girl I later met from the Lebanon, the most beautiful woman I have ever seen). This indiscretion has haunted me ever since and recently speaking at a climbing club dinner some wag shouted out; 'Tell us about the Zamba bar!'

Graham 'Streakie" Desroy performing.
Photo Dennis Gray

Over the past thirty years several generations of Leeds Wall users have come and gone, but one I will never forget is Danny Day, who worked in Centresport, one of the first of the new generation of retail climbing shops, and who died so tragically in winter on the North Face of the Matterhorn. One night he and I were on the wall, just the two of us. The Clash were playing at the Union and the 'Clockwork Oranges' were everywhere. Hundreds were turned away for it was a full house and they began to rampage about the campus and for some reason came down in their masses to congregate outside the PE block. Before I could stop him Danny, who was built like the proverbial brick house and had fiery red hair and a real temper to match, pulled down the window and shouted, 'Why don't you fuck off or I'll beat the lot of you up!' A remarkable piece of bravado which left me quaking, for there were only two of us and many of them.

Ten seconds later the double doors at the bottom of the stairs which used to be the entrance to the climbing wall were smashed in, and literally dozens of kids with brightly dyed hair, waistcoat-type jackets, denim baggy pants and big boots came charging up the stairs. Danny and I locked ourselves in the adjoining table tennis room and began piling chairs up against the door. We could hear their boots kicking in the windows, then banging the wall - sacrilege! and against doors, including the squash court. Then finally our door came in for some attention. Just when it looked like being a massacre the police arrived in van loads and this was the signal for the kids to abandon us. 'Let's get the pigs! Smash 'em. Burn their vans!' and off they went chanting into a pitched battle outside. The ensuing riot made national news headlines and I stopped listening to the Clash after that. Just two weeks later Danny was dead, but I can still imagine him on the wall, chuckling mightily about the night he provoked a riot at the Clash concert.

Many of the regulars at the Leeds Wall in the 1970s developed party tricks. I think the most bizarre was Graham Desroy who used to sit on one of the large holds facing outwards with his hands folded and legs tucked underneath him. It looked very simple but I never saw anyone else manage it. There were rumours amongst his detractors that Desroy, who is universally known as 'Streakie', had an unusually shaped backside that enabled him to carry out this feat. He had a variation on this theme -another trick of placing a small chair on a large jug hold at the top of the wall on which he used to sit with his arms folded. Graham was yet another climber who came to Leeds ostensibly to study but most particularly because of the climbing scene. He reports that when he arrived in May 1977 everything lived up to his expectations, although he did find it intense on occasion!

The Bullshit Books

Over the years there developed a passion for writing up the doings of the Leeds Wall group in what were fondly called 'the Bullshit Books'. Recently I had a chance to study some of these and though they do contain much dross and lots of weak undergraduate-type humour, there is plenty that is pure gold. There are the descriptions of several major new routes, including John Syrett's Almscliff masterpiece, The Big Greeny (named after the Number 56 and 57 buses which serve Leeds 6), and Alex MacIntyre's two great climbs on the Grandes Jorasses in 1976. They give many interesting insights into the climbing scene of that and the preceding era and thus are, I suppose, important historical documents. Naturally, the humour of those accounts appeals to me. Some are still capable of generating a smile despite the passage of time.

One such incident concerns the time Ken Wilson, then editing Mountain, turned up at Almscliff in October 1975 and noted a young climber soloing up and down some of the crags harder routes. In typical Ken fashion he rushed up to the bottom of the North West Face and shouted out loudly 'Hey, are you Ron Fawcett?'

'Christ, am I climbing that badly?' replied Mike Hammill, who in those days might fairly have been noted as a rival of Ron's.

Another is the occasion when two members were moving together in bad conditions, one rope length apart on the second ice-field of the Eiger's North Face. Tim Barnett having trouble with his crampons and becoming gripped, shouted across to his partner Dave Langrish obliterated by the mist. 'Dave...Dave! For Christ's sake where are you?'

'On the North Face of the Eiger. Where are you?' came his partner's laconic reply.

There is much emphasis on black humour in these large ledger-size books. Typical is the occasion Pete Wimbush fell off John Peel, a test piece of the era in The Peak District. He almost took a ground fall, escaping what would have been serious injury. His second man demanded of him, 'When you were falling, did you see your whole life flashing past you?' Pete considered a moment then replied.

'Er...no. Only my last runner!'

Concern about ethics is also evident in 'the Bullshit Books'. Typical are two incidents, the first by Pete Livesey after he had climbed the Cumbrian on Esk Buttress. 'I didn't set out to use aid but somebody saw me hanging from a sling!' The second, two members discussing how best to tackle a repeat of one of the areas hardest grit problems. Pete Wimbush; 'I'm told there is really only one runner placement on the whole route but it's also a hold, so you've the choice of a hold or a runner.' Terry Ralphs decided the answer to this was obvious,'That's easy. Just pull up on the runner!'

In the late 1960s an amazing new climbing facility was discovered after completion of a hall of residence - the Henry Price building situated on the edge of the old General Leeds Cemetery. Underneath the building, which is set on concrete plinths, a gritstone retaining wall remained exposed on the cemetery-facing side. Members of the climbing club soon realised that here was a brilliant traversing playground. Broken up by doorways into four walls, they gave dozens of metres of sideways climbing. 'The Bullshit Books' record some of the happenings when these were first developed. An unusual feature was that you could climb there at night, aided by the roof lights intended to allow flat-dwellers to find their way to their back doors; also the walls stayed dry, protected from the rain by the building above.

One November night of thick mist and pouring rain an over keen member was traversing the wall, when a policeman appeared.

'Hello, hello! I'm arresting you for attempted burglary.'

'Officer, how many housebreakers do you know who climb into buildings sideways for dozens of metres for Christ's sake?'

In the early 1980s I was climbing under the Henry Price Building with Tim Clifford when we were stopped by the sound of fiendish laughter from the graveyard. 'Jesus! What was that?'

'It must be the wind. Oh no, there it goes again!'

'I'm going,' Tim decided .

'Wait for me,' I agreed and as we scrabbled to change our rock boots, a figure rose from behind the gravestones. This was even more terrifying than the laughter, but as the dripping wet form drew near I started laughing - a drunken voice demanded, 'Aye boys, have ye a light?' It was only one of the local winos whose presence became a feature of the Henry Price Wall. The graveyard was a retreat for local drinkers and later, more sadly, glue sniffers.

All this wall activity used to play havoc with the skin on one's fingers, but we found if we treated them with Friar's Balsam in between sessions they recovered

The wall at the Henry Price Building, Leeds University.   Photo Dennis Gray

the quicker. Friar's Balsam is a brown sticky liquid which is actually a patent medicine. Unfortunately I keep getting this mixed up with Gee's Linctus which is a cough mixture. Recently one of the latest crop of Henry Price addicts collared me and asked how we used to manage to climb there so regularly, pulling on the small gritstone edges without wearing out the skin on our fingertips.

'Oh we used to coat them with Gee's Linctus afterwards' I assured him. Off he went straightaway to the chemists and bought a bottle. When I met him a few weeks later he reported that he had tried out the remedy I had recommended, but that his fingers had simply stuck together and he had experienced real difficulty in freeing them. It was then I realised my error, confessing that he should have bought the Balsam and not the Linctus!

Tom Curtis and 'Mad Axe' Wilson

Throughout the 1980s the university club attracted an ever increasing number of members – as I write the membership stands at over 200. It would need an entire book to do justice to all the club's doings over the years, but it would be remiss not to include two final stories from the archive.

Tom Curtis was President in 1986 and if anyone typified the nutty professor image Tommy is that man. Small, squat and wearing heavy glasses he looks like a fugitive from a science laboratory. Despite leaving behind him a trail of chaos – the club even had a 'Tom Curtis Award' for the biggest cock-up each year – he managed to pull off brilliant climbs in the Alps and the Himalaya such as the first ascent of Leila peak in the Karakoram.

A Korean climber walking the chains at   Martin 'Mad Axe' Wilson in action at
Leeds University   Photo Dennis Gray   Buxton.   Photo Ian Smith

At the 1986 Club dinner held at Tyn-y-Coed Tom was enjoying Presidential privilege in the hotel, the rest of us staying in the hut. After closing time Tom wandered back to the hut with us to split our own bottles. Returning to the hotel very late, he couldn't find the keys to get back in. Undaunted, he decided to climb up the drain pipe, traverse along the gutter and clamber into his bedroom, as he could see that the window was slightly open.

Unusually for Tommy, this plan worked like a charm, that is until he started to clamber in through the window when a lady sat bolt upright in the bed and started screaming. Tommy had managed to climb into the wrong room and the resulting fracas took all of his diplomatic skills to sort out!

My final story concerns Martin 'Mad Axe' Wilson who brightened all our climbing lives in the 1980s. As a fresher he immediately impressed me by his juggling and balancing skills, for he could walk the chains near the Henry Price building easily. These were two long strands set together which stopped unauthorised entry by car into the complex, and of course we used to try to walk across them like Blondin. It was difficult to balance across one, but to carry on and do both was quite a feat.

Martin could do this every time, and I was intrigued. It transpired that from a young age he had been involved with the Circus and this remained his interest besides climbing. I immediately recruited him for the BMC's Buxton Conferences and he made two appearances. At the first he appeared in the cabaret and juggled with ice-axes, and at the second he rode a unicycle at speed round and round whilst juggling with ice-axes! On both occasions he brought the audience to its feet, for he was a consummate showman. The trouble with his kind of act is that you have to keep 'upping the ante' and doing more and more difficult or dangerous feats to keep the crowds amused.

In 1989 at the end of Martin's sojourn in Leeds there was a BMC film festival held at the university. One day prior to this event Martin came round to my house and announced he had a new act which would bring the house down and which he aptly named 'the Piton of Death'. He explained that he and his partner Karl had an idea for a brilliant new stunt, where they stood a person in the middle of the stage with a piton held in his mouth. They would then throw ice-axes back and forth to one another, standing apart and in line with the poor sucker in the middle, just missing his body on each occasion. To finish they would then use one of the throws to knock the piton out of his teeth.

'Bloody hell that sounds exciting,' I admitted; 'but who the hell will you get to hold a piton in his teeth?'

'That's where you come in!' he laughed. 'Honest, it's dead safe. We can throw the axes to within fractions of a centimetre in accuracy.'

'Oh no! I'm too old...not that stupid. Bugger off!' But Martin kept at me and persuaded me to stand between him and Karl on the grass besides the Henry Price Wall whilst they threw ice axes at one another, catching them easily and deftly. I closed my eyes and heard them go whistling past, but none came close enough to touch me. So I stupidly agreed.

On the big night there were about 400 people in the hall of the Riley Smith theatre. I stood nervously on stage whilst Martin and Karl selected their axes from a pile in the wings. 'Ladies and gentleman we now present the Piton of Death,' and Martin came over and stuffed an ice piton into my mouth - at least he had not selected a RURP! Then he and Karl stood either side of me about thirty paces apart, and started to throw the axes at one another. Hamming it up, they deliberately missed catching the axes a couple of times whilst I screamed as they shot past my face.

But this was for real. I suddenly realised they had been throwing the axes out wide on the trial run intentionally. Now they were actually grazing my body as they shot past and I froze. I closed my eyes, praying that none would hit me. I need not have worried, for years of circus training meant that they could safely do such tricks as long as I kept still. Finally the last axe came winging over; it missed me like its predecessors, but Crunch! it took the ice peg with it. It also took half of one of my front teeth, for I was so gripped up, I was biting on to it as if my life depended on doing so.

The crowd screamed and Mad Axe Wilson had done it once again. Each time he appeared at a major climbing event he had put on an even greater performance. 'Again!' they screamed, but as I lisped a 'thank you' to our two axe men through my broken tooth, I was adamant I would never do that trick again. It was some relief to me that shortly after this event Martin emigrated to New Zealand where he is no doubt entertaining the locals throwing ice-axes around their bodies and catching them!

University climbing clubs are by their nature, I suppose, only a transitory place for most activists. Nevertheless, because this experience usually occurs in the intensity of a climber's youth, their time with these organisations remains vivid in the memory for the rest of their lives. Shortly before his death the late Jack Longland spoke of his days with the Cambridge University Mountaineering Club with lucidity and humour, fifty years on from those events. Many of the senior climbing clubs (such as The Rucksack in the case of Manchester University) rely heavily on student clubs for recruits. They welcome such members into their ranks once they have finished their studies and move on into a career. But for that short intense period in a climber's life, those who have been fortunate to have been involved in such a group often look back on it with nostalgia and gratitude.

Thus I remain grateful to the Leeds University club for the fun and good times I enjoyed over the years in their company. In the case of their former members Arthur Dolphin, Dave Cook, Alex MacIntyre, Roger Baxter-Jones and John Syrett, who were all my friends and were to die either climbing or around the sport, I wish to finish by paying tribute to their memory.

Chapter Two

Saving the Whales

Turning Pro for the BMC

Every sport in this country is represented by a national body, and there are literally hundreds of such organisations. Some so large that they are major employers and businesses, others so small that they rely solely on voluntary effort for their administration. Mountaineering was in this last category until the end of the 1960s, but a massive growth in the sport and the attendant problems that this brought about made the officers of the British Mountaineering Council at that time decide that a full-time professional officer was needed.

This took some while to organise, for in part it needed grant aid support from the newly formed Sports Council, but on the 1st January 1972 I became the first ever National Officer in the history of the sport.

Many national bodies of sport refer to themselves as governing bodies, but I always feel that climbers are ungovernable and that the two national bodies, the BMC and the Mountaineering Council for Scotland, should always be referred to as representative bodies. It was with mixed feelings that I took up my post and reported for duty, supported by a part-time secretary.

The BMC was then renting a small office in the old Central Council of Physical Recreation HQ in Park Crescent, London, situated in the plush surroundings of Regent's Park. It was soon brought home to me that turning 'pro' was not going to be all serious for on my very first evening in London, working late in the office on my own, I answered the phone.

'Is that the BMC?' demanded the voice of an anxious young woman.

'Yes'.

'Well it just will not go!'

It will not go,' I repeated totally mystified.

'I have already told you so!' Lady getting angry.

'What will not go?'

'My mini car that I had delivered this morning.'

'But why are you ringing us?' I demanded.

'You are the BMC and I want it mended now... tonight,' she responded.

'My dear lady, we are the British Mountaineering Council, you need the British Motor Corporation. Good night!' and I hung up on her ungallantly.

There was much happening at the BMC at that time; a new magazine, Mountain Life, was launched, the Council agreed to take over the administration of the Mountain Leader Training Scheme from the CCPR and two volumes of new climbs guidebooks were being prepared. However, I was nonplussed once I found out how stretched the BMC was financially at that time. It owned no office equipment other than an ancient manual typewriter and an equally decrepit duplicator, whilst the furniture, such as it was, belonged to the CCPR.

Our first electric typewriter was purchased from the profit made on a fund

23

subject was 'Competition and Climbing'. To the best of my knowledge this was the first time it had been debated internationally, and it came about very much at the instigation of the Russian Federation. They were keen to have their style of speed climbing competitions adopted as an Olympic sport. I elected to speak last, but unfortunately the conference was being held in the Lowenbrau beer hall and there were unlimited supplies of the amber nectar available. This was brought to our table by a little old lady who somehow managed to stagger over from the bar carrying ten litres of beer each trip.

It was an impressive occasion, with an audience of 2000 and live television coverage. I was accompanied by a professional interpreter who could speak German, Russian, and French. I had put a lot of effort into researching the background of 'competition and mountaineering', discovering for instance that when Coubertin, father of the modern Olympic movement, proposed sports which would be included as a part of the Games, mountaineering was one of the originals. And that gold medals were awarded to climbers at most of the Olympiads up to the war - our own General Bruce and the 1924 Everest party being awarded the medal for that period.

Anyhow, after what seemed like hours of waiting our turn came at last and the interpreter and I were called up to the microphones which were set on a speaker's dais on an improvised platform. I began my introduction and turned to the interpreter, awaiting his translation. In a very slurred voice he whispered in my ear 'Sh...sorry old boy...but I'm pissed!' and disappeared. To my surprise I found that the old maxim, 'everyone can understand English if you only shout loud enough' was almost true, and I ended up being the only speaker to get by without an interpreter. The result of the debate was that only the Russian Federation voted to adopt competition climbing, all others being against!

In the September of the following year the BMC organised the biggest international climbing meet ever held in this country on behalf of the UIAA. Fifty-seven climbers from nineteen countries met in London, from where they travelled up to North Wales in a hired coach. We quartered them in bunkhouses and, though the weather was abominable, they managed a lot of climbing.

Many of our guests were not used to placing their own protection, and during the meet we had a miraculous escape which made the tabloid newspapers. A very good looking Swiss lady was climbing with a rather portly Austrian gentleman who nevertheless was a Bergfuhrer (mountain guide) on the Main Wall route of Cyrn Las. The crux of this climb is the narrowing ramp pitch, especially when wet. The Austrian, climbing in rather large mountain boots, had just reached the awkward section about ten metres above his belayer when his feet slipped and off he came. He had no running belays between himself and his second, and we 'guides' below watched with horror as he shot over our heads.

I remember Rowland Edwards screaming out, 'Hold him! Hold him!' Then to our consternation the Swiss maid came hurtling over the edge after her leader. I thought, 'Oh God no, not again!' For many years previously I had been at Cyrn Las in a similar situation, when Frank Butler and his girlfriend had fallen off Main Wall climb and they had both been killed. Thankfully, this time the lady had doubled her belays and, despite the fact that one had failed, the other one held.

Though she burned her hands she bravely held on and arrested the falling Sepp (for that was his name) after an amazing twenty five metre plunge. Next day the Daily Mail banner headlines proclaimed; 'Swiss Milk Maid Saves Austrian Boyfriend From Death Fall'.

Shortly after that group returned home, eight members of the famous Groupe de Haute Montagne also came as BMC guests to North Wales. Led by Eric Vola, they included such legendary figures as the late Patrick Cordier, Simone Badier and Jean Afanassief. I climbed with the latter one day at Tremadog when he insisted on climbing Alpine style. I suppose if you are used to guiding in the Mont Blanc range eighty metre routes seem small by comparison. He proceeded to race up everything, coils in hand, easily climbing routes like 'Grim Wall' and 'Merlin Direct'. He even had me convinced as I galloped up behind him, until I found myself on 'the Grasper' . . . . .there ended the lesson.

The most historically significant climbing of that meet was to be the performances of Simone Badier. In 1973 few in the UK seriously believed that women could climb as well as the men. We were quickly forced to revise our opinion as M'amselle Badier floated up some of the hardest test pieces of that period. I'd say it was her example that started the renaissance in British women's rock climbing that has continued to this day.

Alan Blackshaw & Co

When I joined the BMC I was very conscious of the fuddy-duddy image it had with young climbers and resolved to try to change this. By common consent it was agreed that the Council needed to start holding more meetings and functions away from London, including its AGM which up till then had always been held in the Alpine Club. The first two 'away meets' were to be held in the Peak District, and in 1974 we met at the prestigious Maynard Arms in Grindleford. I had always hoped to involve more young people in our proceedings and as an experiment had booked a Manchester rock band as the after dinner entertainment.

The AGM in the afternoon and the Dinner in the evening were the usual wrinkly events, with everybody involved peeing in each other's pockets. But immediately the after-dinner speeches were over we cleared the room for the gig. This was much to the surprise of the old guard who were used to a quiet drink in the bar as the regular entertainment. Unfortunately, the friend who had booked the band for me had omitted to state that they were a heavy metal outfit, and as soon as they started to play I thought, 'Oh my God!'

Within seconds of the music starting the place was besieged with young climbers (those under 30!) Somehow word had got around and by the group's third number there were around 300 bodies jumping up and down on the dance floor. At this juncture my presence was requested by some of the BMC Management Committee, including the redoubtable A.B.Hargreaves. They demanded to know who was responsible for this outrage, and were gobsmacked to learn that we were actually paying these hooligans to perform. It didn't help that by this time a well-known climber had been given a leg-up by his companions and was now swing-

Urbane diplomat and ex-BMC
President, Alan Blackshaw.

Photo Dennis Gray

ing backwards and forwards over the dancers' heads, hanging off one of the chande-
liers!

John Hunt intervened on my behalf,
saying how marvellous it was to see so
many young people enjoying themselves.
Then the manager of the hotel arrived.
He was Italian and very excitable and he
was not amused. He had been assured that
only very well-behaved old buffers ever
attended BMC events, otherwise he would
never have accepted our booking. However, he met his match in our then newly
elected President of the Council, Alan
Blackshaw. Amongst his other accomplishments he had actually worked for some
time in the Diplomatic Service.

Alan's technique was to talk very qui-
etly, so his adversary could barely hear him. He never got excited, never got
involved, even when he was being shouted at by the very angry manager, who
was almost in tears because of what this rabble of climbers was doing to his
beautiful hotel. With some surprise I heard Alan agree that we would pay for
cleaning the place up and for any damage caused. This eventually amounted to
around £400 - a substantial sum in 1974 from a very tight BMC budget.

Alan Blackshaw was a brilliant BMC President, and during his term of office
many decisions were taken that later bore fruit in terms of increased support and
membership, including the moving of the Council's administration to Manchester. His work rate was prodigious for there was an oil crisis at the time and he was
serving as an under-secretary to Lord Carrington at the Department of Energy.

Alan turned up to chair one of our meetings with top secret documents locked
in a briefcase, which in turn was padlocked to his wrist. The meeting was being
held in a London club frequented by high-ranking military types. We were discussing the role of the BMC in training and I recall the consternation of the
other patrons when one of our committee members, Ken Wilson, was moved to
call out, 'Climbing is all about dying!'

Because of his work Alan was familiar with the new management techniques
of 'team building' and 'bonding'. Shortly after his election he suggested we try
such an exercise and so we called up all BMC officers and area representatives to
attend a meeting at an outdoor centre in Nidderdale. This invitation was also
extended to observers from the Sports Councils.

Just as I was leaving home on the Friday night our phone rang and a voice too
low for me to recognise whispered, 'Can you come and pick me up, I've broken
my neck!' It transpired it was the Peak District representative Bob Dearman, who
had done just that, falling off a climb in Dovedale. He made an impressive sight
when I met him later that night on Leeds City station; he was wearing a huge

surgical collar and had been forbidden to laugh or cough on pain of death.

Mind you, there was not much chance of the former happening. Though Blackshaw's attempts to make this weekend fruitful for us all were for real, with well-structured talks and slide shows, certain parties decided to play the Nationalist card and scuppered his good intentions. At our final de-briefing session the representative from the Sports Council for Wales insisted on delivering a long speech in Welsh, presumably trying to emphasise the diverse nature of Britain's heritage and staking Wales' right to be heard in mountaineering circles (despite the fact that apparently everyone else present hadn't a clue what he was saying).

He was to be confounded when he received an equally comprehensive answer in his own language from the BMC's President. Afterwards I collared Alan and demanded of him, 'Where did you learn to speak Welsh?'

'I was evacuated to a Welsh hill farm during the war, and they spoke nothing but, so I had to learn it quick!' he smiled in reply.

In my role as National Officer I had to give many talks and lectures. I had started giving climbing lectures on my own account as early as 1960, first to clubs then to the public, and by the time I joined the BMC I was a seasoned veteran. My biggest audience was at the Preston Guildhall in 1967, when 2000 people turned out, and my smallest only twelve at the Garrison Theatre in Plymouth that same year. At least they were a select audience, all being Admirals. They had been asked by the MOD to look into the future of naval apprentice training. It was subsequently decided that outdoor activities would be a major part of this.

Such gatherings usually go without a hitch. You have your box of slides, your prepared spiel and you simply turn up at the venue and give your talk. If all goes well you come away feeling satisfied at having provided an 'entertainment' for like-minded souls. Occasionally things did go wrong, and my most spectacular evening in this respect was at a lecture organised by the Nottingham Climbers Club as a fund raising event for a club expedition.

This was held in the Co-op Hall and several hundred people had turned up to support the local mountaineers who were planning a trip to the Himalaya. I began my talk and all went well for the first twenty minutes. I asked my projectionist to change a slide. Up came the new image, but it slowly wrinkled and dissolved before our eyes. We tried again and the same thing happened, and again. Before I could solve the mystery the operator yelled that the projector was red hot and he was burning his hands trying to rescue my slides!

Suddenly the ancient Aldis projector burst into flames. It was sitting on a wooden table in the centre aisle of the main body of the hall and within seconds this was also burning. The fire alarm went off and the audience left the building. At that point the fire brigade arrived and quickly got the fire under control.

I was left out on the pavement clutching the remains of my precious box of slides. Hundreds of disappointed people began to besiege the organiser, asking Doug Scott what was going to happen next. It soon became apparent that there would be no lecture that night. The Notts CC had not organised a back-up projector and in any case the fire brigade had now sealed the building and would not let anyone back in until they knew the cause of the fire.

I decided to cut and run and quietly slipped off to my vehicle, revved up and drove swiftly back north. My last view was of Doug standing on the pavement arguing with some of the more vociferous members of the audience who were now demanding their money back!

Buxton

The Buxton conferences were initiated by me in 1974. They were held more or less every two years up until I retired in 1989 and there were virtually full houses on every occasion. The names of those who appeared as speakers over those years makes impressive reading. Ministers of Sport, Chairmen of the Sports Council, Lord Hunt, Reinhold Messner, Wanda Rutkiewicz, Walter Bonatti, Anderl Heckmair, Kurt Diemberger, John Gill, Warren Harding, Don Whillans and dozens more. Inevitably, my fondest memories of Buxton conferences are the more outrageous ones.

We used to hire a hotel for our guests which became the centre of operations for the weekend. Often there were gatecrashers who managed to get in by virtue of being 'friends of friends'. At one conference the American 'Hot' Henry Barber was speaking and Al Rouse, Pete Minks, Mick Geddes and several more of their friends slept on his bedroom floor. The hotel management didn't know about this and next morning Rouse & Co. crept downstairs without waking Pete Minks, having taken all his clothes except for his pants.

Al, Henry, Mick and the rest then drove up to the front of the hotel in Geddes's car, horn blaring. Minks, who was a giant of a man and not one to be trifled with, came rushing downstairs and out to the front steps. Rouse sat in the front of the car with the window down and the engine running. 'What the fuck are you guys up to?' bellowed Minks.

'Pete, this is an initiative test. We're going to Stoney Middleton to climb... see you there!' said Al and promptly drove off. Minks was left standing outside on a raw March morning; barefoot, barechested and all alone to work out his next move. I have no idea what happened subsequently, but having previously seen Pete Minks in action dealing with a load of troublemakers at a party after one of my lectures in Liverpool, I confess I was mightily impressed by Rouse's bravery.

I could fill a chapter with Buxton Conference stories. There was the time when the army brought an outdoor climbing wall and set it up in the grounds of the Buxton Pavilion. Unfortunately, their chief instructor hit the deck from the top when one of the squaddies let go of his rope by mistake. 'Now pay attention you chaps...this is how it's done. .' and whoops! down he came. Nevertheless, he was still directing operations as they carried him off on a stretcher. The man was obviously a born leader!

I recall when one of our speakers decided to take a communal bath in the middle of the night with three other guests (including an attractive young woman) and flooded the place out. But pride of place must go to a Sunday morning at the Old Hall Hotel. I was sat at a table in the dining room congratulating myself that

Al Rouse – a brave fellow indeed.   Mo Anthoine – a ribald sense of humour
       Photo Terry Tullis   Photo Terry Tullis

the event was successfully over for another two years. My son Stephen, who had provided some of the music for the conference and cabaret, was with me. We sat eating our breakfast surrounded by other guests, most of whom had nothing to do with our event. They all looked rich and the wrong side of seventy.

Stephen and I nursed headaches from the previous night's post-conference celebrations. It was a beautiful morning and we were gazing out of the bay windows facing onto the park when we saw Mo Anthoine coming across the curving road at the side of the grass. Mo was one of the great characters of the British climbing scene with one of the most impressive all-round records of his time, but it was his ribald sense of humour that his friends valued most. He hated pomposity and loved to deflate anyone with an ego. Mo immediately recognised us and quickly sized up the scene - middle England at breakfast!

He came up to our window, turned his back and dropped his trousers, mooning us and our fellow guests. Stephen and I were in hysterics but the others were not amused. One elderly lady screamed whilst a blimpish type behind us shouted 'bloody disgraceful behaviour, the fellow should be horse-whipped!' Thereupon Mo slowly pulled up his trousers and nonchalantly disappeared round the corner. Of course, we never let on we knew him.

Later Buxton conferences (those held in the 1980s) became ever more spectacular with the 1984 event having the finest cast list of any that we organised. Bonatti, John Gill, Tom Frost, Pat Ament, Stefan Glowacz and Alex Kunaver were just some of those involved. The latter, a Yugoslav almost unknown in Britain, had perhaps the finest Himalayan record at that date. He and I were firm friends, and his death a few weeks after the conference in a helicopter crash in the Julian Alps (along with the famous Munich climber Toni Hiebeler) was devastating news. The more so because a few days before this tragedy he had been in Britain on business and he'd phoned me. Just after he died a gift arrived through the post; a bottle of his favourite 'Slivowicz'.

Every Saturday night at the Buxton conferences we used to wind things up with the traditional 'My Life and Hard Times' lecture. Distinguished climbers who gave these talks included Diemberger, Heckmair, Harding, Messner, Robbins, Bonatti and of course, Don Whillans. On the occasion that the 'Villain' gave his seminal talk, just as the lights dimmed in the Opera House ready for him to start, a streaker appeared and ran across the stage in front of him.

'Well I'll be buggered!' declared the Salford hard man, 'And come to think of it so will he be if I can catch him.' Don made to run after the naked figure disappearing into the wings of the auditorium, which almost brought the house down. This put Whillans into his most avuncular mood, and he gave the best lecture I had ever heard him deliver. It was so well received that in all the talks given over the years at the Buxton Conferences only Bonatti received a similar ovation.

BMC Manchester

In January 1975 the BMC moved to Manchester, I became General Secretary and we appointed Peter Boardman to succeed me as National Officer. Although he had the physique of a lumberjack, Pete was an English graduate who later proved he had outstanding ability as a writer. His very first book, 'the Shining Mountain', won a major literary prize. He was a mountaineer par excellence and later that year he was to go to the summit of Everest via the difficult South West Face. He was also a keen singer and a member of his climbing clubs group 'the Mynydd Minstrels'. At any climbing function or pub do he was happy to get up and give a solo rendition of the tongue-twisting 'Rawtenstall Annual Fair'. He was neither shy or retiring as some commentators have subsequently inferred, but self-assurred and mature beyond his years.

The new office in Manchester was situated in the university precinct centre, a short distance from Moss Side, Hume and Ardwick; three very deprived areas with massive crime problems and a lot of teenage delinquency. Our premises were frequently burgled and battling with the criminals became routine.

In almost my first week at the office I came out of the building to see my car being driven slowly up to the car park barriers. These were automatic; to get in you needed a special pass but to get out you had only to slow down at the barrier and it lifted automatically. At that time I was still doing some running and I sprinted for all I was worth and caught up with it as it approached the barrier. By sheer good fortune my hatchback door had recently been damaged and would not lock. I yanked this up and dived into the vehicle screaming at the top of my voice. The would-be thief took fright at this, and as soon as he had the car through the barrier he pulled on the brakes and ran off, leaving me wondering what would have happened if he had simply kept on going. I might have been kidnapped!

One night at the end of 1977, just before he left the BMC, Peter Boardman caught a gang of youths trying to break into the office. He chased them and boxed their ears, telling them not to come back. Unfortunately this was not a wise thing to do to Moss Sider's as the very next day they came back with a high powered rifle. They fired through the window, narrowly missing our secretary Rita's head as she sat at her desk typing.

Later that week I was working so late one night I decided to sleep on the meeting room floor rather than face the drive home. At about 2 a.m. I was wakened by the sound of a window being forced open by a crowbar. I jumped up clutching my sleeping bag about me and called out. I confess to having been scared but I reckon the burglar got the fright of his life. He made the fastest getaway I have ever seen and the last I saw of him he was running across the adjacent gardens shouting at the top of his voice. He must have thought I was a ghost! Despite these problems, it was obvious that the move to Manchester had been the right one.

There was a vibrant climbing scene at the university at that time, spearheaded by Dick Renshaw and Joe Tasker, and we had many more volunteers and helpers to call upon for the myriad tasks that had to be done.

Joe Tasker was a tremendous character. He had originally been intended for the priesthood and attended a Catholic seminary, but at fifteen one of his teachers had taken him climbing. He became hooked on the sport and subsequently decided he could not make the Church his vocation. He elected instead to study at Manchester University. He used to come and sit in my office and talk for hours about intended expeditions, both practical and improbable, or we might discuss religion and the meaning of life!

He was a tremendous debater and loved an argument, unlike his long time climbing partner Dick Renshaw. Dick was known as the 'quiet man'. Despite their different natures, or perhaps because of them, he and Joe did many brilliant climbs together including the North Face of the Eiger in winter.

In 1975 Joe and Dick had made an epic journey to the Garwhal Himalaya, driving there in an old Ford van. Against heavy odds they pulled off a first ascent of the south-east ridge of Dunagiri, taking six days for the ascent and another five to come down. During their climb they had seen and photographed the West Wall of Changabang and Joe now had his sights set on this. Dick had been badly frostbitten on Dunagiri, so Joe was looking for another partner. He was a regular visitor to our office and soon decided that Pete Boardman was the climber he required. The snag was Pete had only recently returned from Everest and was not due any time off work.

Undaunted, Joe set about canvassing on Pete's behalf. He started on easy ground, buttonholing me at the office Christmas party. He went on to speak to the BMC President, then to Chris Bonington and finally Lord Hunt and managed to persuade us all that the future of British mountaineering was at stake.

Pete got his time off and the rest is history and can be read about in the aforementioned book the 'Shining Mountain', still one of the best climbing books ever written.

Today, climbing has grown so much in popularity that it is becoming increasingly impersonal. In those days there was still a sense of a climbing fraternity and in my trips around the country to Wales, the North East, the Lakes or Scotland I usually stayed with friends. I have particularly pleasant memories of my trips to Scotland.

One night after a meeting of the Mountaineering Council of Scotland I remember sitting on the carpet in Sandy Cousin's flat in Glasgow, with half a dozen other climbers listening spell-bound whilst the late Sir Robert Grieve told of his early climbing days in the Highlands before the war. With a glass of malt whisky in hand, we then heard a discourse on Gaelic poetry, which Bob was an authority on.

If our evening meetings were somewhere like Bridge of Orchy then during the day we nearly always climbed on the Etive Slabs, the Buachaille or did some Munro bashing. In contrast nearly every time I ventured down to the South West the visit ended in farce, an incredible punch-up or both.

My worst experience was when I attended an Area Committee meeting in Bristol one Saturday afternoon in the Summer of 1977. After the meeting I met up with Arnis Strapcans (the climbing anagram) on the limestone cliffs of the Avon Gorge. Arnis was a leading light among the younger generation of British climbers and I had known him for several years. He had pioneered many climbs of the highest standards of those days and was equally at home on outcrops or major cliffs. Typical of Yorkshiremen, Arnis was no respecter of reputations and was a master of the put-down.

On one occasion I was introducing him to Sir Jack Longland. Before I could say the name Arnis said, 'I know your face. I've seen it often in the mags.' Sir Jack beamed at being recognised by one of the leaders of the younger generation.

'You're that bloke - the climbing plumber,' continued Arnis. Sir Jack spluttered and I nearly choked.

Arnis asked if I would like to go to a party that night at Steve Berry's. Parties in the South West were legendary and I readily agreed. 'Just time to snatch a route before we go to the pub, let's solo Thanatos,' Arnis suggested.

'How hard is it?' I demanded, knowing that Strapcans thought nothing of soloing what were really hard routes by my standards.

'About... 5a.' We set off for the climb, situated on the sea walls area of the cliff and beginning to the left of a large iron grill, blocking the entrance to a cave at the base of the rock face.

'Only the first moves are difficult,' my guide assured me as we began to climb up by way of a corner. I followed right on his heels, thinking if I got into trouble he might be able to help me.

Thanatos is only approximately twenty five metres high and as Arnis had warned the first corner proved to be both awkward and hard. I was glad to join him on a ledge above. We then traversed left along the ledge and I then watched apprehensively whilst Arnis climbed a ramp leading onto a steep headwall. He powered up this, then started swinging left which involved almost a hand traverse. Some strenuous pulls led him into a final groove which he quickly climbed and my young friend was at the top urging me to follow him.

'Hell, ' I thought. 'Here goes!' and made a step onto the leftwards slanting ramp, climbing easily up this to reach steeper ground. A wild pull onto the wall

Arnis Strapcans – fellow Yorkshireman and
climbing iconoclast.
                Photo Dennis Gray

Steve Bell – hit by the biggest bruiser in
Somerset.   Photo Dennis Gray

above and I realised I was now committed. There were good handholds but I was getting tired, and by the time I reached the swing left I was becoming worried.

Arnis leaned down and shouted, 'Good finishing jugs up here,' pointing to some holds at his feet. I climbed into the finishing groove and somehow managed to get bridged into a resting position. The ground was about twenty metres below me whilst above but still a metre away were the big holds. A delicate balance up and I grabbed these and was very happy to pull over the top and join Arnis.

'Bloody hell kid... you'll kill me yet!' I laughed, happy to land on a good ledge with an obvious easy descent route beckoning us back down to the ground. Just a short while after this Chris King, one of Avon's local experts, was also soloing Thanatos. He, too, made the swing left on the top wall but unfortunately a hold broke and he hit the ground, badly injuring himself.

After our climb Arnis and I visited a pub and afterwards, joining up with a host of other south west climbers, we were all hanging around laughing and joking in Steve Berry's flat. The drinks were flowing, the stereo was blaring and everybody seemed relaxed and happy. I was talking to Steve Bell, who was well known to me as he had climbed a lot with one of my best friends, Tim Leach, on routes like the North Face of the Matterhorn in winter.

Suddenly a giant figure loomed over me and 'wham!' The guy hit me in the throat, knocking me flying straight onto a bed in the corner of the room. The blow was so hard I almost swallowed my Adam's apple. I lay on the bed choking and watched as Steve Bell loyally jumped at the guy shouting 'What the hell is the problem?' The massive figure lashed out again, and this time Steve went down. Doggedly, like a boxer trying to beat the count, he got first to his knees, then groggily onto his feet. The fists hit him again and down he went once more. This time the guy only waited until Steve got to his knees before he lent down and uppercut him. All hell broke loose and everyone was fighting and arguing with the giant pugilist. I had no idea what it was all about, but next thing I knew Arnis had rescued both Steve and I and was supporting us out of the flat, down some stairs and out onto the road.

'Come on both of you, that guy is crazy with booze, let's go back to my flat for a brew.' Though he studied in London, Arnis and his girlfriend maintained a basement flat in a large Victorian house in Bristol only a short walk from where the party was being held. We were just safely inside, licking our wounds and wondering why the apparent madman had set about us, when there came a tremendous hammering on the door.

'Go away Dave,' Arnis shouted.

'What the hell is going on?' I demanded.

'It's only Dave...he sometimes gets like this if he drinks too much,' Strapcans calmly informed us.

'Let me in or I'll smash your door down!'

'Dave, go home, you've had too much to drink.' Instead of having the desired effect, this only seemed to enrage Dave the more, and crash! he smashed in the front room bay window with his bare fist.

'Bloody hell,' I gasped, by now frightened stupid. The front door gave way and the huge figure of our earlier assailant came charging into Strapcan's flat. 'King Kong' grabbed our host by the throat, encircling it with one large hand. Steve Bell grabbed the giant's other hand and was hauling at this, but things were looking grimmer by the second for Arnis, who was going redder and redder in the face as the life was being squeezed out of him.

I ran into the kitchen looking for a weapon (desperate situations require desperate actions) and there, lying on the gas stove, was a large iron frying pan. I picked it up, ran back, and - taking aim from behind - hit Dave on the head with the pan. Suddenly he ceased his aggression, let go of Arnis, stopped battling with Steve and looked bemused.

'Where am I?' he demanded.

'Bloody hell Dave, you nearly killed us,' Arnis told him. The giant looked around him at the trail of destruction he had caused and I thought he was going to cry.

'Oh my God . . . . .I'm so sorry. . . . it's the drink . . . I just don't know what comes over me.'

'Bugger the apologies, wait till Hilary gets back from work, our lives will be hell and who is going to mend the door and the window? The landlord will go spare!' Arnis informed him, not in anger, but really worried about what his girl-friend would say when she got in from working night shift as a nurse.

'I'll mend the door,' offered Dave apologetically.

'And I know how to mend a window,' I volunteered. Next day was spent racing around Bristol buying glass, putty, window sashes, a door frame and a new door. We finished repairing the damage just in time for me to set off north for the long drive home to Yorkshire. I never did like DIY and ever since the biggest climbing bruiser in Somerset flattened me I have tried to avoid doing such time-consuming chores. Get out climbing and leave it to the professionals is now my motto.

Yes, my visits to the BMC South West Area were always interesting and per-haps I should have been paid danger money. When Arnis disappeared soloing in the Mont Blanc range during the summer of 1980 his friends could not believe it, for technically he was one of the very best British climbers of his, or any other generation. Arnis has never received the recognition his pioneering efforts mer-ited. He was at the cutting edge of the limestone free-climbing revolution, and his routes at cliffs like Cheddar Gorge, Wintour's Leap and Pembroke bear wit-ness to a brilliant talent. But it was his attitude to climbing and life that his friends valued most, everything seemed possible with Arnis Strapcans and merriment was assured whenever he was around.

Some marvellous nights were also to be had back at the BMC in Manchester. The meeting room was an uninspiring brick construction holding forty at a pinch, but even so we held a Literature Festival there and a Survival Symposium. These were helped along by a barrel of beer provided by a local firm, Troll Products. The 'Survival' evenings were particularly enthralling. My office would become the bar for the occasion and, once speakers and audience were adequately supplied, we would settle down and relive some remarkable epics.

I remember Tony Barley telling of his experience when climbing in a remote area of South Africa. He fell over sixty metres, fractured his skull, barely survived a difficult rescue but lived to tell the tale thanks to the skill of Dr Christian Barnard.

Perhaps the most gripping story was that of Ivan Waller. Ivan was an engineer with Rolls Royce during the war and carried out some secret missions. On one he was on a night flight when the engines stalled as the plane flew over the Firth of Clyde. The pilot told everyone to bale out. Ivan jumped with the others but his 'chute got caught on the tail of the aircraft and he went down into the murky waters of the Clyde. He was carried underwater but managed to cut himself free and float to the surface. He was eventually picked up suffering from hypother-mia. Clearly the man who pioneered the famous Belle Vue Bastion climb in 1927 was made of special stuff.

Looking back now it seems that in the 1970s we did have more than our fair share of crises at the BMC. We were having to learn everything the hard way, by experience! Dominating the work of the Council during that decade was the long running Mountain Training dispute, which ended in arbitration in a court-room format at the Lands Tribunal. There were many other 'incidents' which stand out, some of which have never really been documented. One was the huge rock fall which occurred at Bwlch y Moch, Tremadog in 1978. This not only blocked the road (forcing it to be realigned) but almost destroyed a house in its path. The lady of the house was alone when a massive boulder smashed into her kitchen, pushed her fridge across the floor, and pinned her against the wall.

Tim Jepson and some other climbers were nearby. They got into the house and freed the woman who, amazingly, was not seriously hurt. There were however suggestions that the actions of climbers had made the rock unstable. Geologists confirmed that this was not the case, nevertheless there were calls for climbing to be banned from one of the most popular cliffs in Britain. The matter was resolved when the lady who owned the crag, Mrs Williams, gave the crag to the BMC. Along with ownership comes responsibility for managing the area and all that entails.

During the summer of 1979 one of the most serious incidents in climbing history occurred. This became known as the Tour Ronde accident. The Tour Ronde is part of the Mont Blanc range where a British party of three was descending in the afternoon, via the normal route to the Vallee Blanche. They slipped and fell; possibly snow balled-up on their crampons. We'll never know. Several other parties were beneath them on the slope and they crashed into them, pulling them off in a tangle of ropes and bodies. Some fell hundreds of metres into the bergschrund at the bottom. The final tally was eight dead and as many injured. The only survivor of the British party was seventeen-year-old Christopher Marsh, and the French police wanted to bring a case against him for manslaughter, which was unprecedented.

Thanks to the BMC's increased international role we had very good contacts in France by then. Vincent Renard, a Parisian climber and one of the officers of the French Federation, helped us greatly by arranging for a fellow climber, a barrister from Grenoble, to take on the case. He soon had the young British climber released from Annency, where he was being held. When the case came up for review by the examining magistrate he got the manslaughter charge dropped on the grounds that it was impossible to apportion blame in such an accident.

If the case had proceeded and the charges proven the consequences would have been horrendous. No longer would climbers have enjoyed the freedom that is part and parcel of the sport. By nature mountaineers do not like organisation and regulation. They like to leave all that behind when they go into the mountains. I have never been an authoritarian, and until I joined the BMC had never been involved with the organisation of climbing. The Tour Ronde accident confirmed to me that in today's world climbers have to protect their sport and this can only be done by a body like the BMC. The Council spent several thousand pounds defending Chris Marsh. I hope every climber feels it was money well spent and realises the need to support their representative body.

Chapter Three

The British Union of Mountaineers

Meeting Challenges with the BMC

During my two decades at the BMC in the seventies and eighties climbing changed from being a minority sport to a major activity. By the time I left the Council in 1989 there were many more people hill-walking and rock-climbing than playing both codes of rugby. Every year during those twenty years the membership of the BMC grew, particularly in the case of individual members, a situation that has continued until the present day. This reflects the changing face of the sport, with its participants ever more mobile (on a global scale) and an ever younger intake.

When I started climbing at eleven years of age in 1947 I knew no other climbers of my age, whereas now if you visit any of the indoor climbing centres you will often meet gaggles of young enthusiasts.

Equipment development during those two decades was to be of crucial importance in helping to change the image of the sport. Heavy sweaters, breeches, woolly socks and big boots were common in 1970, but over subsequent years we came to realise the benefit of specialised, lightweight clothes. In rock climbing we enjoyed many innovations which improved safety; new protection devices like Friends; the development of lighter, stronger 'kernmantel' ropes; and improvements in footwear design, including the adoption of 'sticky' high-friction rubber soles for rock boots.

All these developments encouraged leaders to push standards, which in turn caused new climbing areas to be developed, such as the South Pembroke sea cliffs and slate climbing in North Wales and the Lake District. There has also been a revolution in free and bolt-protected routes on Derbyshire and Yorkshire limestone and even in some of Scotland's more accessible glens.

Similar dynamic developments occurred in mountaineering, with the wholesale adoption of front-point crampon techniques, the introduction of plastic rigid boots and curved picks for ice tools. These changes, along with improved snow and ice protection devices such as dead man' plates, screws and drive in pitons, brought winter climbing within the capabilities of more and more climbers.

This had major repercussions at the BMC and there were added complications with the start of climbing competitions and the development of indoor climbing centres. An ever increasing number of climbers were going abroad, some, particularly in the winter months, to the new style 'sport' climbing grounds which had been developed in Spain and France. Others travelled further afield to the USA, Canada and Australia or to the remote ranges of the Himalaya, Patagonia or the Andes. There was a lot of satisfaction in being part of this 'explosion', but in my meetings with representatives of other sports I realised that such increased interest and activity was not confined to climbing.

Soon after I started my work with the BMC I attended a conference organ-

At Buckingham Palace to meet the
Queen.   Photo Mrs. L. Busfield

of the top table and whoosh! – I got the contents of the first bucket full in the face. This turned out to be wallpaper paste and the rest of the distinguished guests got the same treatment from the second bucket.

After this all hell broke loose, and it turned into a scene from a Three Stooges film, with people sliding about on the floor throwing anything they could get their hands on. In the end a truce had to be called whilst the management cleaned up and cleared the room for the inevitable disco.

Subsequently I had to contact the chap who had loaned me the dinner suit and ex-plain that its return would be delayed whilst I had it cleaned. 'What the hell have you been up to?' he demanded.

'Unfortunately it became a little stained at the dinner I attended,' I lied, feeling like a small child.

'You bloody climbers are a coarse lot.' If he had seen his suit before it was cleaned up he might not have been so understand-ing. I was also a little miffed to discover my ukulele sounded like a strangled duck ever after.

In those BMC years I was also able to meet some of the leading politicians and members of the British establishment. Everyone from the Queen and Margaret Thatcher to great sportsmen and women like Seb Coe and Mary Peters.

One unusual meeting was with Jack Charlton the footballer. At the height of the Mountain Training dispute, when the Sports Council officials had cut our grant (acting unilaterally and without any real knowledge of the issues), we de-cided to lobby any appointed member of their Council who would speak to us. Jack Charlton was then on the Sports Council and was also the manager of Sheffield Wednesday FC . We managed to set up a meeting via Geoff Birtles, the editor of 'High' and a shareholder of the footie club.

Big Jack the Geordie laddie met us in his office at the 'Owls' ground, and after introductions Geoff and I launched into a long and, I now realise, over-compli-cated dialogue about the mountain training dispute and the iniquitous bureau-crats in London who had embarrassed us poor climbers by stopping our cash. We were stopped in our tracks by our football hero declaring 'Awa laddies, I'm only a simple footballer, it's beyond me! Let me ring Winterbottom.' He then phoned Walter, the former England soccer manager, who at that time was the Director of the Sports Council.

A lively discussion then took place over the phone, with Jack getting ever more wide-eyed. After he put the receiver down he thought for a moment then, with a shaking of his head, he advised us; 'It all sounds incredible to me, can yer no get together all you climbers and sort it out?' This sounded an awful simplification of the problem at the time, but we managed to choke out a 'we'll try' as we departed.

In the end this proved sound advice for shortly after that meeting in Sheffield we did all get back together, that is all the parties in the mountain training dispute, and opted for an independent arbitration procedure. I liked Big Jack for it was obvious in the way that he dealt with us (good humoured and courteous throughout) that the man's no fool.

One of the 'great and the good' who I used to see an awful lot of during my BMC years was Sir Jack Longland. I met him in many guises; as Vice Chairman of the Sports Council, President of the Alpine Club, Chairman of the Mountain Leader Training Board and also of Plas y Brenin. We were all involved in a fearful row over Mountain Training in the seventies, with Jack on one side and me on the other, but somehow we stayed friends. There was something underneath the 'Sir Jack' image that I liked immensely; mainly his ability to laugh at himself. His range of accomplishments would have made most people envious; athlete, scholar, outstanding rock climber, Everest team member, broadcaster, Director of Education - the list is almost endless.

I had known him since I was about fifteen and over the years I enjoyed many meetings and some lively correspondence with him. My favourite story of Sir

Anderl and Trudl Heckmair with Sir Jack Longland at Buxton.   Photo Terry Tullis

Jack concerns one November night when he and I were attending a boring Mountain Training Board seminar at Plas y Brenin. Though I believe the work the MTB's carry out is vital, it can be just too much of a good thing on a Saturday evening. I sat in the back row of the crowded room, almost falling asleep as a lecturer droned on and on about 'River Crossings'. I heard a whisper in my ear – 'Let's get out of here'. It was Sir Jack. I needed no second bidding and was soon stepping out of the Brenin's front door and into the inky night, with my eyes fixed firmly on the Chairman's receding figure.

His car was parked just outside the centre down towards Capel Curig, tucked into a lay-by at the side of the building. He held the passenger door open for me, I climbed in and we were just about to roar off up the road to the bar at the Pen y Gwyrd when a large figure loomed up, caught in the Austin's headlights. It was the Plas security guard and handyman. He was carrying a huge torch, which he shone through the windscreen straight into our eyes, blinding us. Jack wound the window down. 'Is there something wrong?'

'Wrong... wrong... don't you ever park your car in that place again, Sir, or there will be trouble! It's a no parking area'.

'Don't you know who I am?' Jack spluttered.

'Yes ... I know who you are...don't you ever park there again. If everybody who comes here thinks they can just park where they like it would be chaos.'

'But I'm the Chairman of the Management Committee,' Jack informed him.

'I know and you ought to know better... good night, Sir.' At which he turned his light out and disappeared back into the centre, finally leaving us to make our clandestine trip to the watering hole.

'Bloody hell,' chuckled Jack as we drove along. 'He needs promoting. Such devotion to duty on a Saturday night!'

Debates and Diplomacy

An outstanding character at Plas y Brenin at the end of the seventies was the Director John Barry, a mountaineer's mountaineer. An ex-Royal Marine Commando Officer with the physique of Garth, a brilliant raconteur, a formidable opponent to anyone rash enough to physically provoke him and underneath a heart like a bucket.

He brought a breath (storm) of fresh air to the stuffy old Brenin and its parent organisation, the Sports Council, and frequently had them reeling from his many adventures. I used to be on the centre's Management Committee to whom John reported. At that time serious questions were being posed about the Brenin's future role and whether the climbing world really needed such a showpiece centre. Ken Wilson and I wrote a paper on how we thought this might develop, and eventually a working party was set up to examine the centre's future.

In the process of achieving this Ken, as was his wont, became embroiled in wordy and heated exchanges with Barry. I decided that I ought to try to act as a peacemaker and thought that fences could be mended if we three could get together socially over a meal and a beer or two. I could not have been more wrong!

The venue for this tete-a-tete was an Indian restaurant in Mold, chosen some-how at random because it was halfway between the Brenin and Manchester and we could therefore meet on neutral ground. We had barely got inside and sat down when a row started, with Ken shouting out his message that 'the climbing world via the BMC would decide on the future direction of Plas y Brenin, not a crowd of bloody bureaucrats!'

No one less like a bureaucrat could be found than Barry, and I was gobsmacked at Wilson's temerity in provoking him. I was trying to turn the conversation round to climbing and climbers, but Ken was having none of this. The poor Indian waiters must have thought we were a trio of madmen as they hovered around us trying to set the table, especially when John grabbed Ken by the throat and threatened to flatten him. Incredibly, Ken just kept on going, really into his subject. He just did not seem to realise the danger he was in. I then tried to intervene, got a punch in the chest for my troubles but somehow managed to part them.

'I'm going,' Barry announced. 'I have not come here to listen to this garbage!' and off he strode.

'Bloody hell Ken, be careful ... remember Barry's a trained killer!' I was just observing when John sheepishly reappeared back through the Indian's front door..

'Sorry,' he apologised to me as he sat back down at our table. One of his most charming traits was that he was always ready to apologise if he'd upset anyone. We started again, and even got as far as ordering when Ken once again raised the question of the Brenin's future role. John, new in the job, was defensive and in any case had come for a social night out like me, but Wilson never relaxed once he had an issue to grind. So the BMC's tame rottweiler once again bared his fangs at Captain John.

The effect was electric. The table went over, Ken was grabbed and only the intervention of several turbanned waiters and myself stopped a massacre. Then Barry was gone and this time I knew he would not be back. After re-establishing good relations with the restaurant's owners by paying for all the damage, we climbed back into the car and drove back up to Manchester. Ken turned to me and observed absolutely seriously, 'You don't think I said anything to upset him do you?'

'No, not at all Ken,' I replied wearily, but secretly felt that if Barry had stran-gled him in front of my eyes I would have gone into the witness box at his subsequent trial and pleaded his innocence on the grounds of extreme provoca-tion.

It seems that Ken was always around throughout my period at the BMC. Few sports can have been graced by such a character, such an obsessive debater, such a politician-in-waiting, such a forceful committee member. Over-reacting to almost every situation, he nonetheless cares about climbing and climbers to a degree that would be declared insane in any other walk of life. Immensely tal-ented in his own fields of photography and publishing and running his own successful business, he still finds the time to spend hours on end phoning people the length and breadth of the country, gleaning ideas, lobbying, king-making and generally steering people round to his view on whatever he sees as the current crisis facing our sport.

Normally Ken is a gentleman, capable of having a laugh at his own expense, but once roused by an issue he becomes a steely-eyed, aggressive debater with unbelievable stamina. When we held the first meeting to discuss the design, construction and management of climbing walls in the BMC's Manchester office, we invited everyone who we thought could make a contribution, including a representative of the Sports Council. Come the evening of our get-together, the person who attended on behalf of that body was Peter Sutcliffe, the former Yorkshire cricketer and a member of that famous family. He was a no-nonsense character from the Broad Acres; powerfully built, thinning on top and with a 'reet' good accent, but obviously keen to be helpful.

Twenty-two representatives had assembled from all over the country and after introductions we began the business of the meeting. We were barely into our stride when Ken began to question Peter's bona fides. What was he doing there? What was his role? What expertise did he possess? On and on he flowed and finished by observing that we could not allow some government Quango to start dictating to us in our sport. I tried to explain that Sutcliffe was there as an observer, had come to try to advise and help. This was not good enough for Wilson and it ended with long wrangles about the status of observers and who had the right to be present, to speak, to vote etc etc.

Procedures in committees can be very important, especially when taking decisions on future policies. However, this was only a first get-together to try to decide what kind of forum, if any, would be necessary to prosecute the then relatively new phenomena of indoor climbing walls. I could see that Peter was fuming about his reception, and as soon as he could he apologised and left early. We were old mates so I followed him outside and persuaded him to go upstairs with me to the shopping precinct above the office, where there was a pub for a pint.

'Who is that bloody lunatic who never shuts up? I nearly slotted him one, he wouldn't survive ten minutes up at Headingley.' For once I was really proud of Ken; few other national bodies can have such a dynamo in their ranks that can so upset a former county cricket captain.

'That, Peter, is the incredible millionaire publisher Ken Wilson.' I laughingly advised him, stretching Ken's wealth a little.

'He is so full of wind he could blow over the stumps at 22 yards,' observed my fellow tyke, laughing now. I half agreed with him.

The marathon of BMC debates used to be Management Meetings, held in our own meeting room within the offices in the university precinct. At the height of the Mountain Training dispute, with feelings running high, these might start at 7.30 p.m. and run on into the wee small hours. Delegates would be there from all over the country, and I used to feel sorry for them and myself staggering out on a cold January evening at, say, 2.30 a.m. to begin the long drive home to Glasgow,

Llanberis, London or Bristol. It was not only Ken who managed to keep these meetings at boiling point, for we had other area representatives who equalled him in stamina in debating.

One was from the London and South East Area, Dr Will Butler, a cancer specialist with the Medical Research Council and a Vice President of the BMC. Quietly-spoken, tall and reedy, but immensely impressive he was brilliant in presenting the BMC's case to the independent arbitration panel set up to adjudicate on the Mountain Training Dispute by the Alpine Club. This was held in a courtroom format at the Lands Tribunal, and the clerk to the court thought he was some barrister off the Northern circuit retained to represent us.

This dispute was the most long-winded in British climbing history and at the end, with all the parties exhausted and willing to accept the compromise solutions offered by the arbitrators, the BMC mounted a charm offensive on some of those we had been most in conflict with- including the officers of the Sports Council.

Once again, as with John Barry on a similar occasion, we selected an Indian curry house for a get-together, this one being high class and situated just around the corner from their offices in Euston. Bob Pettigrew, one of our senior statesman and a former President, took over running the event, for he was our expert in Indian cuisine as a man who speaks Hindi (having lived for a decade on the sub-continent).

When the time came for everybody to order Bob gathered up each individual's choice then called a waiter over. Obviously out to impress the Sports Council members with the urbanity of members of the BMC, he then proceeded to deliver our order in fluent Hindi. At which the poor waiter became ever wider-eyed, and eventually, unable to restrain himself, interrupted Bob's flow in a high-pitched Brummie accent: 'I've not a bloody clue what your saying. I'm from Birmingham myself - I've never been to India!' At which even the staid members of the Sports Council erupted into laughter. Typically Pettigrew, a master of the double take, passed this off as a 'just testing ' gambit.

Besides lectures and dinners, I was often invited to speak at various academic centres (such as UMIST) and to learned societies, even to the British Institute of Management at one of their get-togethers held at Westland Helicopters. When I had studied psychology in the sixties I had become interested in risk taking and, surprisingly, it was a topic that caused much animated debate. I illustrated my talk with slides of climbing and climbers, but explained this held good for most other environments. I remember staid members of the BIM almost coming to blows about my suggestions that risk taking means progress, means innovation, means job creation. Swedish academics strongly challenged my ideas after a talk I gave at Lulea University in the north of that country in the depths of winter. An advantage of that trip was that it enabled me to get out skiing and ice climbing during my stay, on an all expenses paid basis.

My most unusual invitation came from the Cork Literary and Philosophical Society, the oldest of its kind in Europe. Accompanying me to Ireland on that occasion was Ian Parsons, a good friend who I had climbed with in the USA and many parts of the UK.

We took the trip rather casually, stopping off in Dublin and staying with the presiding spirit of Irish climbing, Joss P. O'Lynam, enjoying some climbing at Dalkey and attending a marvellous ceilidh after a lecture I gave to the Federation of Irish Clubs.

Thus we arrived in Cork much the worse for wear and at the very last minute. The lady who had organised my talk met me on the steps of the City Hall and I could see by her demeanour she was not well pleased. She had dressed for the occasion in a full evening gown, wearing a tiara sparkling with diamonds.

'Where the hell have you been?' she demanded as we crawled out of the car. We had brought it over from England and this alarmed her no end. 'Don't you know it's dangerous to be driving down here with English number plates?' The IRA were then very active in that area, especially around the high security area of Port Laoise. (Her anxiety was borne out when, on our way back to Dublin after our stay in Cork, we were given a 'warning' when we stopped off at a pub there. This caused us to abandon our Guiness and beat a hasty retreat.)

I rushed into that great hall in Cork and up onto the stage to begin my talk, to be greeted by the serried rows of the great and the good of Irish society. The men wore evening dress and the ladies gowns and there was I in jeans, a sweater and a T-shirt; no one had warned me that the evening was to be one of formal dress. I began by apologising, explaining tongue-in-cheek that I had not had time to change due to delays in our journey and that, as I was half a Dillon, I hoped they would understand. This brought a roar of approval and never did my theory of risk-taking receive such rapturous approval. Afterwards, as I signed their speakers' book, I was more than gratified to find that Charles Darwin, Oscar Wilde, W.B. Yeats and George Bernard Shaw had been among those who had trod those same boards ahead of me.

Two Warriors

During my years at the BMC we enjoyed a succession of Presidents and Vice Presidents that very much enhanced the reputation of the Council in the climbing world. It may seem a mystery how anyone becomes the President of the BMC; in fact any group of clubs or sufficient individual members can nominate anyone they like for the office at the AGM. Usually such officers just emerge by natural selection and there is rarely a queue of climbers standing by ready to take on such a time-consuming and thankless task.

Needless to say, I had hair raising adventures with some of them; such as driving up the wrong lane of the M6 with Bob Pettigrew in a thick fog on our way to a meeting in Glasgow, with cars looming out of the night and just missing us like fairground dodgems, and a brilliant day's 'thin' ice climbing with Johnny Cunningham on Scafell. Some of my most memorable times were with a President who is perhaps not so well-known to the mountaineering public, but who is nonetheless an impressive character, namely Tom Price. An erudite climber and an articulate speaker despite his retiring nature.

Tom had been an English student at Liverpool University in 1939 and had known Edwards, Kirkus and McPhee. When war broke out he had been drafted into the Royal Navy as an able-bodied seaman, but finished up commanding a destroyer on D-Day. After the war he had been warden of Eskdale Outward Bound School, cox of the Workington lifeboat and an advisor to the old West Riding Education Authority. When I got to know him he was Dean of Bingley Teacher Training College where he was responsible for training some of our most famous rock climbers as teachers. Pete Gomersall, Jill Lawrence, Pete Livesey, Bonnie Masson, John Barker, John Sheard and later, when they merged with Ilkley College, Ron Fawcett.

Scholar mountaineer, Tom Price when President of the BMC.

Photo Dennis Gray

My first climb with him came about when he phoned me at home one day just before Christmas. He was a little animated for one so quietly spoken: 'Livesey & Co have landed me right in it! They've climbed the College's clock tower, stuck a Christmas tree on top of the flagpole, and hung a pair of frilly knickers off its tip. I've got the Department of Education Inspectors coming tomorrow….all the students have gone for Christmas, so can you come over and climb up with me and get the bloody things off?'

I drove over to Bingley, only a few miles from where I used to live in Guiseley, prepared for an epic climb. It was freezing cold and very windy, but dry. The thought of shinning up a flag pole, atop a clock tower, above a high building sounded a bit gripping and so it turned out.

We could go up inside the building to reach the clock tower, which was an amazing edifice set at the top of a building several storeys high, built from the local gritstone. From there we had to climb out of a small window, then up a sharply curving leaded roof to reach the flagpole. We roped up, with me belayed to one of the supports of the clock, whilst Tom clambered out through the window and into a blustery wind. The lightning conductor was conveniently near the point where he got out onto the lead, and grabbing this he managed to layback up the smooth surface and even place a couple of thread runners into gaps between the strip of metal and the roof's surface.

Twelve o'clock struck. Once the chimes started I was deafened standing alongside the whirring wheels and clattering bells. After what seemed ages the rope became tight and I clambered out of the window and began balancing up the leaded roof. It was as exposed a position as one could wish, with the wind roaring over us. About eight metres above I could see Tom hanging from his rope tied round the bottom of the flagpole.

'Is it safe?' I shouted up.

'Must be, Livesey and company climbed this in the dark,' came the reassuring reply. I joined Tom and looked up at the flagpole shaking in the wind, with the Christmas tree and its adornment about five metres above my head. Once I grabbed hold of the wood it seemed perfectly sound. I closed my eyes to blot out the exposure and began shinning up the pole like any schoolboy who has ever been scrumping.

Up I went, scared witless as the pole whipped and cracked in the wind until I stopped just below the tree. Then I cut the tree down, using the Swiss army knife I had carried up for the purpose, but not before I noticed there was a message on the knickers for Tom from a certain lady climber. I slid back down the pole like a fireman and Tom top roped me back down the leaded roof. He then followed down with his rope wrapped around the base of the flagpole as a safety net. Back in his office drinking tea it was obvious that, far from being annoyed at this student prank, he had loved every moment of the adventure.

When I came to know him better this turned out to be typical of his approach to life. His whole existence has been one great adventure, including canoeing across Canada, skiing the length of the Alps and still instructing climbing and canoeing in Africa into his seventies.

When Tom was President of the BMC and living in Portinscale near Keswick, his great friend and neighbour was burly Bill Peascod, who also became a Vice President of the Council. It would be difficult to find two more interesting people to climb with. Bill had gone down the coal mines at fourteen years of age and begun to climb as a teenager. He made his mark in the history of Lakeland rock with first ascents such as Eagle Front in Buttermere, then as a young man had emigrated to Australia like many other working-class Britons in that period. He continued to climb in Oz but also became first a mining engineer, then a celebrated painter. In the last years of his life he returned to his native Cumbria, set up a studio with his Japanese wife Etsu, and of course continued to climb.

I had known Bill as a boy before he emigrated, meeting him at Castle Rock in Thirlmere and at Gatesgarth Barn in Buttermere. Bill was perhaps the first climber I ever met who was into training. Midweek after his shift down the pit, if he couldn't get out to climb, he visited a weight training gym and his muscular body exemplified what the modern rock jocks would call 'a way honed dude'.

When he returned to Britain in the early 1980s, thirty plus years on and many pounds the heavier, he was still as keen to climb as ever. We met at the Black Dog Inn at Belmont. He loved being in climbing company, talking routes and telling stories about his adventures in the antipodes, and he ended by staying the night. Next morning, despite a long evening on his favourite tipple, malt whisky, he was out on the local gritstone outcrops.

Tom and Bill did not keep up with climbing fashion sartorially; not for them brightly-coloured lycra. Bill looked more like Herman Buhl than Patrick Edlinger when on the crags (wearing a tyrolean hat, a jacket and breeches), and Tom also tended to be traditionally kitted-out. One busy Sunday I was climbing with them, leading 'One Step in the Clouds' at Tremadog. After successfully completing the first sections of the climb we were all gathered together on the large ledge near the top, which is shared by several other routes. A young climber popped out above the layback finish of Vector and, looking up, gasped in absolute amazement at the sight of the two ancient warriors.

'Bloody hell,' he shouted down to his mate. 'There's some guys up here from before the war...I'm seeing things. I must have had one pint too many last night!' And he somehow proceeded to slip and shoot off back down the groove from which he had just emerged, taking a monster of a fall.

The Great Pie Mystery

In the summer of 1986 we organised the first of our Youth Meets at Stanage. The idea of these events was to bring together young climbers from all over the UK and later from abroad. The second event, also at Stanage, was held in June 1987 at the North Lees camp site and on this occasion we had climbers there from the USA, Malta, Israel, Finland and Germany besides Britain, with around a hundred climbers of both sexes attending.

During the day everyone was out climbing, whilst in the evenings we enjoyed lectures in the upstairs room of the Scotsman's Pack Inn in Hathersage. These would be given by the likes of Johnny Dawes, Andy Pollitt, Paul Pritchard and many other leading British climbers. On the final evening we held a quiz and a social and afterwards, exhausted by the week's activities and retiring late, I fell asleep practically comatose.

I was wakened at about 7.30 a.m. by our National Officer, Andy Fanshawe, shaking me as I lay on the floor of the large marquee tent which was the nerve centre of the meet.

'Dennis, the police are here, they're demanding to speak to whoever is in charge.' Hastily, I crawled out of my sleeping bag, dressed and went outside to be greeted by a Police Sergeant and a Constable.

'Are you in charge of this lot?' the Sergeant demanded pointing around the tents on our site. I had hardly nodded my assent when he continued; 'Last night some persons broke into the George Hotel in Hathersage and stole a host of pies from their kitchen. We've followed the trail of crumbs from the hotel and they've led us to your campsite.'

I was impressed at this piece of detection work, for it is a good thirty minutes walk up from Hathersage, via muddy fields, cart tracks and over several stiles. This feat would have done credit to an Inspector Clouseau.

'We wish to interview everyone in these tents,' the Constable informed me (there were about forty of all shapes and sizes). As many of the climbers were under age I was asked to accompany them in loco parentis. My head was throbbing from the previous night's celebrations and I found it hard to concentrate, but I meekly agreed to trail around.

What followed was hilarious, for it was still only early in the morning and

Mr Enthusiasm himself, Andy Fanshawe with Slippery Vic Saunders in the BMC Office 1988
Photo Dennis Gray

many of the bodies inside the tents were still fast asleep. At each awning the police shouted out, 'Police... wake up!' and of course it was thought this was just some of their mates joking. 'Fuck off!' 'Get stuffed!' were just two of the comments, some in English some in more unusual languages like Finnish. At one tent they undid the door and shook a youth in his sleeping bag, who came round to find two large bobbies looming over him.

'What were you doing last night laddie?' The kid panicked and blurted out: 'I was stood on the roof of a speeding minibus sir, pretending to be a surfer.' The two village officers looked at me in surprise, but I was gobsmacked myself by this response. The Sergeant took me on one side and demanded to know if the lad was on drugs. I assured them there was nothing like that in the climbing world. After this they reluctantly accepted that the great pie mystery would have to remain just that. By then they had been around most of the camp and, though the trail of crumbs from the hotel might come up to our site, they had not found so much as a pie crust in any of the tents. Without such evidence they could not nail the culprits. The bobbies prepared to walk back down to Hathersage, but not before gazing suspiciously at us and declaring they'd be keeping an eye on climbers in the future.

Andy Fanshawe was appointed National Officer of the BMC in 1986, and was very much in the mould of his two predecessors, Peter Boardman and Alex MacIntyre, who had both died in the Himalaya in 1982. The summer before he commenced work he had managed a great success in the Karakoram Himalaya by completing the first traverse of Chogolisa along with some friends. We became close friends over the next three years until I retired, as with Peter and Alex before him. He was Mr Enthusiasm and nothing seemed to get him down; not even his motoring exploits which eclipsed all previous breakdown stories, with blown cylinder heads, blasted big ends and broken drive shafts. Perhaps this was to be expected from someone who would work late Friday night, then jump in his car, pick up a mate en route and drive all night to Lochnagar, or Ben Nevis or Creagh Meaghaidh in time to be in position to pull off a big route on the Saturday.

Wiry and of medium height, he was not the world's best rock climber but, like Alex MacIntyre before him, he was an outstanding performer on mixed ground and in the high mountains, as his first ascent of Menlungste West in 1988 proved. In all my years at the BMC he was the most popular staff member, thinking nothing of turning up at meetings in summer in a T-shirt and faded pink rock pants. Most other climbers identified with him and one felt that they would never accuse the Council of being made up of 'stuffy old farts' with 'Fanny' in the ranks.

Andy died on Eagle Ridge, Lochnagar in March 1992. It brought back memories of Peter Boardman and Alex MacIntyre, two other National Officers who died mountaineering and worked tirelessly for the BMC. In trying to make sense of these untimely deaths, I can only respond by declaring that all climbed in order to enjoy the life-affirming qualities of our sport. They had no death wish, but enjoyed their existence through their own individual approach to climbing. It was a privilege to work with them, and I count myself fortunate to have known them and all the other officers and volunteers at the BMC.

Chapter Four

Foreign Bodies at Home

First Contact

British climbing has developed for over a century in its own unique way, partly because of its island isolation, partly because of the complicated weather and geography of the country. The Highlands of Scotland are arctic in winter, while the hills of the Lake District and Snowdonia, being near to the sea, hold as variable a climate as any mountain area. Our outcrop climbing close to the major conurbations and the sea cliffs around the coastline have been developed in a sporting, adventurous manner that has preserved a fine balance between challenge and safety.

Progress has occurred with little or no direct influence from foreign climbers, although initiatives developed elsewhere in the world of mountaineering have made an impact; particularly in areas such as equipment innovation. However, as recently as the early 1960s our home climbing scene had not received many notable visits from overseas climbers.

There were one or two exceptions before the war, including the visit to Wales by Bavarian climbers in 1936, when they pioneered the magnificent Munich climb on Tryfan, and the Slavs' visit to Ben Nevis in 1934, when they ascended their eponymous route. After hostilities ceased it was difficult for UK citizens to travel to climb in different areas of the country, and it was to be a decade or so before visits by overseas climbers were no longer a six day wonder.

I well remember the fuss made about the 'official' visit by Russian climbers to Wales in 1960, at the height of the cold war, but the first climber I met travelling to the UK alone to sample our scene was Rusty Baillie, who arrived from Rhodesia in 1963. A giant of a lad with gingery hair and the expected accent of the country.

Rusty was great fun whilst attending a Rock and Ice Club meet in the Peak District. The weather was damp but I still recall us struggling up a route – 'High Heaven' at Yarncliffe Edge – along with one of the youngest members of our group, Jimmy Fullalove. Perhaps not the wisest choice of venue in such conditions. In the evening Rusty entertained us in the pub with some impressive Matabele songs and dancing and inspired us with his tales from the land of the Kopjes.

The first European I met on a similar mission was the Austrian guide from Mayrhofen, Peter Habeler. Many of the great alpinists of the immediate postwar period were mountain guides – Buhl, Bonatti, Contamine, Rebuffat and Lionel Terray. The chance to climb with such a mountaineer was not to be missed.

Habeler came to Britain at the instigation of some of the members of the UK section of the Austrian Alpine Club but an old friend, Ian Howell, was invited to partner him for a visit to the Avon Gorge. This led on to Peter and Ian coming up to Wales for the weekend where I met up with them in the Llanberis Pass. The young Austrian was a striking figure and looked every inch the Alpine guide; lithely built, blond-haired and blue-eyed. He was immaculately turned out, in contrast to Ian and myself dressed in torn jeans, holey sweaters and knackered boots.

This was in the Spring of 1965 and, although by then I had climbed a lot in the Alps and twice been to the Himalaya, I had never shared a rope with one of the Continentals. Whenever I had met up with such climbers in centres like the Dolomites or Chamonix it had appeared that the Europeans were not nearly as proficient on rock as our own Rock and Ice leaders. Habeler was to change these perceptions.

Peter was keen to climb on Clogwyn du'r Arddu and, although the weather was inclement on the Saturday morning, we walked up via the Snowdon railway track to finally stop under the East Buttress of the cliff. We looked around us at the mist-shrouded smooth rock walls, trying to decide on a possible objective. By then it had begun to rain so we decided to investigate the sheltered East Gully. We scrambled up the wet greasy slabs that bar the way, each taking his own line. The galloping Tyrolean shot ahead of us, though eventually we reunited under the East Gully Wall -a complicated traversing route up a sixty metre high buttress pioneered by Brown and Whillans in 1953.

To say it looked uninviting was an understatement, with water running down the steep rock faces. If it had been up to me I would have immediately retreated back down the way we had come. My companions were made of sterner stuff; the ropes were pulled out of their rucksacks so I reluctantly tied on and set up a belay. This was before the development of sit harnesses and we simply knotted the hawser laid nylon ropes around our middles using a bowline.

Habeler set out leading in his mountain boots. It was immediately obvious that he was a supremely confident climber from the way he moved up the rock face. On reaching an in situ piton at the crux he balanced up and clipped into it and, pulling up on this, he was soon over the steep bulge above. After a short hesitation he seemed to gather himself and whoosh! he moved up the rest of the pitch so fast I could hardly play the rope out to keep up with him. He pulled himself onto a ledge at nearly the half height of the wall where he made fast and then he was calling down for us to follow him.

Ian set forth and followed with difficulty. He found that reaching for the piton was awkward, for Peter had not left a long sling for him to reach for the karabiner. Then I climbed up after him, experiencing even more trouble. I am ashamed to report I let the side down by shouting rudely at Habeler to 'get that fucking rope in', doing nothing to help Anglo-European relations. After this poor effort I felt I needed to redeem myself and elected to take over the lead.

The second pitch begins with an airy traverse leftwards, and as I started out on this I placed one of my secret weapons, a nut. By that date they had begun to be manufactured in the UK, and Peter was impressed as I slipped a MOAC chock into a convenient crack. In spite of what I've read in recent years, nuts were not developed on the Continent but first used on British crags in the fifties, when ordinary machine nuts on slings were jammed in cracks. However, they were not universally accepted or commercially produced until the early sixties.

My heart was in my mouth as I reached delicately for an arete, then I stepped down around a corner, avoiding a large detached flake, and bridged across into a groove. The greasy rock had me marking time whilst balancing on the vibram soles of my Terray mountain boots, but I knew that once into the groove I was OK. I had climbed the route before and it was easy from that point up to the belay set in a sheltered nook below the final crack. I organised some more running belays, then climbed over a loose block and scampered up the rest of the pitch to gain the safety of the stance.

The others followed with increasing difficulty, for by now the weather had gone beyond a joke. It was hailing and, looking up the final vertical corner crack, I was beginning to wonder if it would go. 'I vill lead,' declared our Austrian guide once both he and Ian were safely with me. Taking some additional slings from us Brits he set forth.

Anyone who thinks that Continental climbers cannot jam should have witnessed the exhibition that followed. It was textbook arm jams, knees, hands. Once again, despite the conditions, Peter flowed up the pitch, stopping only to place a couple of slings over chockstones for runners. Fifteen metres of climbing in bad weather in just a few minutes.

'Bloody hell, Ian, this guy's a genius!' I stuttered with chattering teeth.

'You should have seen him in action at Avon,' my companion responded. We followed the Tyrolean with difficulty. At the top we stood shaking hands in driving rain and made plans to meet up in Austria that summer, keen to attempt some of the routes Peter had pioneered on his homeland cliffs. I was also intrigued that he was an artist, a painter of glass, as this mirrored my own interest in fine art. We did go out to Mayrhofen later that year, but it turned out to be the worst summer in the Alps in living memory. The whole of the Inn valley was flooded and we never did get to climb with Habeler again.

In 1975 Habeler made a breakthrough in the Himalaya along with Reinhold Messner, when together they made the ascent of the North West Face of Hidden Peak in the Karakoram. Habeler went on to make the first climb of Everest without Oxygen in 1978.

The leading American climber, Royal Robbins, came to stay at my parents home in Leeds with his wife, Liz, in the spring of 1966. It is hard for anyone who was not around in that era to appreciate the legendary status that the Californian climber and his peers had built up in world mountaineering circles. If British and Continental climbers had led the field in the fifties, it was the Americans who were centre stage in the sixties. Royal had pioneered great climbs like Salethe Wall on El Capitan in 1960 and the Dru Direct in 1965. One of the secrets of their success was the equipment they had developed for big wall climbing, particularly hard steel pitons.

The chance to meet and climb with Robbins and his wife was another rare opportunity. They stayed for a few days and we climbed on several gritstone outcrops and edges including Almscliff, Brimham and Curbar. Robbins was one

of the calmest, most controlled personalities I have met climbing, matched by
his fellow-countryman the legendary
John Gill. Liz was also a most interesting
companion and very obviously a strong
character who supported Royal to the
hilt in his climbs.

When not climbing, Robbins pre-
ferred to play chess, a game I abhor for I
find it mentally exhausting, and he only
talked when he felt the need. I particularly remember him telling how he instructed skiing in the winter, a sport at
which he had excelled when young, in
order to be able to climb in the summer.
He contrasted these two existences, one
with all the trappings of the consumer
society and the other poverty-stricken,
living out of the back of a van on the
road to climbing destinations all over the
Western USA.

Royal Robbins at Gogarth in 1966.
Photo Dennis Gray

Royal was an equipment innovator like Don Whillans and during his visit he
climbed in his 'Robbins', which were a blue suede 'kletterschue' type rock boot.
He was most impressive crack climbing, where his Yosemite training allowed him
to cream up routes like the Right Eliminate at Curbar Edge, a grunt of an off-
width. He also loved bouldering and one night at Almscliff he had set himself the
task of climbing a slab to the right side of the Black Wall without using his hands.
This was something that was then all the rage in US climbing circles. He tried
this again and again and finally succeeded in the gloom of twilight. Later that
night he confessed in the pub, under the influence of Tetley's bitter to us locals,
'Your climbs are small, but perfect gems!' This was a catch phrase which caught
on and was to be repeated and quoted in several articles in the days ahead.

Tony Barley and myself subsequently returned to Almscliff and worked this
'no hands' problem and eventually we both managed it. In later decades I did try
it again, but could never repeat this feat. I must show it to the younger generation, but doubtless they will spring up it at the very first attempt!

The Good Doss Guide
After I joined the BMC my family home magically seemed to have appeared in
some kind of 'International Good Doss' guide for climbers. Although some who
stayed were on planned visits, others simply turned up. Typical was one night in
the early 1970s, when I had just arrived home late from London and my wife
and I were putting our children to bed. The phone rang and a voice declared, 'We
are eight Swedish climbers and we need some help with information about
places to stay and climb in Britain.'

'Oh?' I responded somewhat wearily. 'Where are you?' thinking they would say Stockholm or Gothenberg. The voice hesitated, then informed me they were in a telephone box around the corner from the house, so I felt compelled to invite them to come to see me. Being Swedes they were enormous and, though we had a small, three-bedroom-box of a house, they ended up staying the night. There were bodies everywhere!

Over the next few years we were to entertain some truly interesting personalities at our various homes in Guiseley. Some characters were involved in such dubious activities that I wonder now why we never attracted the attention of MI5. One who came to stay unannounced was Tobin Sorenson, a young American climber. Tobin was deeply religious and it transpired that his climbing activities were in part a cover so that he could smuggle bibles into Eastern Europe!

He was an accomplished all-round mountaineer and made the fourth ascent of the Eiger Direct climb in October 1977, along with Alex MacIntyre. Though powerfully built, he looked like a choirboy with a round, angelic face. He often wore a suit when he wasn't climbing and on Sunday declined to climb at all, preferring to preach at our local Baptist Church in Guiseley. Once he stepped into the pulpit he was a real life Elmer Gantry, all hell fire and damnation!

I had to journey to a meeting at Plas y Brenin and Tobin decided to accompany me. We picked up Ken Wilson en route and Tobin and myself entered into a debate about religion and the worth of the New Testament. It was the only occasion I have ever known Ken silenced. This heated exchange continued once inside the Brenin, with the result that we actually sent Ken to sleep!

Tobin once confessed that he had heard voices from God telling him to do certain climbs and that he would protect him. As an agnostic I received this information with scepticism, but his climbing career certainly notched up some amazing successes. Amongst other climbs he had made a difficult new route solo on Huandoy in the Andes and many fine ascents in the Alps, including the first ascent of the Dru Couloir Direct, besides the Eiger Direct and the Matterhorn North Face Solo in winter. Add to this list climbs of some of the hardest rock pitches in the world, such as an early free lead of the Naked Edge in Colorado. His test piece, the Edge at Tahquitz in California, still remains just that. When visiting the crag in 1995 I was interested to learn that it still has not received many repeats. Tobin died at the age of twenty-five in October 1981 whilst attempting a solo ascent of the North Face of Mt Alberta in the Canadian Rockies.

Another frequent visitor to my house during this period was the Polish mountaineer and dissident, Janus Onyskiewicz. He and his English wife, Alison Chadwick, had made their home in Leeds where Janus lectured at the university in pure mathematics. We enjoyed some good days out together on the gritstone where the Pole was happy to second routes like Valkyrie and Three Pebble Slab at Froggatt and Almscliff's classic Green Crack, although his Himalayan record was outstanding (including successful ascents of K2 and Gasherbrum II). Alison held the record for the highest mountain first climbed by a woman (and still does), when she summited Gasherbrum III in 1975 with a Polish ladies' expedition.

We enjoyed some good times talking climbing, climbers and politics back at our house. Sadly, the turmoil that was happening back in his homeland and the death of Alison on Annapurna in October 1978 made him decide to return to Poland. (Alison died in a mysterious fall at around 7,000m, when she and her climbing companion, Vera Watson, were killed.) Janus became the Western spokesman for the Solidarity movement, was arrested and spent years in the notorious Bialoleka prison near Warsaw. All his British friends organised petitions and letters to try to secure his release but to no avail, other than a note from Janus himself to assure us that, compared to the bivouac he had endured high on K2, jail was a doddle!

For once good triumphed, with perestroika leading to a revolution in the Eastern bloc and the setting up of democratic structures. Janus became a major political figure in his own country, a member of the government and a Minister to boot!

A South African couple arrived at our house rather mysteriously one night in the late 1970s, one of whom was Dave Cheesmond. Dave was to go on to make some outstanding ascents in the Canadian Rockies but sadly died with the well-known American climber, Catherine Freer, in Alaska. They had barely got inside the house when Ken Wilson, the voice of British mountaineering, was on the phone.

'I hear you are now harbouring white fascists from the apartheid regime in South Africa contrary to the agreed policies of the climbing world!' How Ken had found out about our guests was a mystery - he seems to have informants under every boulder in the country - and just who had decided these 'policies of the climbing world' I decided not to challenge.

It gave me the greatest pleasure to be able to say to him, 'Ken, Ken the poor buggers are emigrating to Canada, they just cannot take the South African regime any longer.' A long silence followed, then a snapped 'Oh, that's OK then!' and the receiver was jammed down.

Throughout the seventies our family lived in a small detached modern house in a discreet close in Guiseley, a commuter town for Leeds and Bradford. The comings and goings of our friends were watched by neighbours through lace curtains with increasing interest. None more so than in February 1979 when six French climbers stayed at the house on their way to and from Scotland for winter climbing, and on both occasions I was away on BMC business. This team included Jean Marc Boivin, Jean Franck Charlet and Rene Ghilini. During this visit Jean Marc pioneered a classic route at Lochnagar with Brian Sprunt; the 'French Connection' on the face to the right of the Pinnacle Gully.

Boivin returned to the UK to speak at the 1980 Buxton conference where he showed films and spoke of his enthusiasm for Alpine ice climbing, hang gliding and the new sport of paragliding. Sadly, we learnt of his death later that decade in a freak paragliding accident in South America.

After the 1980 Buxton Conference the two American climbers Warren Harding and Henry Barber came to stay with us in Guiseley. On the second night of their

Joanna Barry stripping at Buxton.   Photo Terry Tullis

A Musical Interlude

An abiding interest of my family has been music. My father and mother were pianists (my father played many instruments badly), my sister was a professional singer, my former wife and my sons are musicians and my nephew and his Israeli wife are both opera singers. Over the years it was quite a treat to welcome climbers who had similar interests to our home.

Kurt Diemberger entertained us one evening playing on the guitar singing his own compositions, including some songs he had written in Inuit which he had learnt whilst climbing in the Arctic. Pat Ament the American climber was another who sang for his supper, playing the piano and singing songs from his LP's. But the biggest surprise was Yves Ballu.

Yves came to Britain in 1983 when he was head of the French Ministry of Sport, as chef de mission of a group who visited the UK to study the design and management of climbing walls. The party included Christine Grosjean, Patrick Edlinger and Jean Marc Blanch, who was to become the leading French wall designer of his generation.

Graham Desroy and myself drove them the length and breadth of the land showing them every type of artificial structure then in vogue. Throughout Yves remained aloof, occasionally donning rock boots but more usually consulting with his officials about costs and design features.

At the end of the week we fetched up in West Yorkshire and, after a session at the Leeds University wall, we repaired to Guiseley for a farewell supper. After consuming a few beers, Yves sat down at our upright grand piano and began to play a piece I recognised from a recent French film, a technically difficult work with complicated chord sequences. My eldest son, no mean pianist himself, enquired admiringly who had composed this rather unusual music. We were rather stunned when Yves confessed it had been him!.

Music took off in a big way at the Buxton conferences, especially the cabarets: all-singing, all-dancing, mickey-taking events with song parodies written especially for the occasion. My favourite remains the Miss Buxton contest of 1984, won by Donna Whillans. The contest had a serious purpose - to help raise funds to purchase the Alex MacIntyre Hut at Onich. John Barry, Nat Allen, Dave Alsop, John Stevenson, Whillans and myself all appeared in drag, compered by Alistair Macdonald. Judges were a panel of women climbers chaired by Rosie Smith.

After her interview Joanna Barry was carried away by such exposure to fame and decided to strip to her undies, promising the capacity crowd that she would present the full Monty if they would double their donations to our good cause! And he did and ran off to the biggest ovation of the evening. I have always been surprised that such harmless horseplay will always incite 'Disgusted of Tunbridge Wells' to write complaining about the demise of civilisation as we know it. There on my desk at the BMC on the following Monday morning was a letter from an outraged defender of public morals.

Rack of Nuts

One of the specialist committees of the BMC is the International Committee. They look after expedition advice and support and have organised many visits by overseas climbers to this country, either for summer rock climbing or winter mountaineering in Scotland. This, coupled with the biennial Buxton conferences, meant that during my tenure at the Council I was able to meet and climb with some of the leading climbers in the world, including the Italian Renato Casarroto and the Pole Woytek Kurtyka in 1975.

The Italian was a member of a group of eight of his countrymen who visited North Wales in April of that year. In contrast to the time I climbed on Clogwyn du'r Arddu with Peter Habeler, the climb I made on that same cliff with Renato was in excellent conditions. We ascended the East Gully Grooves, a memorable time for me because not only was my companion fun to be with but also, although he had made some of the hardest ascents in the Alps and Dolomites, he had not used a rack of nuts until our climb together. To say he liked them is an understatement, and every time he found a good placement he let out a cry of joy as he pushed in one of my new wires. Unfortunately, like many other climbers doing this for the first time, he then weighted them so heavily that removing the gear after him was harder than climbing the route.

Once again, as in the fifties, it was British climbers who helped to change the face of climbing around the world during the late sixties and into the seventies. Climbers like Robbins took nuts back to the USA and began to use them instead of pitons which scar the rock so badly.

Following the development of the sit harness by Don Whillans in 1970 as a means to a more comfortable and secure means of prusiking fixed ropes in the Himalaya, climbers even felt differently about falling off. Before the Whillans' harness, with the rope tied directly around the waist, every climber feared falling into space. I was at the Tre Cime area of the Dolomites in 1962 when a British climber fell off the Yellow Edge to dangle free from the rock face and by the time a rescue party could reach him he had choked to death. Nowadays, in a sit harness, you would just hang around until you've sorted out some means of extricating yourself.

The original Whillans' harness has been further developed, for it had an alarming propensity for trapping male genitals. I know of one climber who badly damaged one of his testicles after a long fall. Once, climbing in the Belgium Ardennes at a cliff called Darve, I became so constricted that I screamed out loud, much to the consternation of my partner, the late Claudio Barbier. There are now so many types of sit harness that, if Whillans was still alive and getting a royalty on them all, he might be a millionaire!

We must have looked like climbing technocrats to some visiting climbers in the 1970s, but one Polish climber confirmed it was still the man and not the gear that mattered. This was Woytek Kurtyka, who I had the privilege of meeting in the Autumn of 1975, when eight of his countrymen came to the Peak District and North Wales.

It was the first time a group of Polish climbers had been allowed to visit Great Britain. Dennis Davis (who had made the first ascent of Nuptse in 1961), had recently been working in Poland and had returned with a wife and stories of a Pole who was a climbing machine, known as 'the Beast'. He was the hardest physical specimen Dennis had ever encountered. Together they had made a difficult winter ascent in the High Tatra, when their main source of sustenance had been a large bottle of Vodka!

I climbed with Woytek at Stoney Middleton where I was talked into leading Boat Pusher's Wall by Tom Proctor, the local expert. I would never have committed myself to attempting the climb without the Stoney Master on the ground giving me the beta. Although only about fifteen metres in height, it is a serious lead. Steep wall climbing is followed by a harrowing traverse left along a break, to finish with a hard series of mantels on rock which was far from firm. Friends would make this top section well protected today, but at that time I was contemplating a long fall if I made a mistake or a hold broke as I made the final pull out at the top. With modern equipment the pitch is graded E3 5c, so after succeeding in reaching the top and belaying safely I was feeling smug; that is until my Polish partner began to climb.

Wearing trainers on his feet, because the climbers of the Eastern bloc could not obtain rock boots, and tieing directly on around his waist, he came up the route so fast I could not take the rope in quick enough. I ought to have realised from my own visit to Poland in 1967 that there would be climbers behind the Iron Curtain as competent as any in the world.

Dennis Davis later confirmed that Woytek was 'the Beast' who had climbed with him in the Tatra. In retrospect, it is not so surprising that Kurtyka went on to become one of the foremost names in modern alpinism with his first ascent of the West Wall of Gasherbrum IV, achieved with Robert Schauer the Austrian in

1985 and still a benchmark for difficulty in the Himalaya.

In spring 1976 I had the pleasure of taking some German climbers to Almscliff and Ilkley. Among them were Manfred Sturm and Reinhard Karl. Rheinhard was to become one of the most influential German climbers of his generation. The standard of free rock climbing in Germany was not what it was to become in the next decade following the example of Wolfgang Gullich, Stefan Glowacz and Reinhard himself. I have never seen so many leader falls in such a short space of time as on that day at Almscliff.

Over the years I have taken many overseas visitors to our local outcrops and some, such as the Czechoslovakian climbers who visited in 1986, have been impressive whilst others, particularly those from limestone areas, find the roundness and lack of incut holds with elephant bottom finishes difficult to cope with. It did not help that most of the Germans insisted on climbing in high mountain boots. My climbing companion, Tim Leach, was helping me show our visitors around. Once, not being tied down and himself small and compact, Tim was pulled so far up the crag by one of our falling guests when he parted company from Zig Zag Direct, that he met his leader on the way down and they both ended up lying winded on the ground.

I kept in touch with Reinhard over the years and, inspired by his visit to Britain, he really worked at his free rock climbing. Two years after this visit he pioneered the 'Pumprisse' in the Kaisergebirge along with Helmut Kiene. This was the first route to be graded VII in the Alps and later that same year he climbed Everest along with Robert Schauer. Over the next few years he climbed everywhere from Patagonia to the Karakoram and the Llanberis Pass.

In 1982 I arranged to climb with Reinhard in the Frankenjura, after we had both attended and spoken at the climbers symposium during the Trento film festival. By that date the younger German climbers looked to Karl for their inspiration, for not only was he a fine mountaineer but a good writer and brilliant photographer. His books and articles were extremely popular and he won both literary and photographic awards, but on reacquaintance I always found he was still the same unaffected person I had met in Britain.

The weather turned from bad to worse and we abandoned our plans to go climbing and said our goodbyes, for he was leaving shortly for the Himalaya. I was never to see him again; that summer he was killed on Cho Oyo falling into a crevasse.

In September 1978 a joint Swedish/Norwegian group visited the UK and climbed in the Lake District, West Yorkshire at Almscliff and Malham and in the Peak District. This party included Hans Christian Doseth and Ulf Hansen, two free climbers who successfully ascended outcrop routes like the Sloth at the Roaches and the Western Front at Almscliff during their stay. Our team of helpers included British climbers Steve Bancroft, Choe Brooks and Steve Bell, and it was a most enjoyable meet both on and off the crags.

While we were climbing at the Roaches I decided to show our guests 'Brown's Mantel'. The Rock and Ice climbers of the 1950s were as keen on bouldering in the Peak District as the Sheffield freakies of today. Two problems which they climbed stand out, the first at Froggatt Edge set on the slab immediately left of 'Joe's Mantel' (which only Eric Price could then climb, although subsequently a vital finger hold has been mysteriously enlarged though it is still graded 6b/c), and the other a mantelshelf at the Roaches. This was set on an undercut boulder and was a one-handed mantel over a roof which I had only ever seen Joe Brown achieve. Despite the best efforts of Doseth, Bancroft and Hansen they could not get off the ground, and they were mightily impressed when I told them I had seen Joe climb this 'when I wer' a lad'.

This illustrates that no generation has ever made a great leap forward in climbing standards. Progress is slow and though ever-upwards, improvement from year to year is usually slight. The hardest problem I ever saw Arthur Dolphin climb was at Ilkley Quarry in 1952; Earwig Rib Direct straight from the ground, a problem he had first achieved during the 1940s. This has also subsequently had a bastard finger-hold cut into the rock, but is still graded 6a. Dolphin climbed it wearing gym pumps and therefore it must have been at least 6b before it was mutilated. Fifty years on with improved equipment, applied training and much more leisure time to climb standards have improved, but not by as much as some pundits like to suggest.

Breaking Boundaries
Many of the International meets that the BMC organised relied heavily on voluntary effort by many different British climbers. Usually we recruited a host team who helped to drive minibuses, guide foreigners up routes, provide local knowledge or organise social events. Arrangements were usually made in advance, but on one occasion a spontaneous meeting led to one of the more memorable events.

On the evening of August 31st 1985 Al Rouse (a BMC Vice President), and myself were awaiting the arrival of a team of eight French climbers led by Jean-Claud Droyer and including Isabelle Patissier and Alain Gherson. This was at Manchester Piccadilly station and their train was late. The rain was drumming so heavily on the concourse roof it was difficult to hold a conversation and looking around I spied a familiar figure wandering aimlessly, looking up at the walls of the building. I recognised the figure immediately as Johnny Dawes.

He caught sight of us and walked over. I explained I was waiting to take a crowd of French climbers to Wales and introduced Johnny to Al Rouse. Johnny immediately asked Al if he could come along and brushed aside Al's worries about his lack of gear, confident he had everything he needed in the tiny rucksack on his back containing rock boots, chalk bag and harness. It turned out Dawes had been mooching round looking for new routes, having already pioneered some very hard bouldering ascents in and around Central Manchester!

We made the long drive to Plas y Brenin and after midnight that night we crawled into the bunkhouse exhausted after a reception party and disco. Though fully clothed, Johnny Dawes was complaining of the cold as he lay between Rouse and I on a large communal bunk without sleeping bag or blankets of his own. I have to admit that it was surprisingly nippy that night despite the fact it was summer. Then Dawes had a brainwave; he crawled out of the bunk and onto the floor of the hut which, being a Sports Council property, was well carpeted with an expensive brown thick cord matting. He lay out on this and, grabbing its edge, slowly began to roll himself up inside it as a protection against the freezing conditions. Grunting and groaning he squirmed about the bunk house floor until he had accomplished his mission, at which he announced he was now warm enough to sleep.

Rouse was so intrigued by these happenings that he couldn't resist turning his head torch on and pointing it down onto the floor to inspect the end result. This invited some agitated mumblings from our French guests who, understandably, were by now convinced that Dawes was not quite all there. 'Bloody hell Johnny! That's the best imitation of a packet of Rollos I have ever seen,' chuckled Al, who was very witty when on song. 'But how will you get out of it if you need a pee in the night?'

The next day there was much earnest activity up on the crag at Tremadog. The French met their guides; Nick Dixon, Mark Leach, Claudie Dunn and Craig Smith and rushed from Vulcan to Vector. But this was not the Rouse way, nor was it Dawes' style. The pair of them spent the morning sitting in Eric Jones' cafe swapping stories and drinking brews. It was obvious that there was some kind of affinity growing between them and when they finally decided to go climbing later that day they elected to try for a new route.

The sheer smooth wall to the right of Gurr-eagle at Bwlch y Moch had not been climbed, although several parties had tried it. Its steepness and lack of pro-tection had repulsed all comers. Dawes and Rousey decided they would try to put this right and set forth to conquer this last great challenge of South Snow-don. Al climbed up the easy introductory slab of Oberon to reach a good ledge under the unclimbed objective; he then set up several belays and brought Johnny up to him. After this he transferred his own considerable armoury of equipment onto his younger companion's harness, including a hammer and a sheaf of pitons. Dawes adjusted all this gear to his liking and then set forth to climb.

To cut a short story down, Johnny did awfully well until he was about ten metres above Al, where he ran into serious difficulties. He stopped, marking time on a sloping ledge with poor handholds. He could not find any protection and, with no runners between him and his second, his situation might have been described as serious. On Rouse's advice he decided to place a leaf peg in the only possible placement, a nearby hairline crack. Dawes was not used to placing pegs and so, on instructions from his mentor, he gave the piton a few taps into place. Al was insistent that he leave it so it was not hard for him to remove; he had no wish to lose what he considered to be one of his best iron men.

Johnny tied it off and went for it on Al's advice. A couple of metres higher he found himself in even worse trouble and, slapping wildly at the arete above him, announced 'I can't make it. I'm coming off. I'm going to jump for it!' Some way above his head he could see what appeared to be a good hold.

'Is that wise?' queried Rouse, just as Johnny leapt up the crag like an Olym-pian to grab at a ledge high above him, only to find it was a sloping illusion.

Whoops! His hands slipped off and down he came, first onto the piton which twanged before it shot out, stopping his flight slightly for an instant. Then he was hurtling down the rock face once more and falling clear through space. Whilst this had been going on Jean-Claud, Isabelle, Muriel and Alain with their British guides had gathered at the base of Merlin Direct and Gurr-eagle, getting ready to climb. Suddenly they realised their danger as Dawes headed down in their direction and they scattered willy nilly.

Down, down came Johnny and crash! he hit the slab below Rouse and then slid down it heading straight for the deck. 'Whoa boy, whoa!' Al stopped him just before he hit the ground and, amazingly, once he had been lowered to terra firma Dawes stood up in triumph, bruised and battered but not seriously hurt. Soon he was laughing at his amazing escape.

'You know Jean-Claud?' Rouse shouted down to the French captain, happy at having performed a minor miracle by getting in so much rope as Johnny had been falling. 'You cannot fall like that in France!'

'Why ees that?' demanded Droyer.

'It's all those bloody bolts mate, they tend to get in the way!' replied our Vice President.

On these meets I witnessed some fantastic climbing, but a few climbers stand out above all the others. One was sixteen-year-old Jason Stern from New Palz, USA, who led routes like London Wall in the Peak District on the Youth Meet held at Stanage in 1987. He climbed with such maturity it was obvious that he had a great talent as an all-rounder. Despite subsequently being successful in the arena of climbing competitions and even, in one case, becoming a World Champion, some of our other visitors could not have emulated his performances.

Another impressive performer was the young Slovak, Svetozlar Polaczech. He came to Britain with a Czechoslovak party in 1986 and I had the privilege of

Joav Nir (Israel) and Jason Stern (USA) at Stanage in 1987.
Photo Dennis Gray

climbing with them in Yorkshire, the Peak District and Cornwall. Svetio was then 20 years old and as good as anyone I have met. When he was in the UK he not only soloed hard outcrop climbs but 6b routes in Cornwall on sight. My heart was in my mouth on those occasions, especially one night at Sennen Cove when he was having a bit of a struggle fifteen metres off the ground soloing an E6 called Demolition. Fortunately, local guide Mark Edwards arrived when the Slovak had been stuck for some little while and we managed to point him in the right direction by sign language, for Svetio spoke no English.

Along with Svetio on that visit was another great climber, the powerfully built Czech Thomas Czarda, who was responsible for many of the hardest routes on Bohemian sandstone. During his time in Britain Thomas comfortably led climbs like Superjam in Cornwall and Strawberries in North Wales. It was a joy to take them to outcrops like Caley Crags near my home, where they easily outperformed any previous overseas visitors I had been there with.

Svetozlar Polaczech soloing Oedipus at Froggatt in 1986 wearing his carpet slippers, car tyre rubber stuck to the soles!
Photo Dennis Gray

The amazing thing about Svetio's climbing was that it was accomplished wearing carpet slippers. Known to the Czechos as Bochkary, with rubber from old car tyres stuck on the bottom! When he was in the Peak District wearing these he soloed Down Hill Racer Direct and many other hard routes, much to the amazement of the locals from Sheffield. But the really good thing about this group was their sense of fun and good companionship. Thomas Czarda, for instance, found it unbelievable that after a day out on the crags some young British climbers now miss out on a visit to the pub.

In 1988 the surgeon and climber Steve Bollen and myself visited Prague where we helped to chair a medical conference. Afterwards we visited Bratislava in Slovakia to climb with Svetio and his friends and from there they took us climbing in an area in the far east of their country and into Russia. We presented our friend with a pair of Mega rock boots and, overjoyed, the next day he abandoned his slippers and led me up ten climbs on a nearby limestone escarpment. I was shattered and declared defeat but he proceeded to solo some of the hardest climbs in the area, mostly on sight. Thus it was with the utmost sadness I learnt a short while later of his death in a freak accident whilst working repairing the roof of an apartment building in Bratislava.

I am still in contact with many of the climbers who visited Britain over the years. A few, like the German climber Erik Henseleit who died so tragically on

Shivling in 1987, became close friends. Erik came to Britain on his own and climbed with Al Rouse and myself. Right up to his death we wrote regularly to each other and because of such friendships I have no time for those who believe that British, French or American or any other style of climbing and climbers are superior to the other. Each country has developed its mode of climbing because of its geography but climbers have similar motivations wherever they're from.

The Sugar Loaf Pinnacle, Zadiel canyon, Slovakia.
Photo Dennis Gray

Some who came were truly unforgettable such as John Gill, Alex Kunaver and Walter Bonatti and I am sure they left an indelible impression on all who met them. If you travel widely you will find that there is a welcoming climbing community in many countries of the world. I hope that British climbers will always be happy to meet and to help any activist from abroad who ventures to our shores.

Chapter Five

Foreign Bodies Away

Hazard

When I started to climb in 1947 the idea of a visit abroad was so far removed as to be beyond the bounds of possibility. Clothing, food, petrol and many other essentials were rationed and Europe was still devastated by the war, but slowly during the next decade living standards improved. My older companions began to visit the Alps and they regaled us with many epic stories on their return. It required real initiative for working class climbers like Glasgow's Creagh Dhu, the Bradford Lads and Manchester's Rock and Ice to journey to destinations like Chamonix or Cortina.

My first trip to the Continent was in September 1955 as part of an athletic team visiting Austria, which was still occupied by the victorious Allies. We travelled by train to Innsbruck in the French zone; journeying through France was an unforgettable experience as the damage caused by the war was still in evidence. Our ancient steam train broke down at Chalons and we had to sit around for twenty-four hours until a replacement engine arrived from Paris. The last time I travelled by French railways was on the TGV from Paris to Venice. How I envied our Gallic friends' superb modern railway system. What a contrast between those two journeys!

During those early years of the return to the Alps by the British you needed to be keen to travel. Public transport systems were unreliable and there were no motorways to ride on (except for the prewar autobahns in West Germany) for those fortunate enough to own vehicles. In the case of many working-class climbers motorbikes were the only means of transport. Carriageways were badly surfaced and lethally narrow, so driving to a destination like the Dolomites could take several days.

The prize for initiative must go to Morty Smith, who set out as a sixteen-year-old in the mid fifties with only £12 to hitchhike to Chamonix for his annual two weeks' holiday. He successfully reached his destination, climbed five routes, bought himself a pair of Terray mountain boots and hitched home again to arrive one day late at his workplace, with £2 left from his original stake. He was rewarded by almost being sacked!

In 1958 when I accompanied Joe Brown, his wife Valerie and Morty to Chamonix on the train it was a real adventure for me, although the others had already travelled that route before. The weather in the channel crossing from Dover to Calais was stormy and the ferry started bucking like a bronco once out of the harbour. This was before the modern ships with stabilisers and, though Joe was probably as good a climber as any in the world, he was a lousy sailor. He lay out on the deck going greener and greener and becoming sicker and sicker. Some old biddy who was up on the rails parting with her breakfast became convinced we were about to sink and insisted that we join her in a prayer, then

Eric Beard, Dennis Gray and Celso Degasper (Guide) during the filming of 'Hazard' in the Dolomites 1959.

Photo Toni Hiebeler

she sang in a high shrill voice 'Abide with me'. Throughout the next three weeks of our Alpine campaign Joe's greatest concern was about the return crossing of the channel. Inevitably, when this came about the sea was like a mill pond.

In 1959 Eric Beard, Brian Fuller, Eric Metcalf and myself drove out to the Dolomites to meet up with Joe Brown and Don Roscoe who were helping to make a film, 'Hazard'. It took us several days to drive from Yorkshire to Cortina, including driving through the middle of Paris. During the drive we were impressed by the gung-ho attitude of the French drivers, especially in towns and at roundabouts. It did not matter who was on a major or minor road, the rule was that you always had to give way to any vehicle coming in from the right. Out in the countryside this seemed to include cart tracks and on several occasions we were nearly wiped out by other motorists who turned into our path from the most minor roads without warning and at high speed.

We spent a month in the Dolomites filming under the direction of Tom Stobart, the man who had made the 1953 film of the ascent of Everest. Hazard was the story of two climbers who worked in a steel works, one of whom was a careful, safety-conscious type, the other an easy-going careless fellow. For their summer holidays they decide to journey to the Dolomites to attempt a major first ascent, during which the careful climber is hit by stone fall. He is held by his companion through a piton and, though unconscious, is lowered safely down to the belay.

Mr Careless then sets out to bring a rescue party but falls on one of the abseils because he has placed the anchor badly and not tested the single piton from which he is suspended. He lands on a small ledge after a long plunge through space, sustaining multiple injuries.

Meanwhile Mr Careful regains consciousness, realises what has happened and manages to climb solo down the face to alert a rescue party to help Mr Careless. Once he is finally rescued Mr Careless realises the error of his ways and from then on he becomes Mr Safety Conscious both at work and out on the crags.

Hazard was made as a safety film for industry but it went out on general release and, deservedly, received many plaudits for its realism, especially the scene where the piton pulls and Mr Careless falls down the cliff. We climbers took it in turns to double for the film stars, with Joe leading some hard free pitches, but as there were no professional stuntmen we drew lots as to who would take on the fall scene by Mr Careless. I drew the short straw. When I think about it now I realise how naive we were, for the actors were being highly paid for their work whilst we climbers were being rewarded with just a few pounds a day. I was paid an extra £5 for doubling in the fall scene!

The filming was done one wet and misty day at the Cinque Torre. Tom Stobart had found a ledge about eight metres off the ground on the west side of the Torre Grande on which he could set up the cameras. Before shooting commenced Eric Beard and I carried up sack after sack filled with grass and we placed these on the scree, directly below the fall line I would take.

Filming is a terribly slow business and Hazard was no exception. Many of the scenes were shot over again for the actors sometimes forgot their lines or there was a problem with the light or with continuity. Sometimes scenes were shot and if the Director didn't like them once he had seen the rushes they were filmed again. I made it plain to Tom that I was only prepared to do the fall once and that it was up to them to get it in the can.

Once the cameras were in position I tied onto a rope and climbed solo up to the point that had been selected. I hammered home a piton into a crack just above the ledge, making sure that it was badly placed so that the peg would pull out as soon as I loaded it. I then set up the abseil, making up a sit-sling which I forced myself into as I began to tremble with fear. All around were overhanging yellow walls covered by swirling mist which loomed out over our ledge. As I clipped the karabiner from my sling into the double rope and set it over my shoulder the ground seemed to be receding ever further away. Holding onto the abseil I gingerly crept out to the edge of the stance and began to put my weight onto the belay. 'OK!' I shouted. 'Cameras,' instructed Tom. Ping! The peg pulled and I was falling.

Eight metres might not sound a long way, but in the second it took to fall that distance I let out a scream and when I hit the sacks, landing on my back, it felt like I had come from the summit of the Torre. I was so winded by the impact I could not stand up but the Grips, the Continuity Girl, the Best Boy, the Make-Up Man (it was just like Hollywood) and several of the actors came rushing over and pulled me to my feet. It was a while before I realised I had escaped unhurt and, in retrospect, I guess it was a crazy thing to do with only bags filled with grass to land on.

'Are you sure you wouldn't like to do it again?' Tom Stobart pleaded with me, always the perfectionist. I refused. Try as he might, no one else was willing to take it on. Fortunately the chief cameraman, who was an old climber from Bavaria, managed with that single take to get the fall onto celluloid.

Observing these antics were a rival film team from Munich making a documentary for TV about the brilliant Saxon climber, Lothar Brandler, who had escaped to live in the West from East Germany. The year before Brandler had made the first ascent of the North Face Direct on the Cima Grande. The Pro-

ducer of this film was Toni Hiebeler who was to mastermind the winter ascent of
the Eigerwand in 1961 and shortly afterwards helped to found the first of the
modern climbing magazines, 'Alpinismus'. Toni, a round-faced, heavily built guy
was in direct contrast to the lithe Brandler who moved up the rock face like a cat.
Both of them laughed at the antics of der Englander falling down the rock face,
abseil rope in hand. I remained friends with Toni until his death in a helicopter
crash along with the Yugoslav Alex Kunaver in the Julian Alps in 1984.

Sitting in the sun under the south face of the Torre Grande in between filming, Lothar told us about his experiences during the fire bombing of Dresden.
Though only a child he had spent days in the ruins of the city scavenging for
food, trying to stay alive by eating rotting vegetables and stale bread. It surprised
me that he bore no grudge against the British for this act of wanton destruction.

In the fifties Continental climbers could not obtain nylon ropes. British climbers
used to have a good scam going for them in that era; you took out hawser-laid
ropes to centres like Chamonix, particularly those of the half-weight thickness
which were very sought-after by the Europeans for Alpine climbing. One of our
wheezes was to buy a new rope for our holiday, use it on all our climbs then,
shortly before we had to go home, wash it thoroughly in Daz. We would then sell
it to the highest bidder on the Biolay camp site, or swap it with Donald Snell at
his sports shop for a duvet or a Millet rucksack which were then highly prized by
us.

One of my most explosive moments with Don Whillans was during the 1958
season, when I knocked a boulder onto his rope as we descended off the Grand
Capucin. It had already been used on the Bonatti Pillar and the West Face of the
Petite Jorasses, and it was so badly worn that in today's more affluent society you
would not have been seen climbing on such dross. Whillans insisted that he had
a buyer lined up for it down in Chamonix and he was worried that he might
have to reduce the price, due to the fact that the rock I had trundled had cut
through one of the strands!

The Long Holiday Men

The early sixties were the heyday of the 'Long Holiday Men'. We found out that,
with full employment in the UK, it was possible to work for nine months each
year, then spend three months every summer climbing in the Alps and on our
return either resume our employment or obtain a new job. I did this in both
1962 and 1963, spending twelve weeks abroad the first year and eleven weeks the
second. By today's standards we were still poor and used to camp wild or bivouac,
taking most of our food out with us and travelling in my small van.

Don Whillans remained a traditionalist and stuck to his motorcycle. As a nod
to progress he built himself a black box set on a sidecar frame into which he
could put all his equipment. This was quite a contraption and once locked –
typical of Whillans who trusted no one – you would have needed an oxyacety-
lene burner to break into it. One year he travelled out to the Dolomites on this
with Morty Smith , and Eric Beard and I arranged to meet them in the Cortina

area.

When we arrived in the Dolomites it took us a whole day to find them, riding up and down the steep hillsides in pouring rain and thick mist. When we finally did meet up they were camping wild beneath the road leading up to the Tofana. They were down in a small wood and everything they owned appeared to have been soaked by the downpour. We only found them by accident when I stopped the van in a layby for Eric to have a pee and there amongst the pine trees we spied Whillans' tent. It was a truly glum duo who met us when we ran down to greet them.

Don was obviously in the foulest of moods and I began to wish we hadn't managed to find them for he greeted us with a snarled, 'It's a good job you two have turned up!' It turned out Morty had lost the key to the black box and they couldn't get at their gear. I looked at poor Morty in sympathy. Despite Don's uncomplimentary remarks he put on a brave face and laughed out a greeting. I noticed they had been cooking on a wood fire, using a rusty can they must have found in which to boil water. They'd sustained themselves on spaghetti they'd bought in Cortina and luckily the tent was in a pannier.

'Why didn't you drive down to Cortina and see if you could get another key?' I queried.

'Because, you bloody little drink of water, the bike engine's wet through and it won't start,' Don snapped back at me. Luckily the weather improved shortly after our arrival and, with much kicking-over and drying of ignition parts, Whillans managed to get his bike running again. After a thorough search of the ground Morty found the lost key with a shout of triumph but it was to be quite some time before Don regained his normal humour. Later that night, as we stood around a spluttering camp fire with the huge South Face of the Tofana illuminated by a sly moon looming over us, Don quite seriously declared 'It's a bloody good job I'm such an easy going bloke!'

During our stay in Cortina nobody equalled the impact that Eric Beard made on the locals on his visits to town. The Italians love to sing and likewise Beardie. I will never forget one trip we made to the main supermarket which ended with Eric being lifted up onto the checkout by the customers, where he then belted out the popular song Bueno Sera at the top of his voice with a dozen other shoppers forming a backing choir. 'Ciao Erik!' was the cry wherever we went in Cortina.

The Alps were a wonderland for us and it was in centres like Chamonix that we met other British Alpinists of the period. The transition from the UK scale of climbing to glaciated ascents took some getting used to, but in retrospect it was quite remarkable how quickly one adjusted to the demands of this new environment. Nearly everyone who was climbing routes of a respectable standard were members of the Alpine Climbing Group, which had been formed as a ginger group in 1954 to help spread information and advice to British climbers in order to raise the standard of our mountaineering.

I was the Secretary from 1961 until 1965 and the few existing British guidebooks were either out of date or inaccurate. Some of our climbs were akin to first ascents for we might have no description of the route to be followed or the descent. Having made such a climb we passed on the information to other climbers via the ACG bulletin.

A major problem for all British climbers in that era was insurance against rescue and medical expenses. Before the BMC set up its overseas schemes and other UK companies began to offer policies, it was difficult to obtain cover in Britain where the prevailing attitude about Alpine climbing was that it was akin to Russian roulette. In order to overcome these difficulties most Brits opted to join the National organisations of the country in which they intended to operate, such as the Austrian Alpine Club or the Club Alpin Francais in order to be able to insure through those bodies. As Eric Metcalf, a friend of mine, found out in 1959 when he had an accident in Chamonix, the cover offered was often woefully inadequate, especially for medical expenses.

This was further emphasised when I was climbing in 1965 with my girlfriend at the Vajolet Towers. Bivouacking in a large cave close to our camp were a group of young Scots from Glasgow who had journeyed out to the Dolomites by train and bus. One of the Glaswegians, a seventeen- year-old lad, had a bad fall on the Towers whilst we were away climbing in the nearby Catanaccio. By the time we had returned he had been rescued and transported to hospital in Bolzano. He was not too badly injured and three days later he was judged fit enough to rejoin his companions, but the hospital would not let him go until his medical bills were paid. As sometimes happened in those days, the Scot had decided to risk it and was not insured and there was no way he or his mates could afford to pay these expenses.

A week passed and the Glaswegians were getting desperate; it was taking them two days just to visit their incarcerated friend, the bills were mounting and they were getting nowhere with the British Consul in Venice. As my girlfriend could speak Italian, they sought our help and pleaded with us to go and see if we could persuade the hospital in Bolzano to let 'Bonnet', as the laddie was known, go free.

I decided the only course of action was to help him do a runner as none of us had the money they were demanding. My girlfriend and I quickly packed up all our gear, loaded it into the van and set off and drove at speed to Bolzano. Arriving in the early afternoon, we soon located the hospital and the room where the young Scot was sitting. He looked depressed and forlorn, dressed in hospital pyjamas. It was obvious that he was bored out of his skull and goodness knows how long they would have held him if we had not intervened.

'Look Bonnet, you can't stay here for the rest of your life,' I began. 'We'll go back outside and drive my van round to this side of the hospital. You climb out of the window and, as soon as you see us, run and jump in by the back doors and once your inside cover yourself with sleeping bags!'

To cut down on the verbiage, it worked out like a Tarantino heist and we drove out of the hospital grounds with Bonnet inside my van as if we were on our way to a fire. Nobody pursued us and once clear of the town we slowed down and began to think that, in typical Italian fashion, the authorities must have shrugged their shoulders, laughed good-naturedly and put it down to the *Inglese*. We could not have been more wrong!

We reasoned that if we took Bonnet back to his mates at the Vajolet, they and us might get into trouble so we decided to head over the Brenner Pass and take him to Austria instead. From Innsbruck he could use his train ticket to get home. We had brought his passport and travel documents from his fellow Scots, plus all his gear and clothes.

We chugged along up the road leading towards the Brenner Pass. It began to get dark and lorries coming the other way had already put their lights on. Driving along I glanced in the mirror -bloody hell! Overtaking everything came a trio of jeeps rushing up the hill behind us, sirens blaring, lights flashing.

'Oh my God it's the caribineri! They're not after us are they?' we chorused. They certainly were and within minutes we were surrounded by vehicles whose occupants made it plain that if we did not pull over they would drive us off the road. Wearily I pulled the van off the carriageway into a layby and the next second I was hauled out of my driving seat as if I had stolen the Venus de Milo.

There were caribineri surrounding me on all sides, armed and looking very menacing. Other vehicles were stopping to see what was going on but were quickly sent on their way with an 'avanti, avanti!' All three of us Britons were then lined up in the road and unceremoniously searched, then marched off to be presented to the man who was obviously the officer in charge. Pushed in front of him I could see he was none too pleased. He was shouting at me unintelligibly, but then my girlfriend answered him fluently in Italian explaining our predicament. We were only good Samaritans helping a poor British climber in distress; a boy who needed to go home to his parents and had suffered at the hands of the authorities after being injured in a bad fall on the Vajolet Towers!

For some reason the officer visibly began to soften, scratching his chin and shaking his head in disbelief at Bonnet's apparent youth. The caribineri Captain then began to laugh - we must have looked funny dressed in our climbing clothes. He motioned that we follow his jeep in the van.

We three runaways walked back up the road and did as we had been told. Hoping they weren't taking us off to jail, we followed the jeep down a winding road into a village which lay below the main carriageway. Surely we ought to be taken back to Bolzano for trial? The jeep up ahead with the Captain aboard stopped outside an albergo in the village and we were politely ushered inside. We were invited to take a seat at a large wooden table and within minutes there was bread, butter, cheese and a large bottle of chianti spread out before us.

We couldn't understand what was happening until, laughing, the Captain told us that he was a climber too and spent all his spare time either in the Dolomites or the Alps. He was in a real predicament and, as he decided what to do, we began drinking toasts to 'la montanera'. Later that night Bonnet and I waved a sincere goodbye to our friend from the caribineri. I was more than slightly inebriated at the wheel of my van for we had toasted 'la montanera' many times before the Captain had agreed to release us!

We delivered Bonnet safely to Innsbruck, saw him off on his train and heard

no more about the incident from the Italian authorities, nor did we hear anymore
from the young Glaswegian. That is until one night some years later I was giving
a lecture in Exeter at the Northcott theatre and a young chap came up to me
after my talk. 'Yer dinna recognise me dae ya?' It was Bonnet, now Deputy
Manager of the theatre!

'Bloody hell Bonnet, you owe me a pint! If it wasn't for me you might still be
sitting in a room in a Bolzano hospital with a billion lira bill around your neck!'

Good Relations

I hope I am not looking back at the sixties with the same rose-tinted spectacles
that many music and fashion commentators do, but for working class climbers
like me the world really did open up for us then. I was able to travel ever more
widely to Spain, Poland, Mexico, the USA, the Andes and the Himalaya.

One of the most interesting things about these travels was meeting the climbers from other countries. On our way home from the Alps in 1965 we stopped
off in the Belgian Ardennes and climbed at Freyr, where there was a vibrant
climbing scene which centred on Marcel Gailly's bar in Falmignoul. Some of the
most active climbers there were actually from Holland and during that visit I
made many friends from the low countries. As a result, in November 1969 I was
invited to undertake a lecture tour of Belgium and Holland.

These were mainly slide lectures about climbing in Britain, but in Amsterdam
the organisers wished for a showing of the film 'the Magnificent Mountain'

depicting the first ascent of the North
Ridge of Alpamayo in the Peruvian
Andes. This was climbed by a six-man
British expedition which I led. The
show in Amsterdam was my final pro-
gramme and I arrived there late from
Antwerp, tired after ten days on the
road. When I turned up at the hall in
the middle of the city I was surprised
to find it was a very ancient building
sporting two storeys including a balcony. It was already filled with a capacity audience of 650 people.

I rushed straight onto the stage and
gave an introductory talk about the
making of the film, which had won
a major prize at the Trento film festival in 1967. Then I asked the projectionist to start showing the film;
the hall had no fixed equipment for
this and a projector had been brought
in and set up on the edge of the balcony rails. The lights went out and

Climbing in the Belgian Ardennes in 1965.
Photo Dennis Gray

the film started to roll.

Showing a film is much easier than lecturing with transparencies; all you have to do is introduce the work, sit back whilst it is shown, then take any questions at its conclusion. By the end of 1969 I had seen 'the Magnificent Mountain' many times and I usually just switched off once it was safely running. That night in Amsterdam my mind was on the journey back to the UK next morning, so I was paying little attention to what was happening on the screen or in the hall. About ten minutes into the film I suddenly became aware of a commotion in the stalls. Some of the audience sitting directly under the balcony were shouting, 'Put on the lights, stop the projector!' I snapped out of my reverie and wondered what on earth was going on.

The projectionist had not caught the end of the film into the re-reel spindle and the rolls of 16mm celluloid were simply going off the end of the balcony, down into the crowd below. Tens of metres of film were now wound around dozens of pairs of feet, bodies and chairs. As the lights went on the projectionist had the presence of mind to stop his machine. I was convinced my copy, a print I had paid for out of my own pocket with hard-earned cash, was now a write off. However, Dutch people are wonderfully disciplined and everyone in the hall urged those entwined in the film to stay perfectly still. A rather buxom lady then got up on the stage and began to direct operations.

The down end of the film was located by a team of helpers and gingerly released from obstacle after obstacle as the projectionist took it back up onto the reel by hand. Fifteen minutes later this operation was complete and the whole film was rewound back onto its original spool. But was it damaged? There was only one way to find out and that was to run it through once more.

So it was 'lights out' again and this time the projectionist made sure his machine was taking up the film as it ran. Breathless, I sat there as the images came and went on the screen, half expecting many of the frames to be damaged. But apart from the first ten minutes of the film needing a clean, 'the Magnificent Mountain' ran without a hitch. When it was finished the audience stood up and shouted as if they, too, were standing on the tip of Alpamayo, the most beautiful mountain in the world.

The Dutch are incredibly keen on climbing and even in 1969 there were over ten thousand activists in their country. Every weekend hundreds of them drive for hours to reach the limestone in the Ardennes and the sandstone cliffs of Berdorf in Luxembourg and they now have an almost unequalled network of indoor climbing walls.

A friend I made in the 1970s was the Swiss Jean Juge, president of the UIAA (the world body of mountaineering), of which I was then the British delegate. Jean was one of the keenest climbers of my experience and he lived for the mountains. He was already in his sixties when I first met him; lean and of medium height and athletic physique, he was still very fit and looked ten years younger. He had a house at the foot of the limestone cliffs of Mount Saleve above Geneva and just outside of his garden there were boulders on which he

climbed almost every day. In 1976 at the age of sixty eight he climbed the North Face of the Eiger, confessing that until he had retired from his work as a Professor at the University he had not had the time to concentrate on his mountaineering! But now he intended to ascend all those grande courses he had not been able to tackle when young and he certainly was an impressive climber.

One cold Spring day of pouring rain in April 1977 I was in Geneva and visited him at his house. I should have known better for within half an hour we were on our way up a route on the Saleve, Le Balcon, a Grade V climb of eight pitches.

Jean always climbed in Alpine equipment; not for him a T-shirt and tracksuit bottoms, even when the sun was shining. On this freezing wet day of our climb he was wearing breeches, a ski jacket and mountain boots. The crux of the climb was the third pitch, a highly-polished

Jean Juge in 1977 who perished the following year after climbing the North Face of the Matterhorn at the age of 70.
Photo Dennis Gray

ochre coloured wall above the balcony which gives the climb its name and this was graded V+. At the Swiss's insistence I set out to lead, starting out by stepping off the large block which is Le Balcon. The limestone above was wet and slippery and a few metres above Jean I stuck on a small ledge. I hung there trying to warm my hands by sticking them down my pants, losing all my motivation.

'Deni, put the left foot so, the right hand so, the right foot so and you find a good grip up on the left.' Jean knew the Saleve as well as anyone for he had been climbing there for several decades. A good second will often talk his leader up a route, but I have never been so sleep-walked up a pitch as that day on the Saleve. Once I had started climbing I just kept on as Jean shouted out instructions. When I awoke from my dream there, below me, was the wall with all the in-situ pitons clipped as protection. I traversed left to the foot of a deep chimney, made fast and shouted for the Swiss to start on up.

I watched fascinated as Jean climbed, for like all great climbers his footwork was precise and neat, maximising every hold en route and only loading his arms when the steepness of the limestone forced him to do so. Soon the Swiss had joined me and then, with him in the lead, we climbed the awkward chimney above and some steep slabs known to the locals as Le Paturage because of their openness. I belayed, impressed as Juge climbed these obstacles quickly and safely. In following I was to find a section that was even harder than Le Balcon, a steep wall that was wet and greasy. I had to admit as I followed him up a final difficult slab, just below the summit of the crag, that this man Juge was a phenomenon.

He was then sixty-nine years old, four years past the official retirement age in Britain, and yet as he climbed up the rock face he moved as if he was twenty or thirty years younger.

Jean was a great traditionalist and I remember how he dismissed the trend in modern rock climbing to concentrate on the move, which from his point of view was too narrow an outlook. For him climbing meant mountains, the two were synonymous. His death in his seventieth year in August 1978 was sad but poignant. Caught in a freak storm just below the summit of the Matterhorn after climbing the North Face, he died after many hours of struggle against the full force of the blizzard. His demise was met with disbelief by all of us who had known him, for we had expected him to be climbing actively for another decade. I think Jean Juge himself would not have argued with his fate, for few climbers can have loved the mountains more than this Swiss.

Another climber who I made friends with in this period was the Russian Yevgeny Gippenreiter. Tall and urbane, he was a sports physiologist who popped up in many disguises; visiting London with the Bolshoi ballet, attending International forums over the combating of drugs in sport, acting as an interpreter for his country's gymnastic teams and an official at the Olympics. This was at the height of the cold war, but Yevgeny was an Anglophile and I shared some unusual experiences with him.

On one occasion I met him at a climbing hut in the mountains near to Salzburg. After a meal we started yarning over a few beers and quite late in the evening three ancient Austrian climbers from Vienna who somehow knew Yevgeny appeared mysteriously in our midst. The old boys then told me their story; they had been young Communists in Vienna at the time of the Russian revolution and had started to agitate for such an event in their own country. They had actually been involved in the Commune of Vienna but when this had collapsed they had to flee their land. Many of their comrades were killed or imprisoned.

They escaped to the Caucasus where they lived and climbed until the outbreak of the last war, pioneering many new routes. By the end of the conflict they were marked men, for the German Panzers had attacked the USSR via the Caucasus, guided by their mountaineers who had climbed in the area before 1940. Though still loyal communists, the Viennese had come under suspicion for being collaborators because they spoke German. Stalin acted with utter ruthlessness at the end of the war for what he saw as this act of treachery by the Georgians (although he was one himself), deporting and killing whole swathes of the local populace. The three Austrians had escaped back to Europe before the axe fell, but all the new routes they had climbed had subsequently been removed from the records. They showed me diagrams of Ushba, Dykh-tau, Shkhelda etc. with dotted lines up the faces illustrating their first ascents. All had subsequently been climbed and credited to Soviet and other climbers.

'Is this all true?' I whispered to Yevgeny in a break in our conversation, which had been carried out in a mixture of German and Russian with my friend acting as an interpreter. 'Yes it is all true,' he smiled.

Brief Encounter

Though conceived in a spirit of idealism and international co-operation, the UIAA (Union Internationale des Associations d'Alpinisme) more often than not proved how difficult it was to reconcile the different aspirations of its seventy member nations during my twelve years as this country's delegate. Most of the delegates were the Presidents of their particular federations, and it was unusual to find men like Jean Juge filling such roles. Many were ancient warriors who aptly fitted the description of climbing politician.

One representative who didn't quite fit the bill was the tall, bulky American Bill Putnam, who with typical Yankee get up and go often upset the European applecart by his demands for change and progress. Clubs with massive numbers such as the French, the Swiss, the Italians and the Germans were used to the UIAA toeing their party line – all members pay a capitation fee and it is fair to report that in the seventies it was the Continental's cash that kept the show on the road.

In October 1979 the Americans offered to host the General Assembly of the UIAA at Pinkham Notch in the White Mountains of New Hampshire. However, they made it plain that delegates would have to pay their own way and stay in the refuge under Mount Washington belonging to the Appalachian Mountain Club, where the meals would be rudimentary and cooked by volunteers and it would be back to basics sleeping in Alpine bunks. This was in contrast to some of the recent annual meetings which had been held in such expensive locations as the Hilton, Mexico City in 1977 and a luxury beach hotel the year before at Lagonissi near to Athens.

To attend this meeting I flew from Manchester to Boston on the first leg of my journey – the same day that the Pope was on a visit there. When we arrived over the city we were forced to circle the airport for hours due to a security alert and it was early in the evening local time when our plane finally touched down. Getting through immigration was equally delayed. When I was finally cleared I was met by a a youthful-looking lady with a notice board held above her head on which was spelled out my name. I walked over and introduced myself, imagining a large limo waiting in the car park ready to spirit me through the night the hundreds of miles north to New Hampshire.

'All the transport we had organised for lifts up to Pinkham Notch has now gone, and Bill asks that you meet the French and Spanish delegates who are delayed and will be arriving later tonight. Please book them into a hotel then get them across town in the morning to catch the bus to North Conway, leaving the central bus station at 6.30 a.m. It gets in tomorrow night and he will get you picked up and taken on to Pinkham Notch.'

I was staggered by this news and could only guess at how the presidents of the French and Spanish alpine clubs, their wives and entourages would react at having to travel by bus all the next day, fatigued as they would be. For the sake of Anglo-American relations I agreed to take this on, knowing that the American Alpine Club, like the BMC, was only relatively small and not a wealthy organisation.

Just as I had anticipated, when they finally did arrive the continentals were gobsmacked at the news that they would have to make their own way by bus up to the White Mountains. By this time I had booked them and myself into the Airport Hilton, so at least they had somewhere to stay. The security around the airport was intense that night for the Pope was expected back again the next day to fly on to another US destination and we had real difficulty in transferring to the hotel.

Once inside the Hilton I impressed on the French and the Spaniards that we had to be up and breakfasted early the next morning. I was up again by five, dressed and packed and then, after a quick cup of coffee and some waffles, was sat in the entrance lobby of the hotel waiting for our taxis to arrive. The French and Spaniards had grumpily insisted on enjoying a full breakfast before leaving and were still in the restaurant.

Sitting on a sofa set around the entrance in a square made up of chairs and tables, there was just one other person waiting that morning besides me. I could not but help notice her. She was a truly beautiful, flaxen-haired woman of about twenty-five, expensively clothed and deeply tanned. She kept looking at me apprehensively so I decided to try to calm her fears, thinking she might be worried because there was no one else around, 'Good morning,' I ventured. She smiled in acknowledgement. 'Have you far to journey?' I went on.

'Yes, I am going back to the Lebanon,' she replied. My curiosity aroused, I tried to find out some more details about this mysterious woman. After talking about the weather I was just into discussing Kahlil Gibran, the only Lebanese writer I have read, when suddenly five guys shouting and carrying sub-machine guns burst into the lobby. Heading full-tilt at us I heard them shout, 'FBI! Hit the floor.' I sat there mesmerised, stricken with fear whilst the FBI men ran into our square and began kicking over the chairs from around me. Looking menacing and shouting loudly they proceeded to manhandle the young woman I had just been talking to!

She fell onto the floor face down, to be held by two burly guys who pulled her hands up behind her back and handcuffed her.

'What's going on?' I gasped, but other than one of the agents waving his gun in my direction they ignored me. The FBI men pulled the bedraggled girl to her feet and one of the police officers read the charges from a sheet of paper.

'We suspect that you are a member of the PLO. We are arresting you for being implicated in a plot to assassinate the Pope! Have you anything to say?'

'No!' said the girl defiantly. She was run at speed out of the hotel and pushed unceremoniously into a van with blackened windows that they had parked up on the pavement. They drove off at high speed, tyres squealing. I never saw the girl from the Lebanon again, nor did I ever find out what happened to her subsequently other than to read a report about a suspected PLO plot to assassinate the Pope in a Boston newspaper.

The journey with the French and Spaniards was accomplished as planned, taking all of that day to travel up country to North Conway in New Hampshire. True to Putnam's promise, a transit van was waiting. When I met up with the

Yankee later that night I complimented him on the reception he had organised in Boston for a poor old Limey.

'Oh, that was my Secretary,' Bill laughed, thinking of course I meant the lady who had met me off my plane. 'She doesn't happen to come from the Lebanon does she?' I ventured.

'No she's from Springfield, Mass. But why do you ask?'

'Oh, I just happened to meet a fantastic-looking woman from the Lebanon this morning who was surrounded by five FBI men. It wasn't a stunt you Yanks pulled to try to impress us Europeans was it?' I could see from the look on Bill's face he had no idea what I was talking about, but ever since the vision of that young lady from the Middle East has stayed with me as the most beautiful woman I have ever met.

I know that some readers may find it difficult to credit how freely the FBI were running around armed with weapons in the events described above, but I was not. In 1975 Ian Parsons and I were hitch hiking around the Eastern USA and were heading back from Boston to the Shawangunks to climb, when we were picked up late one night by two youths high on drugs. The inevitable happened and they crashed the vehicle, hitting a wall. As neither was hurt we swiftly abandoned the scene, bidding them goodbye whilst picking up our gear out of the damaged car's boot. We then set off on foot towards the distant lights of a village.

On arrival we walked into the local saloon - a typical American bar in a low ceilinged single room. At the counter we noticed a sign above it, 'bowls of stew 50 cents' and as we were hungry (we'd been on the road since early morning) we demanded two helpings of the brown stuff from the lady who served us. One good thing about America is you can always get something to eat day or night, and the bartender disappeared into a back room to get our order. There were just two other guys inside the place besides us playing pool at the back of the bar.

I could see that they were looking at us suspiciously as we walked in. Not surprising I suppose, as we were practically in the middle of nowhere and two chaps coming in off the sidewalk with huge rucksacks at ten o'clock at night, in a part of the world where they might not see many strangers, was bound to raise an eyebrow. I smiled in their direction but at this one of the pool players glowered at us quizzically, then stopped his playing and slowly walked over to stand in front of Ian and myself, eyeing us up and down. We could not help but feel intimidated by this for he was in all truth a mean-looking fellow, huge with a large beer belly, wearing a bib and brace outfit.

'Are you guys Limeys?'

'Yes, yes we are,' I responded, thinking he might be keen on us Brits. But Jesus how wrong can you be for the next second he produced a gun in his right hand, pulled out from a holster under his arm.

'Well we don't like Limeys round here and if you boys don't beat it I'll fill you full of lead!' This was said with such venom by Fatso that I, for one, did not care to hang around to argue with him. Despite our fatigue and our hunger, Ian and I picked up our gear and hit the road outside that saloon. Not daring to look back over our shoulders we quickly walked off up the street and back onto the open road where we spent the whole of the rest of the night trying to stop a lift to get away from the place.

That is why I was not as surprised at the rumble in the Hilton as I might have been; guns are commonplace in the US and on three occasions now I have had weapons pointed at me whilst on climbing trips there.

Tour D'Ai

I have already reported how much in awe we were of Alpine guides, but I never dreamt that I would be an instructor one day. My early experiences in this respect were of winter climbing in Scotland, but my first guiding abroad was when I worked alongside Bill Wayman and Tim Jepson, helping on a beginners' alpine course at Ailefroide in the Dauphine. Such work is demanding and dangerous; with novices you can never afford to relax for one second. However, my most epic guiding was in Switzerland working for Peter Boardman, when he was Director of the International School of Mountaineering in August 1981.

Above Leysin are some wonderful limestone peaks and I set out one day of unsettled weather to climb the Robbins route on the Tour D'Ai along with one of the students, Joe from Colorado. We reasoned that we could get off this route quickly if bad weather set in. Joe was enormous; 6'8 in height and weighing in at around 220lbs. He was then in his forties and a successful businessman. He was a fine rock climber but wished to improve on his Alpine technique. It wasn't unusual for experienced students to ascend major climbs like the Swiss route on the North Face of the Courtes, or hard rock routes in Leysin or Argentiere.

The crux of the Robbins proved to be a difficult crack which yielded to gritstone jamming and bridging techniques and Joe had no difficulty in seconding this pitch. The weather was deteriorating as we climbed, with huge black clouds racing in from the West, so once up that section we charged up the rest of route to arrive breathless on the summit as the first peals of thunder and lightning flashed and rolled around the Tour D'Ai.

Ever since I was knocked out by lightning belaying on the summit of the Brenta Alta in 1963, I have had a real fear of being struck again and was so worried by this possibility that we began our descent off the tower straight away.

After descending about forty metres the storm really hit us and within seconds we were soaked. Our ironmongery began to hum like a telephone line and the bombardment intensified with crashes of thunder like cannon fire and lightning strikes that seemed to hit the rock face just above our heads. Water rushed down the walls and slabs all around us.

In the storm we somehow managed to lose the way and ended stranded on a ledge well-supplied with pitons which showed that others had been lured that way, but we guessed that the normal descent route was somewhere to our right.

In between these two points was very steep rock and Joe was becoming more worried by the second for it was getting colder and colder and we were both beginning to shiver. I tried to reassure him.

'We must set up an abseil and work our way across the face to reach the easy ground,' I shouted, pushing our fifty-metre double ropes through a sling which I tied off through two stout pegs. Throwing them out into space and down the cliff, I instructed Joe to follow me once I had managed to traverse the face. Normally you would send the student down first and give him a safety rope, but in our situation this just was not feasible.

I set out hanging on the ropes, running back and forth across the vertical walls until, after descending about thirty metres and with the ropes running at almost an angle of forty-five degrees, I reached large ledges where I grabbed at some flakes and landed on a good stance. This had obviously been well used for it was equipped with several pegs for security. I was back on the normal descent route!

I tied our ropes off through two anchors, belayed myself and called for Joe to follow. It was obvious he wasn't happy from the time it took him to get ready, but after a while he set forth and began to slide down the ropes towards me, hanging above many metres of space. For some reason the American could not get the hang of walking his way across the rock face, for every time he tried to move right he swung back left, and each time he did so he crashed heavily into a pinnacle. By now it was snowing and getting colder and colder. I was shouting myself hoarse trying to get him moving, but he still hung there in space making feebler and feebler attempts to run across the wall.

'Go further down,' I screamed. 'Abseil down a bit then I can pull you across.' Eventually, after another five minutes of shouting out into the falling snow, this message finally registered and Joe slowly lowered himself until he was almost level with me, but still many metres away to my left. I then began to pull him with the rope running through a karabiner in a piton. At first I could not move him for he weighed too much, but once I had the rope taught he could also help to pull himself. Heaving together, he began to swing his way across. He was almost with me when the rope caught behind a flake above and to his right, which left Joe hanging in space. I was holding his weight but the rope was jammed and I just could not pull him towards me any more.

The snow was now falling in huge flakes and our situation was becoming more serious by the second. Shit, what could we do? I was almost sobbing, but then I decided I had to take a gamble on the American being willing to take a fall and trust me to hold him. I tied the abseil off and gathered the rope ends from my ledge which I had already knotted together. I then tried to throw these across to Joe. At the third attempt he caught them. 'Tie yourself on.' Though he was so obviously tired and his hands must have been frozen, he did as he was told. I then pushed the ropes through my stitcht plate and took them tight to my partner. He was about three metres to my left and still hanging on the abseil.

'Undo yourself from the abseil rope,' I commanded.

'No!'

'Joe, please, we must get down. I'll hold you, don't worry.' He hesitated, but I think my trembling voice must have made him realise how desperate things were becoming and I watched with absolute terror as he began to unclip himself. This was no easy task for he had to pull himself up, hold his weight, then undo his screwgate karabiner. He fumbled and fumbled, fell back exhausted, recovered and then tried again whilst I shouted out encouragement. Suddenly he was off and into space, falling in a curving arc.

'Bloody hell!' When his weight came onto me it was like holding a jumbo jet and I was pulled hard against the anchors. Fortunately my plate locked and the next moment Joe swung onto easy ground about five metres below me, landing safely on a large ledge where he soon made himself fast. With his weight off the ropes it was an easy task to flick them free from their obstruction and soon we were on our way again, climbing roped down easy ground. This time we made sure to follow the well worn descent route and, as we lost height, the snow turned to rain and the air temperature rose and we regained some warmth descending reasonably fast.

So much did the conditions ease as we descended and as the storm moved away towards the Valais Alps, that by the time we reached the scree at the base of the Tower we had almost forgotten the incident on the abseil rope. Joe did turn to me as we coiled the ropes and muttered something like, 'that was one tough cookie!' Subsequently the situation came back to haunt me, giving me terrible angst. What if the belays had failed? What if Joe had blacked out? What if my frozen hands had failed to hold him?

However, you can pose questions about mountaineering incidents forever – although it is wise to analyse mistakes to try to make sure you do not repeat potentially lethal ones. As I headed back down the wet green alps to Leysin, with Joe following in my wake, I think we both felt a sense of joy and release at our escape and still being alive to tell the tale.

Bouldering at Fontainebleau

One place abroad that now fills me with nostalgia whenever I read or hear of climbing developments there is the forest of Fontainebleau, the sandstone bouldering capital of the world just south of Paris. It is a place I have been to many times. Just to pick up the guidebook and look at the list of the climbing sites described, such as Bas Cuvier, L'Elephant, Franchard, Malesherbes, brings memories flooding back. Particularly climbing at Bas Cuvier in the seventies with local experts Claud Deck, Patrick Cordier and Eric Vola and at Isatis with Jean Marc Aselin, Vincent Renard and Catherine Destiville in the eighties. They knew every problem by heart, like a classical violinist playing a concerto. Besides meetings with the locals I have had some memorable visits there with British friends and even the great pleasure of introducing some of them to the delights of this wonderful forest.

On one occasion I was there with Peter Boardman shortly after his ascent of the South West Face of Everest in 1975. Travelling in his car, he had his Everest lecture slides with him to give a talk in Paris on the following day. After climbing, eating and drinking we decided to bivouac in the forest. We drove off the metalled road via a sandy track, parked and climbed a nearby hillock in order to try to get some cooler air as the night was stiflingly hot. Taking only our sleeping bags and mats with us, we stupidly left all the rest of our belongings in his vehicle.

The next morning we rose early in order to do some climbing, before heading into Paris. On descending the hill and reaching the track where we thought we had left the Renault, we were horrified to find there was no vehicle, only deep tyre marks in the sand.

'Oh no my slides. The buggers have got my slides!' Peter was more concerned about his precious pictures than our gear and the motor. I suggested we get the police at Milly-la-Foret and we started to walk away along the track in hot sunshine. Instead of quickly reaching the main road as we had anticipated, this path just seemed to wind on and on through the forest.

We had drunk a few beers the night before in Milly and perhaps we had not taken keen notice of our whereabouts, but even so this route did not tie in with my memory. 'How far do you think we've walked?' I ventured.

'A couple of kilometres,' Peter suggested. 'But we only came a few hundred metres into the forest last night. What the hell is happening?'

We were beginning to feel the heat and decided to retrace our steps. Half an hour later we were once more at the deep tyre marks where we thought the Renault should have stood. 'Let's go back up the hill,' the Everester suggested and, struggling up through the deep soft sand, we climbed once more up to the site where we had spent the night.

Casting around hesitantly, we decided to go down the opposite side of the promontory in order to take a look on that side. It was becoming obvious by then that every side of this hill was exactly the same. Down we ran again through soft sand and ancient pine trees and, sure enough, at the base of the mound there was a sandy track with recent deep tyre marks but no vehicle. Totally bemused by this we turned back up the hillock and reached the top once more. By this time our exertions had us lathered in sweat. We took a turn of forty-five degrees and then ran down the hill once more.

This time when we reached the bottom there was the Renault sitting on a sandy track identical to the other two. Miraculously untouched, with all its contents intact! Our French friends laughed heartily when we recounted the story of how we had been lost in the forest, prompting Vincent Renard to enquire mischievously in his impeccable *anglais* 'Is route finding at Bleau more difficult than on Mount Everest because there are no fixed ropes?'

Besides losing a car I once witnessed a wonderful case of mistaken identity on the road at Fontainebleau when, in October 1981, Graham 'Streakie Bacon' Desroy and I stopped off to climb there on our way to the Ticino Alps. One of the reasons I am so enamoured of the Foret is that it is possible to purchase good wine, cheese and bread very cheaply in the surrounding villages. One lunchtime, before setting off to continue our journey southwards, Graham and I were sat at the side of the N7 road by his ancient vehicle with a large bottle of wine between us, munching our way through huge cheese butties.

Streakie was dressed in a white T-shirt, flared jeans and trainers. On his head he had a straw boater like old Etonians wear. Tall, dark and very angular, I had never thought he looked like anyone else, but a bus full of young Italian girls on their way home after visiting Paris pulled up alongside us and the next moment they were streaming off it and screaming, 'Freddie, Freddie, Freddie!' We looked around wondering who the hell could be so lucky as to be called Fred, but there was nobody about except us and the cars and lorries that were rolling past like demented hornets.

The first of the girls came closer and closer still chanting 'Freddie'. One can imagine their disappointment when they got close enough to realise their mistake - they thought Streakie was Freddie Mercury of Queen. What they thought he was doing sitting by a roadside in France, travelling in an old banger, eating a large cheese butty instead of hitting the scene in gai Paris I'm not quite sure! But Graham still signed a few of their autograph books, writing Streakie Bacon - 'Le Roc Star'.

In summer 1993 I was at Fontainebleau climbing with my young friend Jumper Scarth, a fellow Yorkshireman who looks very unlikely until you see him in action. He is best described as an athlete, being a fine hurdler and a talented boulderer.

Graham 'Streakie' Desroy at the side of the N7, near Fontainebleau where he was mistaken for Freddie Mercury!

Photo Dennis Gray

I have climbed with him since he was fifteen years of age and many an adventure I have shared with him in the last six years. He had just ascended a test piece and I then managed the only really hard problem I have ever managed at Bleau - a variation on one of the Whites at Bas Cuvier, near to the famous problem the Butcher.

Somehow I wobbled my way up this and noticed that I was being keenly watched by a well-honed rock jock, who it transpired came from Norway. When I descended back down to the ground he was waiting anxiously to enquire, obviously impressed by my performance, 'Are you ze boulder freakie from Sheffield?' No one climbs less like a boulder freakie than me, so I curtly replied 'No, I am the Himalayan climber from Leeds.' From the look on his face he was obviously disappointed. God knows who he thought I was - maybe Ben Moon?

An Unlucky Break

In case any reader feels that I have led a charmed life whilst climbing and always escaped without injury, unlike so many of my friends, I am afraid I might have misled you with my tales. I've fractured my left ankle on three occasions, the last time in August 1994.

Jumper and I had been climbing in southern France and decided to call in at

Climbing at Fontainebleau, August 1994 just before I split my heel.

Photo Nigel Scarth

Fontainebleau on the way back to Britain. We had a good session bouldering at Bas Cuvier despite the fact that conditions were poor due to the hot and humid weather; the best time to climb at Bleau is in the winter in cold dry spells, when the friction is at its highest. Before finishing for the day I decided to ascend one last blue problem. These can be quite hard and the one I chose was perhaps English 5b, but it was a number I had climbed on other occasions and so I set forth confidently whilst Jumper took up a position directly below, ready to field me if I needed to jump down.

After a bit of a struggle I had almost reached the top of the boulder, which was about five metres high, at which point I had to stand up by the way of a sloping and highly polished hold. The constant use of resin on the hands and boots at Bleau over many years has rendered many of the classic problems into shiny horrors. I rocked over onto my left foot and was just about to stand up and shout 'cracked it!' when I was off and into the air. Instead of falling vertically I shot off to one side away from my catcher's waiting hands. I have never hit the ground like that in fifty years of climbing. The total force generated by the fall was taken through my left ankle. I crumpled and shot backwards to head-butt the boulder set behind the one I had been ascending.

'Are you OK?' Jumper enquired anxiously as I sat up. I was in absolute agony! When I tried to stand up I found that I couldn't and Jumper and a Dutch climber who had witnessed my fall had to support me back to our vehicle. Once inside this I found I couldn't operate the clutch so we appeared to be marooned in the car park until my ankle recovered sufficiently. (Being under twenty-one my companion was too young to drive my vehicle on the Continent, although he had passed the driving test in England.)

After sitting around for some time worrying about our predicament I had a bright idea. 'Jumper, you lie under the dashboard and push the clutch in with your hand whilst I change the gears. I can operate the accelerator and brake with my right foot!' Being a bright Yorkshire lad he did exactly as he was told, but as we pulled out into the high speed traffic on the N7 heading into Paris my heart was in my mouth. We arrived at the camp site without crashing and then spent the next two days getting my ankle sufficiently rested and bound up to drive back to Yorkshire.

It was in all truth a hell of a mess - hugely swollen and black and blue from internal bleeding - but I knew from experience that this did not mean a lot. It was what had happened to the bones, ligaments and tendons that mattered and only a hospital and X-rays could tell me that. I was determined to get home first before I sought medical help, convinced by my previous experience of damaged ankles that I could drive back to England if I took my time. I realised we could not drive all the way from Fontainebleau to Leeds with Jumper lying under the dashboard, nor would I be able to drive for long periods, so I decided to try to journey for about three hours at a time.

On the third day after my accident we set out on the road home with me taking anti-inflammatory drugs and pain killers like I was eating Smarties. Every gear change was an agony to start with, but as the drive progressed it became somewhat easier. It still took us three days to get from Bleau to Yorkshire. By the time I arrived home I had convinced myself that the ankle was definitely only sprained. The next day, certain that it was ligament and tendon injuries I had sustained, Jumper came round to my house and drove me to a physio friend of ours. Maureen then treated me for a fortnight, but I realised at the end of this period that I was not getting any better - if anything I was getting worse and could only move around on crutches.

I contacted my friend Steve Bollen, orthopaedic consultant at the Bradford Royal Infirmary, and drove over to his hospital. 'Bloody hell Dennis!' he laughed as he scanned the X-rays once he had examined me. 'You've been hopping around with a fractured calcaneus.' He could hardly believe his ears when I told him that I had driven like that from Fontainebleau to Leeds. I spent the next five weeks with my left ankle and leg in plaster and it took a further six months of physiotherapy twice a week before I could climb once more.

More Good Relations

During the years that I have been mountaineering the sport has developed in many directions and more and more attempts have been made through photography, books, videos and films to capture the essence of our activities, both as a record and as a means of interpreting them to a wider public. Photographic and painting exhibitions, book fairs and many film festivals have been held, the grand daddy of them all being Trento, in Italy. I had the honour of being a member of the jury at Trento in 1988. Anyone who mistakenly thinks this is a doddle has no idea what it entails. Each day for five days we began viewing films at eight in the morning until late in the night; by the end of our task we had looked at eighty films. There was everything from hard core rock-jocking and Himalayan mountaineering to basket weaving in the Alps!

Trento is really special, but I retain the keenest memory of a lesser known film festival, Adrspach, in Czechoslovakia in 1987. This used to be organised by the late Miri Smid, the giant Czech mountaineer and bon vivant, yet another friend who was to die whilst climbing. Adrspach is the finest of the Eastern bloc sandstone climbing areas. There are hundreds of rock towers of all shapes and sizes

Playing right back for the rest of the world
at Adrspach 1987.   Photo J. Wolf

surrounding the town, many of which
are difficult to climb by any route.

This gathering used to attract
climbers from the old Soviet satellite
states; Romania, East Germany, Hungary, Poland, Czechoslovakia, Bulgaria
and of course Russia itself. Compared
to Trento the films were diabolical, but
nobody seemed to care and it was the
socialising that seemed to be the most
important feature of the event.

The Czechs proved that they really did know how to do this. Each
night of the Festival they held a different get-together, from a rock concert to a Western Swing dancing session. The highlight of the social calendar was the soccer match, made up
of teams of climbers. It was Czechoslovakia versus the Rest of the World,
held at the town's football stadium in
front of 5,000 spectators.

I was selected to play for the visitors by Miri and was positioned at
right back. My team mates were from
several of the Eastern bloc nations and, although it had then been many years
since I had played football, I was assured by Miri that this did not matter – the
game was 'only for a laugh'. I should have guessed as we were being kitted out in
a matching strip and modern, lightweight boots that it might be something more
serious than that.

In all truth it was the best game I have taken part in. The Czechoslovaks were
like professionals, so pin-point was their passing. Our side somehow managed to
keep in touch, mainly through the efforts of our strong half-back line who tackled like Norman Hunter's, although the match was played in a friendly spirit
throughout.

With only a minute to go we were losing 3-2 when the Czechs conceded a
free kick just inside our half. My fellow full-back was a huge Pole and he rushed
forward, took the kick and passed the ball across the field to me covering on the
right flank. I pushed it on to our Russian centre half and ran forward and the ball
was immediately returned to me. I passed again to our Hungarian inside right
and continued running and bloody hell the ball came back to me yet again. I
really did not know what to do with it with two giant defenders in front. I
turned and played the ball on my inside to our Romanian centre forward, who
dribbled with it someways going round the first of the full-backs who barred his
way. Back came the ball to me. By now the goal was only a short distance away

and so, what the hell, I booted it as hard as I could and ʾwham! to my utter amazement it shot into the top right-hand corner of the net.

A few seconds later the whistle blew and we had managed a draw against all expectations. This proved to be the first occasion that the visitors had not been overwhelmed by the locals. Our supporters in the crowd went bananas. I was a hero for the rest of that night and subsequently did not get back to the apartment I was staying in until three in the morning, noisily drunk as my team mates had insisted on buying me many litres of Pilsen. I suppose there can be few climbers who can say they have played football at international level and scored a goal but, knowing Miri as I did, I suspect it might have been a put-up job!

A crowd of climbers that I met in June 1994 taught me the need for some in our sport to become more liberal in their thinking. Earlier that year I was at the Foundry Climbing Centre in Sheffield and saw a notice declaring that 'Sports climbing is now to be included in the Gay Games. You don't have to be gay to take part, only gay friendly.' Intrigued, I phoned the UK contact of the games, Phil Judson, and was sufficiently impressed with the details of the event that I tried to persuade some of the members of the British team to take part. I suppose I was being naive, but their responses depressed me and one of the women I approached exhibited such homophobia that I decided I would volunteer myself. It turned out to be one of the best decisions I have ever taken.

The Gay Games are the brainchild of the late Dr Tom Waddell, who finished sixth in the Decathlon in the Mexico Olympics of 1968. By 1994 they had grown into the biggest sporting and cultural event outside the Olympics. Gay Games IV were held in New York over a period of two weeks in June and it proved impossible to attend at more than just a few of the hundreds of concerts, discos, exhibitions and sporting contests associated with the gathering.

I will not tell of how our British team won a gold, silver and bronze medal in the Sports Climbing competition. Nor of all the new friends I made or even of what a fantastic place New York turned out to be, surely the most exciting city in the world where travelling on the subway late at night, alone, feels much more menacing than crossing a Himalayan ice fall! Even of the million-strong Stonewall march through the streets of Manhattan, held in conjunction with the Games, with participants there from half the countries on earth. (During the walk I turned to another of the British contingent marching along who I recognised as the portly figure of the actor Stephen Fry. 'What event are you taking part in during the Games?' I gasped. 'I'm only here to give my support,' he laughed. 'They haven't included my sport in the Games yet, but I live in hope' 'Oh, what is that then?' I demanded. 'Flower arranging, dear boy, flower arranging!' and with this riposte he pushed on forward as we headed towards Central Park.)

I will just focus on one incident to illustrate what I mean by the need for some climbers to modify their attitudes towards homosexuals.

Because of flight availability I travelled out ahead of my team mates, and found on arrival in New York that my hosts for the Games were two gay guys who had an apartment overlooking West Central Park. They, like thousands of others in

Bouldering in Central Park, New York 1994.
Photo Dennis Gray

the Big Apple, had agreed to put up free of any charge a participant from abroad for the duration of the event.

This turned out to be an incredible piece of luck for me. I could walk out of their front door and be in the park in seconds. There I could listen to the musicians, including the finest jazz funk band I have ever heard, go for a run around the Reservoir track, watch the roller bladers in action in the Mall and the soft ball players in the Meadows. Many of the events of the Games, like the cycle road race, the soccer matches, baseball and the marathon, were all held there. But most important for a climber, there is good bouldering to be found in Central Park, with the best site being situated just north of the Columbus Circle entrance.

The boulders are of volcanic rock and, though neither extensive nor very high, still offer some excellent problems. Here I met Chuck from Boulder who was working on a construction project in New York. He was built like a quarter-back, blonde haired, blue-eyed. Truly an all-American boy. When I met him he was trying a difficult traverse and on his invitation I joined in. Over the next few days we met early each morning and had a lot of fun enjoying each other's company, talking over places we had been and describing routes we had ascended. We usually climbed until it became too hot and greasy for comfort - June in New York is sizzlingly hot - after which Chuck disappeared back to his work.

On the third day of working it we both managed to complete the traverse we had been attempting, which was about English 6a/b. Typical of Americans, Chuck was buzzing at this success and invited me to return to Boulder with him to climb and stay as his guest. He was truly buoyed up by our success when two guys came running past and his mood suddenly changed. They were wearing T-shirts carrying the Gay Games logo for the marathon on their fronts, obviously out training.

'Take a look at those fucking faggots. I just do not get it Dennis, they'll be on the rocks next and I'll be moving out! God how I hate gays,' Chuck declared angrily as the runners jogged past. Words I heard in utter disbelief as he said them, for I just could not credit that someone who I now thought of as a friend could be so narrow-minded. I bit my tongue and said nothing in response until we were packing up after finishing our climbing for the day. Chuck turned to me, 'You never told me what you're doing in New York, or where you're staying. Maybe we could meet up for a few beers tonight?'

I hesitated and nearly choked as I replied, 'I'm here for the Games Chuck.' He mistook this to mean the Soccer World Cup which was then in progress, with Ireland playing Italy that very afternoon.

'You Brits will go anywhere to watch a game of football,' he laughed.

Trembling by now I corrected him; 'No, Chuck, I'm here to take part in the Gay Games.' The look of utter amazement that came over his face at this news wasn't that surprising, but then he became totally embarrassed and tongue-tied.

'I'm sorry if I offended you. I had no idea you were gay. I just assumed you were normal like the rest of us climbers!' he managed to gasp out. I mumbled it was OK, but as we said our goodbyes I was thinking to myself that we couldn't now be friends with such a gulf of misunderstanding between us.

Subsequently I never saw Chuck at the boulders again, but that incident illustrated for me just how much prejudice a gay climber might still find from his or her fellow participants. I resolved to try to help to change such attitudes and joined the Gay Outdoor Club and Stonewall when I returned to the UK.

On the Road Again

For my sixtieth birthday I decided, along with my young friend Jumper, to plan something special. A four-month climbing tour of the Western USA, starting and finishing in Denver where I knew we would be welcome to stay with my old buddies, Ann and Dez Hadlum. We flew out in September 1995 and, with our

Nigel Scarth, Dennis Gray and the $800 Buick. Photo Dez Hadlum

Nigel 'Jumper' Scarth on Chili Sauce, Joshua Tree 1995.   Photo Dennis Gray

friends' help, bought a car for 800 dollars – a ten-year-old Buick Skylark – and set forth. It was Kerouac and Gary Snyder and Gregory Corso and Gasoline and we were on the road, free to go anywhere we pleased.

We climbed at fourteen different sites in Colorado then on to Utah, Nevada, California, Arizona, Texas and New Mexico before heading home via Denver with 12,000 kilometres of driving behind us. The Buick proved to be a marvellous buy and Dez was so impressed by its performance that he bought it off me for 600 dollars when we arrived back in Denver!

As can be imagined, we had many adventures on the road and climbing, including me spraining my injured ankle again at Joshua Tree in California. There we met Smoking Joe, a boulderer from Tahoe who introduced himself to us by pointing to the Lazers on Jumper's feet and declaring, 'Boy, where I come from we call those boots losers!' But the most humorous incident occurred when we were climbing at the Red Rocks in Nevada. Alongside us on a parallel route were the oddest couple I have yet seen on the rocks. The leader was a huge black lady and her second a tall, worried-looking Arab gentleman from Egypt. They had both been drawn to nearby Las Vegas by the gambling industry and worked as crap dealers in Caesar's Palace.

The black lady was about fifteen metres above her second man and was obviously in difficulty, for she began to shake and wobble like a jelly. Oh my God! She was off, and down she headed for the platform on which her belayer was stood. The Arab gentleman hung manfully on to her rope and, despite the difference in their respective weights, managed to stop his leader just before she hit the ground. Her rope was held through a bolt but, because the second had a lot of slack in their system, he then ended higher up the crag than his leader. It took quite some time before the swinging couple safely regained their belay.

'Are you OK?' we shouted anxiously across.

'Yeah. I guess it's a momentum thing with me; when this lady gets a-going she sure takes some stopping!' the black lady assured us. We could hardly disagree with that statement!

Travelling to climb abroad is still as exciting a prospect, still gets me tingling with anticipation as I pack my gear, as it did when I first travelled to Austria in 1955. It is so much easier to journey now than it was then and today most climbers must be able to travel if they really wish to maximise climbing opportunities. Wisely did Robert Louis Stevenson advise us: 'Youth is the time to go flashing from one end of the world to the other both in mind and body; to try the manners of different nations, to hear the chimes at midnight and to see sunrise in town and country.' Surely no truer words have yet been written?

One I still recall was the story of the electric or stinging-nettle tree. I was told if you ever get hold of it, it's hard to let go and sends a shock through your body like a hundred volts. Once again, I dismissed this as exaggeration until one day I was climbing on the Main Wall at Lukenya, the biggest crag of that massif, ascending a multi-pitch route. Whilst leading at the top of the second section I had difficulty in getting landed onto a belay ledge and grabbed a tree trunk which was most unusual looking. It was made up of a dark green hairy substance, similar to the stem of a nettle, but about as large in circumference as a hawthorn tree in the UK.

Immediately I had grabbed hold of it I realised this was Bill Woodley's nettle tree. It was stinging and shocking me at the same time and I couldn't let go.

'Bloody hell!' I screamed.

'What's wrong?' shouted up my second man, the American climber Phil Snyder.

'I can't let go of this fucking tree, it's stinging me like hell.'

'Kick it hard at it's base,' he advised while I gasped in agony. I lashed out with my foot at the tree trunk and immediately the stinging current lowered in intensity and I managed to let go. My right hand was tender and swollen once I had withdrawn it from that triffid.

'How the hell did you know to kick it to let go?' I demanded of Phil once he had climbed up to join me on my ledge, giving the stinging tree a wide berth.

'I didn't, but if I had hold of something which wouldn't let me go I'd give it a good kicking,' he laughed.

Almost every climb we made in Kenya was equally as adventurous, either because of the remoteness of the cliffs or the fauna to be found out on them. On another occasion I was leading Phil Snyder up an off-width crack. A single pitch route of about thirty metres on another of the Lukenya outcrops which necessitated arm and knee-barring around a Y-type configuration, taking the right hand branch of the fissure. The upper section was so constricted that the side of my face was pushed against the rock. Immediately I did this it felt like a needle had been stuck into my face causing me to scream out in pain. I shuffled up a bit higher and the same thing happened again and this time my screams alerted Phil about twenty metres below me.

'What's wrong?' he anxiously demanded.

'I don't know, but something keeps stinging me in the face.'

'Oh, there must be hornets nesting on the crack walls,' he advised. Pushing my head out of the crack and peering in I could see that he was right, for there, sticking onto the rock, were the tell-tale nests. At least I now knew what to try to avoid. I decided not to retreat; reversing the off-width that bent away down below me looked much harder than continuing upwards. Gritting my teeth and trying to keep my face out of the chimney as much as possible, I battled upwards but still was stung another three times in the face before I reached safety. Phil managed to get away much lighter than me, being only stung twice, but hornets make a hell of a mess of you. I looked in the mirror when we returned to my vehicle parked down on the Mombasa road and my face looked like I had taken a duffing off Mohammed Ali!

Another hazard which came to the fore during my stay in Kenya was the danger posed by bees. A short while after my arrival in the country news arrived at the Mountain Club that three climbers had died on a reconnaissance trip down in neighbouring Zambia. Those concerned had been out scrambling when, without warning, a massive swarm had attacked and stung them to death. This intrigued and frightened me and a short while later I was down at Likoni on the coast, when a swarm of bees descended on an African woman and began to sting her viciously, whilst she ran around screaming, trying to get them off. Though this happened in a crowded street nobody else was attacked.

My friend Ian Howell, who knows the mountains and cliffs of East Africa better than anyone else, seems convinced that it is something to do with the smell emanating from human hair that excites the bees and makes them attack. I was climbing with him at Ndaya, making a repeat ascent of the Party Grooves, one of the hardest rock climbs in the country, when we came into contact with such a swarm.

The cliff is around sixty metres high, made up of firm, clean volcanic rock and the route follows a succession of cracks. That Sunday I was leading. I had managed to overcome the difficult first pitch and was high on the second when I heard a peculiar buzzing sound. It became louder and louder. 'What the hell is that?' I shouted down to Ian.

He cocked an ear then suddenly decided, 'It's bees, killer bees!' the second part of the sentence was said with such emphasis that I sensed Ian was not kidding. In front of my face was a pocket, a two-finger hole. This was the famous crux move that on the first ascent (led by Martin Harris in March 1966) had held up the party for a long time.

The noise came nearer and nearer and the situation was getting desperate. I almost fell off, I was shaking so much but, pushing the middle fingers of my right hand into the pocket, pulling as hard as I could and then walking my feet up the rock face, I almost leapt into the air, grabbed a ledge and was up. I climbed the next ten metres to the top as if the hounds of hell were after me and, without belaying, simply ran as fast as I could across the cliff top, holding the rope until it came tight. Ian needed no instructions from me, as soon as the rope came taught he started to climb and I just kept moving away from the cliff edge as he ascended. Until the bee threat we had been finding the climbing quite difficult and it had been taking us a long time, but now Ian raced up the cliff and he joined me within seconds.

'For Christ's sake, run!' The sky was now black with bees and I needed no more urging. We ran across the top of the cliffs then descended some way down the easy hillside at their southern edge and were relieved to see the bees carried away on a slight breeze over our heads. I had only been stung a couple of times but these hurt like hell. Ian grinned with relief but then went on to recall the horrific story of how he had been attacked on the Main Wall at Hell's Gate, Kenya's most impressive and committing cliff. Despite being continually stung, he and his partner had managed to once again race upwards to safety, for he seemed convinced that if they had stayed put they would almost certainly have

Climbing on Table Mountain, Africa Crag.
Photo Michael Scott

died a most painful death.

By the time I left Kenya at the end of 1971 I had learned that climbing in Africa was as much about being at one with the environment as it was about being a technically proficient rock jock or mountaineer.

On the way home from Nairobi to London we flew for hundreds of miles over the Sahara on a superb clear day. Looking down from the sky at the vastness of that desert I wondered why anyone might wish to travel and climb in such a bleak environment, not appreciating that from 15,000m the subtleties of such a landscape would be totally hidden from view and what appeared as hillocks might be considerable peaks, whilst the small rock faces were actually huge cliffs.

My next African journeys were to be in South Africa in February 1981 to take part in a mountain rescue exercise in the Drakensberg mountains of Natal and to make a lecture tour throughout the Republic. My previous experience in Kenya did help me considerably whilst climbing there, especially in dealing with the snakes and baboons, although the cliffs of South Africa are generally much freer of vegetation and animal life than their northern counterparts.

I managed to climb in the Drakensberg and at Monteseel (both in Natal), on the Lion's Head and Table Mountain whilst in Cape Town and in the Magaliesberg range near to Johannesburg, besides visiting many other areas such as Du Toit's Kloof, the Hex River mountains and the Paarl Rock Dome. It was a truly memorable trip travelling through some of the most beautiful country in the world, particularly in the Eastern Cape. I was impressed with the quality of the rock (except for the Drakensberg which is basalt) and it is no surprise to me now that South Africa is becoming an 'in' place for today's leading activists to visit.

Morocco

In October 1987 a chance visit to Morocco to attend the UIAA General Assembly in Marrakech made me change my mind about the worth of desert landscapes. I had never been attracted to the Arab countries of North Africa before, but I was enthralled by how exotic Morocco was; so near to Europe, yet so different with its own unique brand of Islam and its Berber population.

The weather was superb with hot days and cool nights, but it was the light that fascinated me. As you move south towards the Sahara it becomes ever more intense, until the blue above you, the sunsets and the starlit nights make all the other skies you have seen look like pale imitations. I was won over and I set about getting to know this wonderland.

Morocco is a mountaineer's country, with impressive winter climbing and skiing in the Atlas ranges, superb rock climbing at Todhra Gorge (both traditional and sports), wonderful trekking in the mountains and deserts, a bouldering paradise in the Anti Atlas range at Tafraoute and, in the Ameln valley below that, quartzite cliffs reminiscent of climbing on Gogarth. Add to this the Atlantic coast at Mirleft, where there are sea cliffs which are a mini version of Pembroke.

After fourteen trips I feel I know Morocco fairly well. It is a country that it is easy to travel around by bus or taxi without ever losing a sense of adventure or wonder. I have subsequently led several trekking groups both in the mountains and deserts, but sometimes I have been there alone and during these journeys I have enjoyed some unusual experiences. Until I began travelling solo I realise I knew little of true adventure, for with a party or companion from your own culture you are cushioned from the harsh realities of facing up to an alien lifestyle. On your own you must come to terms, join in or remain an outcast.

In the winter of 1988 I decided to explore the Rif mountains in the north of Morocco, a vast limestone mass up to 2500m in height with dense upland forests. I flew to Gibraltar then travelled by ferry from Algeciras to Tangier. From there I caught a bus to Chaouen, despite a warning how dangerous the Rif area can be as the centre of the hashish trade.

In Tangiers I met a young Japanese who was in a terrible plight. He could hardly speak English and no French, and he had been at Chaouen intending to visit the Rif when he had met some Riffis who had pretended friendship. They had invited him to their home for a meal and picked him up in a car outside his hotel. They had driven for miles up into the mountains where they had taken him into a house and fed him on drugged food. He'd been held hostage for several days until he handed over his money, bank cards and travellers cheques signed up and dated. They had then gone off and cashed them. Returning, the Riffis had driven him up into the hills and dropped him at night in a remote district. He had no idea where he had been nor any clear description of the fraudsters and the Moroccan police, with nothing to go on to trace the gang, had simply run him down to Tangiers.

I listened sympathetically to his story, then lent him some money to get the ferry across to Spain and set forth determined not to suffer the same fate. I arrived in Chaouen and was excited to note a cliff of white limestone outside the town. After checking into a cheap hotel, I set off with my rock boots in hand and a chalk bag around my waist to take a closer look at this challenge. On arrival at the base of the crag I was surprised to find in-situ pitons sticking out of the cracks. These looked so ancient and rusty I guessed they must date from pre-independence days, perhaps placed by French climbers in the early fifties? The crag was about forty metres high and composed of firm limestone but set at slab angle.

I picked out an obvious line to follow, changed out of my trainers into Fires and got going. About twenty metres up the rock steepened and I was stuck for a long while trying to climb an overlap. Retreating to a ledge for a rest I noted that at the base of the cliff a young Berber had climbed up from the path below and sat watching me with interest. I was gobsmacked when a moment later he shouted up in nasal scouse, 'Are yer all right up there?'

'Yes, yes!' I assured him. Just the fact that someone was below and I was no longer on my own gave me the confidence to start climbing again and to bridge up delicately in order to reach a good pocket and pull over the obstacle which had been stopping me. The rest of the climb was a doddle up an easy groove well supplied with holds and rusty old pitons. I traversed off the top of the cliff and descended down a ramp back to its base, worried my trainers might have disappeared along with the English speaking local. I was wrong, however, for he was still waiting for me by my Nikes and he introduced himself as Mr Lahcen from Ketama. At the mention of that name the hair rose on the back of my neck, for anyone you meet from there in other parts of Morocco is almost certain to be involved in the hashish trade. Many are the dire warnings given in tourist guidebooks about the need to avoid such contacts and to give the area itself a wide berth. I tried to keep an open mind and gave my name to this new acquaintance, intrigued as to how he came to speak fluent English with a Liverpool accent.

It transpired he had just spent three years in a Spanish jail in Malaga for smuggling hashish and his cell mate throughout the whole of that period had been a Scouser who had taught him his own unique brand of English! He was twenty-three years old, stockily built with the usual Berber mop of thick black curly hair and dressed in Western garb - jeans and a sweater. He wanted me to go with him to Ketama to meet his friends, for he was obviously impressed by my ascent of the cliff face above him, assuring me that there were many higher and steeper crags close to his town.

After talking to Lahcen for some time I decided I could trust him and, in any case, if I really wanted to see the Rif mountains and to journey via Ketama I was better off with him than on my own - a prey for the local mafiosi who cruise the byways of the range in black Mercedes, forcing unsuspecting visitors to buy huge quantities of kif and then set them up with the local police who they are in cahoots with!

Kif or hashish grows wild all over the Rif area, but it was the Spaniards who encouraged its production when, along with the French, they were the colonial powers in Morocco. In the early 1970s the hashish trade really took off in Northern Morocco, when an American developed the technique for producing it as cannabis resin. This made it easily transportable, and the locals had a much sought-after product. Inevitably, big business moved in, but it is illegal to possess or use kif in Morocco, as many tourists have found to their cost. I never touch the stuff and have seen enough on my travels in the Mahgreb to believe that those who say it is harmless are fooling themselves. Everything depends, I suppose, on how often and how much one indulges, but the long term effects can be devastating health wise.

Ketama turned out to be an anti-climax when Lahcen and I finally reached there. Nestling in the heart of the Rif mountains in a glorious setting, no one tried to kidnap me and no one offered me huge amounts of hashish. In typical Berber fashion, once my companion had offered his hand in friendship, he was very protective. The scenery was stunning and, though the Rif mountains are mainly covered by Cedar forests, there are large cliffs sticking out of some of the hillsides. Arriving late, for our bus was much delayed en route, I stayed the night with Lahcen in his tiny one-roomed apartment at his parents' small house in the town and then moved off to visit Fez, catching a local bus early the next morning.

Before I left my Berber guide took me to a cafe for breakfast to meet his friends. After introductions all around we had coffee and omelettes with bread and several of those present actually ate pieces of cannabis resin along with their meal! They cut slices from a huge block of the stuff which one of them had produced. Lahcen asked me if I would like to try some but I declined, thanking him profusely whilst assuring him it was against my religion to do so in order not to offend someone who only meant me well. Moroccans can understand one refusing on such grounds, but to decline simply because you do not like something is not only seen as bad manners but, with groups like the Riffi tribesman, it can be insulting and thus dangerous.

Unfortunately I also had a very bad experience in North Africa the year after the above events. Inspired by discovering the bouldering area of Tafraoute and the cliffs of the Ameln valley in the Anti Atlas range of Morocco during Christmas 1987, I became convinced that there must be other finds to be made in the neighbouring country of Tunisia.

Starting out at Sousse in the winter of 1989, I travelled across the Tell (the high upland farming area of that country), to the Algerian border without so much as discovering a boulder. I had almost become convinced that Tunisia was another Holland when I met two young Arab students at Maktar, that wonderful Roman ruin. The two nineteen-year-olds informed me that near to their village, Elgeira, were big cliffs full of snakes and scorpions. Thus I arranged to go there the next day for it was en route to Kairouan and they agreed they would meet me and show me around.

When I got off the bus from Maktar at Elgeira, Mohammed and his cousin Abdul were waiting there to greet me. They were both dressed in light djellabas, the full-length hooded robe worn throughout North Africa, and wearing sandals. Both had their wavy hair cropped short western style.

As I descended from the bus I was excited to see a line of cliffs which were reminiscent of the Buoux escarpment in Southern France, just as they had promised. I walked down to these rocks accompanied by the two Arab youths and began to look for possible routes.

The base of the cliffs were guarded by some of the biggest cacti I have ever seen and in any case the faces were so steep and high that I did not dare to attempt to climb them solo. Above and to the right of the main crag was a small valley and there I noted a fine, barrel-shaped buttress of clean limestone about twenty metres in height. I decided to try to climb that and once again changed out of my trainers into rock boots, buckled on my chalk bag, and left the canvas shoulder bag that I was carrying with Mohammed.

The first ten metres passed without incident, climbing up steeply pocketed limestone, but then I was confronted with a crack; a fissure of hand width into which I pushed some jams, only to quickly remove them when I realised that this contained many scurrying insects. They were baby scorpions! I had seen several such arachnids by then in Kenya and down in the Sahara, but I had never experienced a crack full of them before. They are not as dangerous as popular myth makes out, but if they do sting you it hurts desperately. Once I did get bitten on the hand collecting brushwood and I am not too keen to repeat the experience.

I traversed right to reach a groove leading up to a finishing chimney. Once again I climbed easily up pocketed limestone until I reached the finale. This turned out to be harder and steeper than it looked and I nearly retreated from the last section, which was almost overhanging. With my body jammed inside the fissure as I climbed up, and my hands on the outside edges, I found good holds and was just pulling over the top when I felt an incision on the back of my left hand. A tiny red spider had bit me – I must have disturbed its nest – and the hurt was out of all proportion to the size of the wound. My hand was swelling even as I descended down the slope at the side of the buttress to rejoin my two Arab acquaintances. They seemed impressed by my climb but genuinely concerned by my injury and invited me back to Mohammed's parents' farm nearby to wash and dress my hand with antiseptic.

The house turned out to be a ramshackle red brick collection of buildings and barns, in a most run down state of repair. There was only the youth's younger brother, sixteen-year-old Thami; the rest of the family were away working and living in France. After washing my hand in hot water and applying liberal amounts of antiseptic and binding it up in a dressing, both of which I had been carrying in my first aid kit, I was about to depart to catch my bus to Kairouan when Mohammed suggested I stay for the evening. He insisted that the spider's bite could be dangerous and advised me to have a meal with them and rest up until the morning .

I gladly agreed to accept this offer as my hand was extremely painful and I could feel that the wound was throbbing away beneath the bandage. I hadn't much time left before my flight back to the UK, but if I left early the next morning I decided I could easily reach Kairouan by lunchtime and Sousse that night, ready to depart from Monastir early on the following morning.

Mohammed and I then sat around talking whilst Abdul and Thami disappeared into the kitchen to prepare a meal. At that point I had no reason to doubt the intentions of these Tunisians. There was no electricity at the farm and no glass in any of the windows, so as darkness set in it began to feel very cold. The only light was from a paraffin lantern and this did not give out sufficient illumination to see anything clearly. When the food eventually arrived it looked fine; a good helping of couscous was handed to me on a plate which had been ladled out in the kitchen beforehand. I was very hungry and tucked into the meat, vegetables and steamed semolina with gusto. As I ate I noted a strong taste which I took to be a spice, a common enough additive in North African cooking.

Within minutes of finishing I began to feel giddy and was slurring my words as I spoke. It was just as if I was drunk. Mohammed came up to me, grabbed me by the hand and led me into a bare room in which there was no furniture other than an old fashioned brass bed like my grandparents used to own. 'Tu es fatigué mon ami. Dorme bien, dorme bien!' He motioned towards the bed and disappeared out of the room. I undressed and quickly snuggled under the piles of blankets on the bed and fell into a deep slumber.

When I awoke some time later I just didn't know where I was but realised what was happening. Mohammed was on top of me and he was breathing heavily into my face! He had my legs up on his shoulders and he did not intend to seek my permission. Despite being drugged (for I now guessed they had liberally spread my food with cannabis seeds) I brought my legs right up to my chest and, recoiling with all my might, managed to throw him off me through the air, to rebound off the end of the bed and down onto the brick floor. I heard him gasp and swear in Arabic as he hit the deck with force but once again I lapsed into unconsciousness.

The next time I regained my senses it was just getting light and there in the bed beside me was Mohammed, totally naked. Recoiling at his presence after his attempts to rape me in the night, I grunted and climbed out of bed, dressed quickly and, grabbing my bag, wandered out into the yard to the water pump. I stripped off and washed myself thoroughly, although the water was freezing cold as the sun was not up yet. I was just finishing my ablutions when I heard Mohammed shouting out to Abdul and his brother, no doubt boasting about how he had taken me the night before.

I decided to get away from that place as quickly as I could, furious at my naivety but, just as I was leaving and going out through the farm gate, Mohammed came chasing after me. He called me his *cheri* and begged me to stay for breakfast. I assured him I wasn't his *cheri* and in my rage told him that I had AIDS. I've never seen anyone change their attitude so fast.

He then followed me all the way down the track from the farm leading to the main road, pleading with me to take him to the hospital at Kairouan for tests. He appeared certain that he would now develop AIDS himself. Maybe it was a cruel thing to do, but I felt no remorse as I climbed aboard the bus to Kairouan leaving Mohammed on the roadside almost weeping with fear. I guess it was a case of the biter being bit, although I did promise myself, as I sat uncomfortably on that hard bus seat nursing my injured hand, that I would be more circumspect about what I ate in future!

Out With the Boys Again

The very best rock climbing in North Africa is to be found in the Tohdra Gorge situated in the Central Atlas range of Morocco. It rivals its French counterpart at

Verdon, with everything from 300 metre traditional climbs to modern single pitch sports routes. I have been there many times in the last decade and during those ten years I have witnessed an amazing period of development. At the time of writing eighteen separate sectors have been opened up with over 200 routes, but there is still room for many times that number.

The rock is firm ochre coloured limestone, and on my first visit to the Todhra in the winter of 1987 I had an epic adventure with two Italians I met by chance, although I suspect they were in Morocco more to smoke dope than climb seriously.

I arrived at the small hotel El Mansour at the mouth of the Gorge determined to do some climbing. Todhra is at altitude and in December the nights are very cold, although during the day it can be pleasantly warm climbing in the sun. When I arrived it was evening and the two Italians were sat smoking hash on the hotel balcony, but they confirmed that they were climbers and told me on the morrow they were going to attempt the Pilier du Couchant. I was impressed, for this is one of the major features of the Gorge and the climb they intended is graded V and 260 metres in length. They invited me to go along with them and, without thinking, I agreed.

It took the Italians, Roberto and Mario, an awful long time to get sorted the next morning and it was past ten o'clock before we commenced climbing. My companions could not have been more different; Mario was dark-haired, tall, bespectacled and slight, whilst Roberto was small in stature but powerful, with dyed gingery hair. Once we had managed to set off for the climb they showed their fitness, almost running up a steep stony slope to the base of the Pillar.

We decided that Roberto would lead on two ropes and then, in order to save time at the end of each pitch, simultaneously bring up Mario and I climbing just behind each other. Even using such methods our progress was slow and by the time we had climbed four pitches it was obvious that we would have to bivouac out for the night unless we speeded up our ascent.

Roberto was leading the fifth pitch whilst Mario and I watched his ropes. He had almost reached the belay, but as he pulled over to gain the ledge, grabbing at a piton, it shot out of its crack and the next moment he tumbled off backwards. Falling in an arch, he hurtled down ten metres until his rope (held by me through a peg) stopped him. But as it did so he swung into the rock face and hit his left shoulder against the rock. Ouch! I could sense his pain and instinctively knew he was badly hurt. Immediately I started to lower him back down to the ledge where Mario and I crouched together, trying to avoid being hit by any debris dislodged.

There was no question of going on now and our roles were reversed. Roberto's left arm hung by his side and Mario and I agreed that we needed to lower him back down the cliff, then we could follow him by abseil. Whilst the two Italians performed first aid on the injured shoulder, making a sling out of climbing tape, I joined our two fifty-metre ropes together. The length should be sufficient to lower Roberto to the ground.

I was impressed by the Italians' calmness in the face of adversity. Here we were in the middle of Morocco, with the nearest hospital hours away, but they were making light of it and joking about a friend back in Bologna.

We began to lower Roberto, with me holding his rope and Mario backing up on a second belay so that when we came to the knots at fifty metres I could tie off the system, then take Roberto's rope out of my Sticht plate below the obstruction and replace it above. It worked like a charm until it came to the change over, when somehow my plate became jammed and I could not get it off the rope. I had Roberto tied off, hanging on the belay. Struggle as I might, I just could not get my Sticht plate free and my hands were becoming increasingly numb, for by now it was late afternoon. Mario was wearing gloves and leaning down, hanging by his waist belay, he reached the offending friction device and pulled it off the rope for me. Soon we had Roberto moving once more and he reached the ground a hundred metres below us just as the sun set, with absolutely no rope to spare.

By the time Mario and I had followed him with three difficult diagonal abseils it was pitch dark. Descending the slope below the Pillar by the light of our head torches and helping the injured man down proved to be the most difficult part of our descent. On one occasion Mario took a terrible tumble falling over a boulder, on another all three of us catapulted into space, which made Roberto squeal out in pain as we landed together on the rocky slope. By the time we reached the safety of the El Mansour we must have looked a sorry sight, supporting each other after wading through the waters of the freezing river just opposite the hotel doorway.

Just as we arrived back at the hotel a Grand Taxi turned up from Tinerhir, far down below in the Dades valley, transporting some locals up to the Gorge who had been down in town for the weekly souk. After some hurried chasing around, picking up money and passports, the two Italians were transported down to the valley at speed. The Moroccan Peugeot 404 taxis really do get a bat on, especially with a Berber tribesman at the wheel. I did not see my friends again for three days after that, but when they returned Roberto had his injured limb in a sling as his shoulder had been operated on. It transpired he had badly dislocated it and it had needed to be put back under an anaesthetic.

Their journey had taken two days of hard travelling by taxis and buses to a hospital situated at the northern end of the Dades valley and back. The scale of the geography in the Atlas ranges is immense, as I was to find out in succeeding years leading treks there. When I left the Gorge the following lunchtime Roberto and Mario were once again sat on the balcony of the El Mansour smoking hashish.

The Ait Atta

My most recent climbing trip to the Gorge was at Easter 1997. There are now four hotels catering mainly for tourists, but most climbers prefer to stay at the El Mansour or L'Etoile. My young friend Jumper and I climbed at the new sector, Le Petite Gorge. This is a long way above the main Gorge and away from the bun eaters, about one hour's walk each way up and down from the hotels. It is beautifully situated in a small valley with palm trees and boasts many fine routes of all grades on perfect clean rock, mainly pioneered by Spanish climbers.

Up there we kept meeting an old Ait Atta Berber who was herding camels which he moved up and down the Gorge at will as his tribe have ancient grazing rights in the Central Atlas. He jumped out on us from behind a boulder, his wizened turbaned face creased with smiles, demanding as he shuffled towards us, 'Photo? Je suis un nomad! Donnez moi cinq dirham!' We gave him one dirham and took his picture and he did not complain, for the hustlers at the Todhra Gorge are not like the ones in Marrakech or Fez, who either get you to pay up or starve to death. This ancient tribesman had his camels to keep him alive.

The Ait Atta live in the mountains of the Sarhro which run south from the Dades valley into the Sahara. In the winter months of the period 1989-92 I led six treks through these mountains, a beautiful range of jagged peaks, high desert plateau and deep valleys. On each occasion my guide was Alilouch, a nomad who lived in a goat-hair tent surrounded by his three wives, children and flocks of goats and sheep. A fifty-year-old man with the stamina and physique of an Olympic middle distance runner, so fit was he.

At the end of the eighties the whole area just north of the Sahara was suffering from a disastrous drought and some of the Ait Atta who came along as helpers on our treks, such as Omar, had been forced to settle down, building rude houses out of stone in order to be near to the wells which were their only source of water. However, on Christmas Day 1989, on my first trek in the Sarhro, the sky clouded over in the late afternoon and it started to snow! Within minutes a blizzard had set in and it became colder and colder. Fortunately, we had not yet penetrated deep into the range and were still in a region with some pastoralists. We managed to find shelter in a bare brick building with a mud floor which was used to house sheep at night to safeguard them from predators.

As we staggered into the building wet through, tired and cold one of the trekkers, a young lady from New Zealand, appeared to be exhausted. Once inside she collapsed and my immediate thought was hypothermia. No hot baths out in the Sarhro, so we pushed her into our sleeping bags laid on a groundsheet. As I did so I happened to catch her breath - I was surprised to realise that she smelled like a distillery! Lying on the floor with a dozen anxious trekkers gathered around her, the Kiwi first began to giggle then to sing.

'She's not hypothermic,' decided my co-leader, Ann, a real no-nonsense Aussie. 'She's bleeding drunk!' And so she was. As we had trekked along the New Zealander had been taking sips from a festive bottle she was carrying, and by the time we had reached the shelter she had drunk most of a full one.

The Sarhro mountains are truly a wonderful area and I hardly saw a cloud on any of my five other treks. During each trek we climbed three mountains; Amlal, Bou Gaffer and Amalou n' Mansour, the latter being the highest at 2,712 metres. One of the areas that we trekked through, the Bab N' Ali region set on the plateau of Tadaout n Tablah, is a stunning place. The whole region is littered with spectacular conglomerate towers, many a hundred metres high. Whilst the other two mountains we ascended might be dismissed as mere slogs, Bou Gaffer is a beautiful granite mountain reminiscent of the Buachaille Etive Mor in Glencoe. To reach its summit by the easiest route you need to rock climb, albeit at an easy standard, but when you do get up there you can look down on the Sahara, flicking its fingers towards the base of the peak.

It was at Bou Gaffer in 1933 that the Ait Atta made their last stand against the French and when we used to climb the mountain on our treks Alilouch, whose grandfather had been there, used to reenact this event as we climbed up the peak. It was one of the great battles in the history of warfare; on one side you had 1,000 tribesmen used to guerrilla action together with their wives and children, in all about 7,000 persons. On the other a modern army of 83,000 men of the Foreign Legion backed up by four aircraft squadrons.

The battle started on February 2lst and ended on the 25th March. One can imagine the Ait Atta creeping down off Bou Gaffer in the night, crawling into the French encampments and killing silently to return back up the mountain again by dawn. The carnage was terrible and, though the Ait Atta lost half their fighters, for every man they lost the French lost many more.

In the end the Ait Atta surrendered, but only after they had been offered a treaty of friendship under which they still lived when I was trekking through their land. They govern themselves via their tribal leaders, make their own laws and pay no taxes. I used to have a young Ait Atta from Nkob village called Adi along with me on the treks who had been to school and could speak French. The Ait Atta speak Berber, which has three main dialects in Morocco. There is no written language, and there is still a tradition amongst the locals to sit around in the Sarhro at night, telling each other stories from their history over a brush-wood fire. The Ait Atta would not be able to understand a Berber from the Rif for their language is now so distinct, although it has the same roots. The dialect they speak is known as Tashelhait and it was via Adi that I would give instructions about camping, cooking and route finding. By talking to him whilst we walked along I learnt about the region, its history and about his tribe, who are without doubt amongst the hardiest mountain people I have been with.

At night in the Sarhro in winter it is bitterly cold and I have known water freeze inside the tent. Yet I have also seen Alilouch and his friends bed down for the night in those same conditions out under the stars, wearing only their djellabas, white turbans and sandals to sleep like babes. In summer at Nkob it can be as hot as fifty Celsius and, though it is on the edge of the mountains and in a valley, it can still freeze there in the winter. Thus the Ait Atta live in one of the most challenging regions on earth. During our treks it became clear to me how important water and the wells are to these people. You might find water in the Sarhro in the winter to keep you alive but in summer, if you do not know where the wells are situated and aren't good at navigating between them, you might soon be dead. After being with the same five Berbers for six treks I felt they were my friends and I trusted them implicitly. We had many good laughs together and some anxious moments, but the proudest was when they dressed me up in a set of their clothes and pointed at me and shouted delightedly, 'Ait Atta!'

Most of those who came on Sarhro treks were climbers or hill walkers from the UK or the Commonwealth. Occasionally people would show up and I'd wonder why they had decided to take part. There were the two vegan ladies who complained when our Berbers returned from a village with a sheep, which they proceeded to slaughter halal fashion. There was a full plate of meat for any trekker who wished, but for those who did not the Ait Atta could cover. Five of them would eat a whole sheep in a single sitting, staying up half the night cooking and eating. They were like camels themselves, for when food was plentiful they would stoke up as much as they could, but when it was short (which it often is in the Sarhro), they could manage for days on a handful of dates.

On another occasion a young punk girl from London turned up at our pre-trek rendezvous in Marrakech. I doubt she had been much further than the Tottenham Court Road before that trip and she certainly turned some heads in that city with her dyed red hair, Doc Marten's and wearing a punk outfit.

The first night in the Sarhro she came up to me and demanded to know where the snakes and scorpions were. This was desert and by her reckoning the place should be teeming with them. 'Oh you never see them,' I assured her tongue in cheek, 'they hide under the boulders but there are masses of them about.' She walked away obviously unconvinced, but stopped at the first rock sticking up out of the sandy ground and turned it over. With a squeal she was off like Linford Christie for under that boulder was the biggest scorpion I have ever seen. For the rest of the trip she treated my every pronouncement with a respect that embarrassed me.

One other lady who caused me to worry when she arrived in Marrakech was a famous TV scriptwriter, who confidentially took me on one side and confessed she was on the verge of a nervous breakdown. Her doctor had advised her to have a complete rest with a long spell at a health farm but she could not afford to be away from her desk for that length of time, so she had decided to come on a trek instead. She was hugely overweight and unfit, although she had done some climbing in her youth. Somehow she doggedly chain smoked her way around the route, including climbing all of the three peaks in the process.

We had some histrionics on the way, with denunciations of the Director General of the BBC and myself, who she accused of being a small time Adolf Hitler! We parted the best of friends and she returned to London quite sanguine, many pounds the lighter and down to smoking ten cigarettes a day. It proved in the end to be much cheaper than a health farm!

Grand Atlas Marathon

I was to find that trek leading gave me a good level of fitness. Walking over rough ground at altitude brought physical benefits and so, at the end of the New Year Sarhro trip of 1990, I decided to stay in Morocco and take part in the Grand Atlas Marathon. This is one of the great runs of the calendar and, although not as big as the New York, London or Tokyo events, it is nonetheless the most famous in North Africa. Thus it was that on the 14th January 1990 on a beautiful clear day many thousands of us assembled in the huge Place Djemaa el Fna in the centre of Marrakech, with runners taking part from all over the Mahgreb plus a sprinkling of overseas participants.

Moroccans love sport and athletics in particular and their hero, the Olympian Said Aouita, was supposed to start us at 9 a.m. Also at the start as we lined up were hundreds of Berber tribesmen in their traditional costumes, some of whom were carrying rifles; Gnaoua drummers, Chleuh dancers (men and boys dressed in women's clothes), snake charmers, jugglers, acrobats and chanters. It was truly colourful and it could only have been in Morocco.

Lining everyone up seemed to take ages for the din from the spectators was deafening and it was hard to hear any of the announcements. Unfortunately, one of the tribesman became impatient and fired off his rifle. Many of the runners thought this was the signal to start and set off on the course. Others, like me, were not so sure and we hung around for a while, but as nothing was happening to arrest the pack I set off after those in front and was soon into my stride. After hesitating the officials then decided to bring everyone back and to start again.

False starts are unheard of in a marathon and by the time the police caught me up on their motorbikes I had run over two kilometres. Those in front must have covered twice that distance but we stopped, turned around and jogged back to the start. When the race was restarted it was after 10 a.m. and the difference that this would make to the slower runners like me was only obvious once I had passed the half marathon post at 21.097kms.

We ran out through the palmeries and into the desert and, though Marrakech is on a plain, the backdrop was fantastic with the snow-covered High Atlas looming up on the horizon. The course was as flat as a snooker table and it seemed to suit me up to reaching halfway. I still continued to run strongly up to the 30kms marker but by then the heat was beginning to take its toll. Even in January it can be hot in Marrakech and as we approached midday I began to tire. Though I took on water at every station, I just could not get enough of the stuff down me in order to avoid becoming dehydrated.

I had fallen in with a group of Moroccans from Casablanca, mainly Arabs and, running in their slipstream, I was being taken with them towards the finish. Suddenly I hit the wall so feared by marathon runners and my legs began to feel wobbly. I could no longer live with the pace and I started to fall back, whilst every part of my body racked with pain and cramp. It was just like being at 6,000 metres when you are unacclimatised and your head is aching, your tongue is sticking to the roof of your mouth, your heart is beating irregularly and you feel like you just cannot put one foot in front of the other.

I actually considered dropping out at that point but a chirpy little Berber from the High Atlas came up alongside me, grinned and pointed up ahead. He was small in stature but with powerful legs, wearing a football shirt, long shorts and plastic sandals on his feet. I was later to learn he was only seventeen years old, although you are supposed to be at least twenty before you take on a marathon because of the physical demands it poses.

Somehow I managed to keep going, partly because all the way round the course there were masses of spectators, drummers and chanters who cheered us every bit of the way, but also because the young Berber at my side kept shouting,

'Aiwat!Aiwat!' (Let's go). I could not respond other than to grunt an 'OK.' Although he could easily have gone on ahead, so strongly was he running, he stayed beside me urging that I keep going forward.

By that time we were back in the middle of Marrakech running down the long straight of the Avenue Moulay Rachid. The 40kms marker arrived at last and I knew as I reached that point that I was going to make the finish, and so I waved my young companion on gasping at him a 'Shokran', at which he was off like a hare.

I began to feel better and even picked up some speed myself, passing several runners who were in an even worse state than me. Up ahead I could see a large crowd of spectators and found I was then back in the Place Djemaa, where I finally reached the finishing tape, managing a weak sprint to see off an American runner who was a long way from home.

There to greet me with a loud cheer were my friends, the staff from the Hotel Foucald where I was staying, but also the little Berber who seemed more delighted by my efforts than at his own impressive performance. There are kids like him all over Africa who live at altitude and have to run to complete their daily round, developing an amazing stamina and fitness. It is no wonder they are now dominating world middle and long distance running. My time was just under four hours so I was more than satisfied, though I do believe, if it had not been for the problems posed by that false start, I could have bettered it. I walked over to the little Berber, gave him a big hug and thanked him for his help, for without him to pace me I am sure I would have given up.

Later that night I sat alone on the roof of the Foucald gazing up at the vastness of the African sky. A myriad of stars were shining and I was happy to note that it never really goes dark in Marrakech in such conditions. The next morning I was so stiff I could not walk and I had to go down the stairs on my backside! My legs had taken such a pounding out on the course of the Grand Atlas Marathon that they never really recovered. I had intended trying the New York run next, having already completed the London twice, but I had to call it a day for at fifty-five my body would not stand it any more. I was content with my performance; I had run the Marrakech by leading two treks, one immediately after the other, as training. To break four hours, a long-cherished ambition, was proof for me of just how fit you can get by arduous hill walking.

My greatest effort in this respect was when I agreed to lead the first double crossing of the Atlas Grand Traverse in the summer of 1991. This entailed starting in the Ait Bougamez valley beneath Jebel M'Goun then climbing that peak, the highest in the Central Atlas, and twenty days later finishing on the summit of Toubkal at 4165m in the High Atlas (the highest mountain in North Africa). In between these two mountains was twenty days of hard slogging, climbing up and down high passes, ascending many lesser peaks and in some cases huge scree slopes, negotiating gorges and wading fast-flowing rivers. Once we had completed the traverse we retreated to Marrakech, said goodbye to the first group of trekkers then picked up a second party and started out again in reverse.

On the first crossing we had a marvellous group who were tolerant of the fact

Berbers in the High Atlas singing the night away.   Photo Dennis Gray

that we were working out the route as we trekked, especially with regard to camp sites replete with the essential drinkable water. This trek took place in July and August and throughout the first leg it was the hottest weather I have ever known in the mountains. No one complained, even though it was at times physically demanding, and one Irish lady seemed as determined to complete the route as any of us. Hiking along she would curse and swear, take a tumble, then pick herself up and be on her way again. Diminutive in stature, she was very fine company with that wonderful way the Irish have of telling a story to her own disadvantage.

When we finally reached our goal and had completed the traverse South to North, she came up to me in triumph once we were back at the Hotel Foucald in Marrakech with an affidavit, which she asked me to sign as trek leader. This was to be witnessed by two of the other members of the party and stated that she had completed this difficult route successfully. It transpired she was in the process of getting divorced and, as a part of her settlement with her wealthy husband, she had taken on a bet with him that she, a novice mountaineer, would complete the Atlas Grand Traverse. If she did this successfully her former spouse had agreed to pay for a free trip around the world for her, staying in luxury hotels; if she had failed she would have needed to fund him on a similar venture. I was happy to sign this for her but as I did so I understood the real reason for her determination to complete the route!

Three days before the end of the first trek I stumbled on some rough ground close to a village, put out my hand to stop myself and a thorn penetrated the first finger of my right hand. The one thing that the Berbers have never done is to develop proper sewerage or toilet systems, and in summer it is most insanitary around any of their dwellings. They are probably immune to most of these infections but I was not. I bathed my hand in Dettol as soon as I reached camp that evening but within a day my finger was turning septic. A nurse from Anchorage was on this trek and, utilising our ample medicine chest, we tried to stop this infection spreading, but to no avail. Despite taking antibiotics and even trying to lance the swelling ourselves, sitting in a tent working by the light of a Gaz lamp, the poison continued to spread. So much so that by the time I had reached the summit of Toubkal two days later my finger was double its size, yellow throughout its length and I had tramlines of infection running all the way up my arm and was feeling awful.

The moment we were down the mountains and had reached Marrakech I phoned the hospital, worried that if it was not treated immediately I might lose my arm or worse. I was surprised by the reply that it was a Muslim feast day and that they were not seeing any patients until the morrow. I insisted that I speak to a doctor and eventually a surgeon answered. Once I had explained he agreed to see me, but warned that if he needed to operate he had no anaesthetic available until the following day. By then I was most concerned and set out to see him on the hottest day I have ever known in Morocco, for it was in the high 40's.

When the surgeon saw my finger and arm he decided he must lance it and drain the infection immediately. However, as the hospital dispensary was closed I first had to go off in a taxi to purchase the bandages, antiseptic and antibiotics he decided he would need, clutching a prescription written out in Arabic for me. The first chemist I arrived at could not supply these and I began to feel desperate; I was soaked in my own sweat and feeling dizzy through the double effect of the infection and the heat. Nobody normally moves around in Marrakech during midday at the end of July. They sent me to another chemist, who sent me on to another who could thankfully supply all my requirements. Then it was back in a taxi to the hospital and one of the most gruelling experiences of my life.

The surgeon was waiting for me when I returned and he led me into an operating theatre where he introduced me to a huge figure of a man, Mustapha, a male nurse who worked in the hospital. His task was to hold me down whilst the surgeon cut my finger open with a scalpel, then worked my arm to drain out the infection without any form of anaesthetic. Once they started on this operation my screams would have woken the dead. With my body racked in pain and soaked in sweat (there was no air-conditioning), I screamed so loudly and pulled so hard to escape my restraint, that the surgeon remonstrated with me, 'You're soft!' He then went on to tell me how any Atlas Berber would have been able to remain perfectly still whilst he carried out his task. When it was finally over and my finger stitched up and encased in bandages with my arm placed in a sling, I weakly thanked him and paid the fee for the operation, which was about £50. He then advised me to take the antibiotics he had prescribed and stay in bed for a week to let my body recover.

Later that night, being too ill to attend the end of trek party, I was lying feeling sorry for myself in a room at the Foucald when a knock came on the door. I wobbled out of bed, crossed the floor and opened it up and there before me were some of the members of our Atlas Grand Traverse party, clutching a full bottle of whisky. 'Here, drink this Dennis, this will get you up the hill again!' They were right; three days later I was on my way back again to complete the second traverse of the main Atlas range, changing my own dressings and cleaning my wound as we went. However, despite the fact that the surgeon had made a good job of draining the infection, my elbow remained damaged for several years after this event, for the poison had affected the joint. I needed to climb for a long time afterwards wearing a plastic brace as a support.

The Painted Rocks

When I first became interested in Morocco I read every book I could about the country and one writer in particular impressed me more than any other, Paul Bowles, an American who lives in Tangiers. One day I was reading something he had written when my eyes became riveted to this sentence; 'The area around the Tafraoute Oasis is like the badlands of Dakota only writ large, with fingers of granite and high peaks all around'. I looked this place up on the map and found it on the south side of the Anti Atlas range, an old French Foreign Legion Post on the edge of the sub-Sahara. I decided to check this out at Christmas 1987 and set forth from Yorkshire, travelling by bus to London, then on to Paris, down through Spain, across to Morocco, arriving in Tafraoute several days later.

I have never been more excited than at the sight which greeted me as the bus from Tiznit rolled down what is now the old road, across the Tafraoute plateau and into the Oasis. For many kilometres before we arrived we had passed cliff after cliff, some several dozen metres in height and the whole area was littered

The Tafraoute Oasis in Morocco.   Photo Dennis Gray

Ron Fawcett solo climbing a thin slab at Tafraoute
in Morocco.   Photo Dennis Gray

with hundreds of boulders in front of a backdrop of the Djebel el Kest rising to 2359m above the Ameln Valley to the north. I asked the locals if they had ever seen anyone climbing in the area but no one had.

They initially thought I was crazy, running out into the desert each day to boulder and solo out there on my own. I just could not believe my luck. I had discovered a major area, which I now realise is almost on a par with Joshua Tree in California (which I visited in 1995). The difference is that there are many more boulders to develop at Tafraoute than its American counterpart, and you can live in southern Morocco for a mere fraction of what you need to spend in the USA.

I returned to the UK intending to keep quiet about this extraordinary place but I mentioned it to a friend, John Beatty the wilderness photographer, especially informing him about 'the Painted Rocks' and showing him some of my pictures of these. He immediately wished to go there. In 1984 a Belgian artist, Jean Verame, working in the desert a kilometre or so from the Oasis, covered a huge area of rock faces, pinnacles and slabs with primary colours using eighteen tonnes of paint. This was an amazing feat, both because of the weather conditions and the inaccessibility of many of the rock features. When I was first at Tafraoute this action was relatively unknown but ten years on they are a tourist attraction, despite the fact that the colours are now fading. Several of the mainstream climbing magazines in Europe and the USA subsequently carried pictures of rock athletes in action on red, blue or purple coloured pinnacles!

In March 1988 Ron Fawcett, John Beatty and I spent just over a week in Tafraoute exploring the area, bouldering and of course taking photographs. The resulting articles and pictures which appeared about our trip encouraged several other parties to visit the Oasis. A friend who I told about the place, my old buddy Joe Brown, has been developing the quartzite cliffs in the Ameln valley along with a group including the late Trevor Jones, Claude Davies and Les Brown and they have pioneered some fine routes on these huge crags.

My own most recent visit was at Easter 1997 when my young friend Jumper and I spent eight days climbing at Tafraoute. We were both limited by injury on this particular trip for he had hurt his fingers through over-use climbing and I had developed a post-cancer infection which caused my left arm and shoulder to give me grief.

Each day during our stay as we walked out into the desert we passed under a buttress of pink granite, split by a superb crack of hand-jam width. We called this, tongue in cheek, 'the Super Crack of Tafraoute' as there are hundreds of such fissures all around the hillsides. We decided we could not leave without attempting this single pitch route which would not be out of place on Yorkshire gritstone.

In order to attempt the climb we had to wait until the sun had moved off the buttress, for even in early April it was much too hot to attempt in the heat of the day. We sat around waiting at the hotel Redouane where we were staying (paying only a £1 each a night) setting out just before the sunset of our final day for the Super Crack. We arrived at its base and Jumper kitted himself out with an apron of Friends whilst I set up a belay. Then he set forth sinking in hand-jams as he climbed.

Ten metres up he stuck; filling the crack at that point was a huge cactus. Placing a Friend for protection he tried to climb over this but just could not stand the pain and decided to swing out on the wall to his right. Grabbing a good hold with his hands he swung bodily across and then pulled up onto a ramp which led him back into the fissure. This looked very easy from below but when I reached that point I was to find out it was thin. A two-step move up the steep wall and he had his hands and then his feet back in the crack, which he climbed almost non-stop, jamming and placing Friends as he moved upwards. A trying move on some loose ground provided a fitting finale and this outstanding pitch was behind him. I followed him with less grace, but managed to climb the whole route without any help from the rope despite my injured arm. We decided it could not be so hard if two cripples could climb it, so being generous we graded it Hard Very Severe 5b. There are many thousands of such beautiful pitches just waiting at the Tafraoute Oasis, enough to last a lifetime of climbing and the scenery is breathtaking. The sunset that night as we walked back into the village was something to behold.

I was advised by Moroccan friends to visit the Hammam in order to get a massage for my bad shoulder. These are like a Turkish bath and they are found all over the country. I therefore went along to the one in Tafraoute and booked a session with the masseur for a £1. When he arrived he was a small, stocky fellow, a Berber from Taroudannt, who like all of his kind turned out to be impressively strong. If you have never had your limbs pulled almost out of their sockets, your body pushed into positions that you thought impossible to achieve and your skin rubbed so hard that you feel you're on fire while very hot water is poured over you, then can I recommend such a massage. It was so good I was back the next evening and it certainly improved the movement in my injured limb.

A final destination for us at Easter 1997 was Mirleft in southern Morocco on the Atlantic coast. This was another rock climbing area I had discovered in the late 1980s when I found a line of limestone sea cliffs close to the village of that name. On my first visit there I solo climbed a beautiful ochre slab, twenty five metres high, straight out of the sea which was Severe in standard. Just up the coast from that feature was an amazing pinnacle formed like a sea horse, sticking out of the ocean about forty metres high.

On the first day of our stay we walked along the cliffs seeking out the best way to approach this stack, impressed by the fishermen who were perched danger-ously out in the sea balancing on water-washed boulders, casting their lines with long bamboo rods as huge waves crashed about them. The Atlantic tides in Spring off the Moroccan coast are immense and on this occasion the seas were as high as I have ever seen and awesome to behold.

The next morning when we awoke it was raining heavily, but the locals as-sured us that this was normal at that time of year. I had never been there before in April and thus we had to defer to their judgment. After waiting around until lunchtime, frustrated by this inclement weather, we decided to go and take a look at the pinnacle just in case it might still be dry on one of its faces if this had remained sheltered.

When we arrived above the stack the waves were crashing into its base and running high up the rock walls. I was for leaving it be, but as it had stopped raining Jumper insisted we climb down to the neck of the horse to see if we could find a route.

Climbing down the wet slabs to reach that point wearing trainers I was wor-ried, but not as frightened as I was when we reached the base of the edifice. It looked pretty impressive from the saddle we were on and the spray that was being thrown up was continually wetting the rock. The only reasonable route appeared to be a traverse out above the sea to reach two disjointed cracks on the seaward face, and then a climb up by them to reach the summit. But how would we get down again, for we had no pitons and neither of us wished to abandon any of our expensive gear such as Friends.

We decided that Jumper would try to lead the route, placing lots of protection in the cracks as he climbed and if it became too hard he would back off. We were also concerned about the quality of the rock; it looked friable but proved as firm and clean as you can expect unclimbed sea-washed limestone to be. If our leader was successful I would then second the pitch but leave all the equipment in place then, when I reached the top, climb down again re-clipping the rope as I de-scended. Jumper would then retreat removing the gear as he came, protected by the next placement below him.

Once I had arranged a belay Jumper geared up and started out, first climbing a delicate slab to a roof and then a traverse left to reach the base of the first crack, which was of finger width and situated on the seaward face of the pinnacle. In seconding the pitch I was to find that the situation was exposed, for it felt like the sea was literally under your feet whilst the huge waves rolled in.

Jumper climbed the first crack and was moving right to reach the second, hanging onto the vertical limestone, when it started to rain heavily once more. It proved impossible for me to communicate with him because of the noise of the waves hitting the rock face which drowned out our shouts. I understood he had decided to keep climbing whilst I cowered under the shelter of the overhangs and tried to keep dry. The second crack proved to be wider than the first, but fortunately I had brought a large Friend and after placing this Jumper managed to fist and hand-jam up the top crack until he reached a final mantel. He quickly overcame this and then was up onto the top of the stack and trying to arrange a belay. The only way he could solve this was to tie himself with the rope around the whole of the top rock.

By the time I started climbing up to him it had ceased raining, but it was still tricky for the rock was wet through. In dry conditions there might be no moves harder than 4c but it was with real relief that I joined up with my leader on the top of that incredible pinnacle off the coast of Morocco. No one else was around and I doubt that there was another climber within hundreds of kilometres of us. When I was descending back down the first crack I began to wonder what would happen if we had an accident but it didn't bear thinking about for too long.

Pioneering climbing is there for everyone of whatever ability to enjoy. Africa is now wide open to anyone with a yen for adventure and many of the countries of that continent have hardly been explored for their climbing potential. But, as I hope I have shown by relating my own experiences, going there regularly is more likely to result in an obsession with the place rather than simply moving upwards on a mountain or a rock face.

Chapter Seven

Thai Break

Japan

During the seventies information began to appear in climbing magazines about an area of the world which was as little known as the Himalaya had been to earlier generations; the Far East. In that decade British climbers continued to develop rock climbing in Hong Kong and others were hard at work pioneering in Australia, but the activities of mountaineers in countries like Japan and Korea were not widely known.

With the general increase in mobility in the eighties, new climbing areas were discovered in Thailand, Taiwan, Vietnam and, of course, China. As time goes on the Far East will, undoubtedly, assume increasing importance in our sport, both because it has so much further potential and because there are already so many activists in Japan and Korea.

Climbing in Japan is a mixture of home-grown and western styles. It was a region I had always wanted to visit, so when the chance came to climb in Japan in 1981 I enthusiastically agreed to take part. This was as a member of a party of six British climbers who visited the archipelago as guests of the Japan Mountaineering Federation.

We managed to persuade Cathay Pacific to do us a deal on cheap flights and, once aboard, we must have seemed a riotous crowd; on a half empty flight the free service from the bar was excellent and we arrived at our journey's end with monster hangovers. The start of this 'official' visit proved as amusing as the rest of our tour. The driver of the minibus who picked us up at Nairiti airport became lost in the chaotic Tokyo traffic and spent hours trying to find the place where our arrival reception was due to be held. Typical of the Japanese, our tardiness was not mentioned when we did reach our destination, although it proved necessary to hide our hangovers. We then had to join in the many toasts to Anglo-Japanese climbing and friendship by knocking back glass after glass of sake and Sunto whisky!

As we travelled around Japan, it took us some time to appreciate that the teams we were socialising with were a separate group to those we were climbing with during the day. The latter were mainly young and fit, whilst the former were older and more sedate, but Premier Division drinkers. I suppose the experience we had gained when the Japanese visited Britain in 1980 might have forewarned us that this would be so. When I picked up their six man party at Manchester Airport and drove them to Joe Tasker's shop (the Magic Mountain at Hope in Derbyshire), for a reception our guests politely informed us, via their leader Mr Takahashi, that they did not wish to imbibe in order to be fit to climb on the next day. This proved to be a shock as Joe, with the help of Pete Boardman and bank-rolled by a sub from BMC funds, had been to a cash and carry and laid in sufficient supplies of beer and whisky to ensure a memorable party. Fortunately,

Joe had anticipated that this might be the case and in his kitchen, ready and waiting for our Japanese guests, was a huge pot of tea. This drink is universally appreciated in their country, where it has both a ceremonial and spiritual signifi-cance, so while an army of Brits (who mysteriously appeared out of the night) demolished the ale and spirits, our Oriental friends politely sat around drinking char from elegant china tea cups.

Because I was driving and I was needed to chauffeur our guests to the Downes hut where we were to stay the night, I also decided to drink tea. At first taste I thought it boasted a most unusual flavour but, as someone who normally drinks only Yorkshire brews, I put this down to it being a somewhat esoteric brand that Joe must favour. As I was pouring my second cup I noted out of the corner of my eye that Tasker was trying to relay some message to me across his very crowded sitting room (he used to live above his shop). I thought that he must be merry so I simply waved back at him. As I took my third cup of tea I realised that I was feeling somewhat giddy and began to wonder why, but could only assume that it must be because of the crowded nature of the room. A short while later I was astounded when a young Japanese who had been at my side suddenly slid down on to the carpet and started rolling around like a puppy dog, kicking his legs in the air and giggling uncontrollably.

'Bloody hell, Joe! What's in this tea?' I shouted to our host, at which he and several other Brits fell about laughing. I was feeling more and more mellow and grinning from ear to ear as the truth dawned on me. They had been out and gathered a load of magic mushrooms and that was what was in the pot we had been drinking from!

Driving the minibus from Hope to Froggatt to reach the Downes hut later that night proved to be difficult. As we sped along I could sometimes see three roads but, somehow, I always managed to pick the right one –even at major junctions. Like my Buddhist companions, the middle path was the one I chose and fortunately this proved to be correct.

I think ours was the first visit to Japan by British climbers and the hospitality was overwhelming, especially as the Sunto whisky company had donated huge quantities of their product to the meet. The nicest thing about the Far East is the deference that everyone shows towards age; as I was the oldest member of our party, I was accorded a respect I was not used to previously.

At that time climbing in Japan was still mountaineering-orientated. Climbing at Gozaisho, a superb range of granite mountains near Nagoya, in the company of Takao Kurosawa, I was intrigued when we came upon a duo kitted out in full alpine equipment. It was a hot summer's day in July and they were carrying ice axes and wearing double boots and crampons on their feet on a pure rock route. My companion explained that many Japanese climbers often wore such gear as practice for winter climbing and Himalayan ascents!

Climbing standards were not so high then in Japan and throughout our trip we were able to make several first free ascents and even, on occasion, pioneer new routes. My own contribution was when we were climbing at Rokko moun-tain near to Kobe and Takao showed me a fine two-pitch route, the crux of

Dennis Gray leading the first free ascent of The
Groove at Kobe, Japan.   Photo Mr Iwada

which had never been climbed free.
I resolved to try to do this but, as
the first part was easy, my Japanese
friend led up that and then took
up a belay at the foot of a steep
groove, which was a major feature
of the second pitch. Once I had
joined my companion I rested for
a while, conscious that a large group
of local climbers had now gathered
to watch the action. The cliff was
reminiscent of Carreg Wastad in the
Llanberis Pass and composed of
similar volcanic rock. The groove
above my head reminded me of the
Ribstone Crack route on that crag
for it, too, was split by a fissure.

I pulled into the groove and easily climbed up the first ten metres,
which proved to be straightforward,
but then the rock steepened and I
was happy to clip the pitons that
were in situ. The next section was
obviously the crux; as I climbed the
groove it became steeper until it was gently overhanging.

Fifteen metres above my second there was another piton and, clipping my
rope through this, I bridged widely to try to reach over a steep bulge above my
head but could not find any holds to pull over this. I looked straight down
between my legs and saw many anxious faces urging me upwards. Encouraged, I
bridged even higher and from there my fingers reached a good hold. I grasped it
and pulled with all my might then, bringing my feet up to my hands and standing on a small foothold, I balanced up to reach the easy ground above. The cheers
that floated upwards were more than a little embarrassing for this ascent was, in
all truth, a most modest success, being perhaps a British 5b.

Later, when I tried to explain via Takao that this climb of mine was no big
deal, and that several of my friends could have led it quicker and easier than me,
the locals were having none of it. It transpired that the thing that impressed them
was my age; at that time in Japan when you reached a certain mature age a
climber either retired gracefully to follow a career and marriage or was dead. The
accident rate among their climbers was unbelievable. A single mountain, Tanigawa-
Dake north of Tokyo, (known throughout Japanese climbing circles as 'the killer
mountain'), had already recorded over 800 fatalities when we visited. All were
buried in a communal graveyard at the base of the peak and, unfortunately, many
more will have joined them by now. This, plus the dozens of other rescues each
year on the same peak carried out by a professional rescue team, whose head-

quarters are at the base of the mountain, made you apprehensive about the Japanese approach to the hazards of our sport. Perhaps such considerations help you to understand why those young climbers at Kobe were so impressed by an old fart turning up at their local cliff and bumbling his way up what, to them, appeared a hard lead.

One other memory from that visit was on our final night in Tokyo, when our Japanese hosts, led by Naoe Sakashita, took us on a tour of the night life area of Shinjuku. We ended the evening at a disco where the bouncers were Sumo wrestlers, dressed in their traditional garb. Several of them were up on a stage in front of the bopping hordes doing a kind of stomp to the beat of the music, slowly hopping from one foot to the other. These guys were huge but in the wee small hours, emboldened by drink, our group of British iconoclasts decided we would like to have a dance with them. In retrospect it is a good job that we had no idea how dangerous this might have been. In Japan such sportsmen have a status accorded to Royalty elsewhere.

With Japanese climbers on Tanigawa-Dake, the killer mountain. Photo Dennis Gray

Richard Haszko, Nigel Gifford and I jumped up on the stage to gasps of amazement from the crowd and, each singling out a wrestler, started jiving around in front of him! I could see that, initially, the guy I had chosen was a little perplexed about how to react but then he responded by dancing in tandem with myself, as did the other two. The punters on the dance floor loved it and, when we jumped back down off the stage at the end of the set, after bowing to our respective Sumos, it was to roars of approval from the young Japanese.

I was surprised by how tolerant the Japanese are towards odd-balls; a feeling that was subsequently reinforced by visits to other Buddhist countries. For instance, when we first arrived in town we were taken by Tokyo climbers to their favourite practice wall, which was actually one of the flanks of the Emperor's Palace. I cannot imagine London climbers finding a welcome if they started traversing the bastions of Buckingham Palace; they would either be quickly moved on or arrested.

British climbers entertain in Japan, L to R, Mike Trebble, Paul Dawson, Nigel Gifford and Dennis Gray whilst Naoe Sakashita looks on.   Photo Takao Kurosawa

Korea

My first visit to South Korea was in 1984 and I really did not know what to expect. Of all the countries I have been fortunate to visit, Thailand is the most freewheeling, floating gently along on the breeze of Theravada Buddhism. Korea, which follows Mahayana Buddhism, has outstanding rock climbing. They are two countries with vastly different climbing histories; the recently developed climbing scene in Thailand is very French, in Korea which has a long tradition of participation, it is similar to Japan.

The Korean mountains are very similar to the Japanese Alps; deeply wooded, with superb granite faces. The Sorak mountains in the north east of the country are almost on a par with the Yosemite Valley and just outside Seoul in the Bookhan San National Park there are granite faces (like Insoo Bong), which are over 300m in height. On any Sunday or holiday in South Korea, as in Japan, the mountains are more crowded than anywhere else I have been. It's hard to believe, but the Korean Mountaineering Federation, an umbrella organisation like the BMC, boasts a membership of over a million.

On my first visit to the country I ran a rock climbing course for the Korean Alpine Club and, through the contacts I made then (particularly Rae Park and his Taiwanese wife, Vita), I was invited to return in May 1992. After a few days around Seoul I set off alone, travelling by bus to visit the various climbing areas. My first stop was at Masan on the south coast, where I knew some of the local activists. Perhaps because there are so many climbers, the sport had changed dramatically from my visit eight years previously. When the peoples of countries

like Japan, South Korea and Taiwan
embrace a sport they really do ap-
ply themselves and the rise in
standards was impressive. In Masan
I was to learn that there were seventeen climbing clubs, co-owners
of an impressive headquarters
which included a pub and a climbing wall. In the town there were
several climbing 'boutiques', all on
a par with retail outlets one now
finds in western cities. Just outside
the urban limits was a small outcrop in a river bed, on which we
spent a pleasant mid-week evening
climbing before retiring to the
climbers' pub for beers. Not for
nothing are the Koreans known as
the Irish of the east, for they love
music, song and the drink. At weekends (which means leaving work
on a Saturday evening as Koreans
have full employment, putting in a
nine-hour stint, six days a week),

Dennis Gray climbing at Pusan, South Korea.
Photo Mr I. Lee

the Masan climbers head for the hills to the north which boast many fine cliffs.
Despite the proximity of some testing cliffs, the climbers of Masan were not as
fortunate in this respect as the climbers of Pusan, further along the coast to the
east, which was to be my next place of visit. Pusan is a rock jocks' town; I could
see a climbing wall on the side of one of the department stores from the bus
window as I arrived in the city. My friends in Masan had arranged for locals to
meet me and, within minutes of alighting from the bus, I was climbing up this
artificial structure.

On the following day I went climbing up in the hills overlooking the huge
city with some of the members of the Pusan Rock Climbers' Club. Despite the
country's massive industrialisation in the last thirty years, there seemed little pol-
lution up in the hills above the cities and the granite cliffs I climbed on above
Pusan were very reminiscent in scale and quality to Cornwall.

Throughout this visit to the south of the country my friends insisted I should
go to Kyongju, the ancient capital and seat of the formidable Silla dynasty when
the Romans were ruling Britain. When I arrived there I could hardly believe my
eyes; there is an amazing open-air museum with large tombs everywhere of the
Silla kings, Buddhist statues, rock carvings, temples and shrines containing many
works of art. Up in the mountains surrounding the town are some of the finest
Buddhas in the whole of Asia.

However, my visit had another purpose. Some of my Korean friends are Tae

Kwon Do experts and one of the greatest exponents of this martial art, 'the Master', lived in Kyongju. When, at last, I found him at the hostel (which he owned and which I booked into for the night), I was surprised to find that he was sixty-eight years old, but looked fifty, and was tall for a Korean, with a shaved head and angular features. He spoke English fluently, wore a robe of grey - the colour Buddhist monks wear in his country - and, besides Tae Kwon Do, he was an artist in calligraphy.

Immediately I met him I was impressed by his calmness. He greeted me with warmth and invited me to watch him working out that evening in his training ground, a kind of courtyard surrounded by the hostel. To do this I simply sat on a chair and watched through a glass observation panel set in the wall of the reception area as he allowed no one inside his domain while he was exercising.

I will describe what I observed of this. To begin with he sat for perhaps ten minutes cross-legged in the lotus position with his eyes closed, meditating. Then he rose and began to go through a warming up routine, stretching and kicking. Then he was away and the speed at which both his feet and fists moved was breathtaking, jumping and kicking ever higher. If I had not seen him, the notion that an old age pensioner could have done such feats would have seemed unbelievable. The workout continued for a solid hour, then he slowly wound down, stretching and shaking his limbs to finish once again sitting in the lotus position, meditating. He did this twice a day, every day of the year, between five and seven in the morning and evening.

I watched him again the next morning before I left for Seoul and, as I bowed before him and said my goodbyes, I felt privileged to have met him. He had changed my whole perception about what is possible for a sixty-eight year old. This was to be further reinforced the following year in Chiang Mai in northern Thailand when I met a seventy-three year old Chinese Kung Fu master. Both men had the speed and agility of youth because of their assiduous training.

It is no wonder that Koreans respect age. My friends in Seoul informed me that no one had ever managed to beat the Master in a bout of Tae Kwon Do, although he never took part in formal competitions or championships as he disdained such activities.

Back in Seoul I prepared to travel to the Sorak Mountains in the north east of the country. Before I left I spent some enjoyable evenings at the Kolon sports centre with Rae and Vita on the climbing wall there. I also made a memorable two-day trip to Mount Dobsang to the south-east of the city, where I was led up a hard modern free route 400m in length. The crux was a crack like the famous fissure of the Arc en Ciel on the Saleve above Geneva, and I confess I could not have led it.

Everyone, I suppose, has now heard about the student demonstrations which are a regular feature of life in Seoul, and the day before I left town I found out that there was to be such an event in the afternoon. I decided to go along and see this ritual for myself and it turned out to be quite a spectacle. It took place in the middle of the city, along the main thoroughfare known as Chongro, which is the Oxford Street of Seoul. This stretches a long way and is designated into sectors;

Chongro One, Two, Three etc. The students lined up in Chongro Four, while the police and military lined up in Chongro Two, arriving in dozens of buses, getting dropped off in the side streets and then rushing forward to form up in their prearranged positions.

The thing that surprised me was how organised the students were. Like their opponents, they wore body protection, gas masks and their front rankers carried huge plastic shields. There were hundreds involved on both sides and the two marched down Chongro in serried ranks chanting slogans until they clashed head on in the number three sector.

The battle then commenced, with the students throwing bricks and bottles, then attacking with clubs once they were close enough for hand to hand fighting. Their opponents responded with tear gas canisters and by firing rubber bullets.

Dennis Gray pioneering a new route at Insoo Bong, Nr Seoul, South Korea.
Photo Rae Park

Caught up in the middle of this confrontation outside the Pagoda Park, I suddenly realised how exposed I was to injury, wearing only a T-shirt and track suit bottoms and with my eyes already streaming from the tear gas. I decided I ought to beat a retreat and ran into the park, but just as I did so two large water cannons mounted on armoured vehicles rumbled into Chongro from a side street. They wheeled into the middle of the conflict and, once in position at the head of the forces of law and order, began firing huge jets straight at the student leaders, who were simply knocked over by the force.

This was the signal for both sides to retreat back the way they had come. Still chanting, the students picked up their fallen comrades, turned around and moved slowly back to their starting point in Chongro Four. The police and military let them go and they, in their turn, returned to sector two and dispersed. As far as I had seen there were no arrests, although several of the combatants on both sides had sustained injuries and there was quite a lot of blood lying on the road surface after they had gone. If such a demonstration could be said to be sporting, I suppose this was it, but it was a Catch 22 situation for both parties. The military were, in the main, conscripts merely carrying out their orders. The students were on the side of democracy and freedom, plus the reunification of their divided country.

The Sorak mountains in the north east of the country are an impressive range

of granite peaks, but I had two problems when I arrived there on my
own by bus from Seoul. First and
foremost, I needed to find someone
to climb with, for Koreans do not
take time off work lightly and mid-
week there was no one about. Sec-
ondly, as with many mountain areas, it seemed to rain a lot. On my
second day I managed to climb an
easy route solo to the summit of
mount Sorak-san, at 1,708m the
highest peak in the range. This
proved a long scramble up an easy
ridge, while all around me were
magnificent granite walls hundreds
of metres in height. It was an unusually clear day and I had a breathtaking view from the summit. I descended by the tourist route down
a man-made walkway replete with
ladders, bridges and steps.

The Towangsong Falls in winter with climbers
in situ.   Photo Rae Park

The very next morning, as I had
promised Rae I would, I set forth to pay my respects at the Towangsong water
falls. During my visit in 1984 I had climbed with him and three of his friends
from Masan, ascending a classic rock route on Insoo Bong. The following winter
these same four men had tried to climb the Towangsong Falls, a challenge which
provides 500m of steep ice climbing of the highest quality. Unfortunately, due to
the extreme cold in Korea in winter, there is a real threat from powder snow
avalanches, and one caught my four friends before they could even commence
their climb at the very base of the iced-up falls. All were buried beneath deep
snow. By a miracle, when the rescue team arrived and dug them out, Rae was still
alive but badly injured; the other three, sadly, were dead.

Accompanying me on my pilgrimage was Mr Son, who, like myself, was staying with some Korean friends who owned a hotel in Sorak-dong at the foot of
the peaks. Mr Son was a famous composer who only a few years previously had
been well-known in his country, but was now staying in the mountains to try to
regain his health after a total breakdown due to overwork and related alcoholism.
He told me that he found the inspiration for his music in the Korean countryside, particularly in the mountains. After remembering my dead friends by throwing
flowers into the foaming waters, we retraced our route down the bridges and
walkways we had climbed to the base of the waterfalls.

On arrival at the hotel the composer hesitantly asked me if I would like to
hear some of his music. He went to his room and came back with an LP, which
he proceeded to place on the record/tape deck in the room we were sitting in. I

did not know what to expect, for some modern Korean music is very imitative of western styles, but this was highly original. It was haunting, melodic and truly uplifting, inspired by the mountains of the Sorak range. Over the next two days of incessant rain I played this record again and again and as I listened I could see myself with the Masan climbers in 1984 ascending the route on Insoo Bong and laughing at our difficulties caused by communication problems (they spoke no English and I no Hangul). On the the day I was leaving to catch a bus back to Seoul and then my flight home to Britain, Mr Son came shyly up to me and presented me with a pristine copy of his LP. A generous gesture which I feel is typical of Koreans who live in Chosun, the land of the morning calm.

Mai Pen Rai

I first heard there was climbing in Thailand from my friend, the desert climbing specialist Tony Howard, who visited the country in the late 1980s with some French mates. They had travelled the peninsula looking for rock climbing areas and had discovered an area in the south, around Krabi - the cliffs that are now such a popular venue for sports climbers from all over the world. I quizzed Tony when he returned to the UK, and he spoke with such warmth about the Thais and their country that I resolved to go there.

I arrived in the Spring of 1991, through my connections with a trekking company, for there is a huge amount of this activity based on Chiang Mai. Compared to other trips I had led it proved to be an easy amble along well-made trails through jungle terrain in the hills and tribal villages near to Pai. There were some highlights observing an elephant working, crossing a river on a bamboo raft and the time when the participants of the trek had the chance to puff on a pipe of opium during the final evening's stay in a Karen village.

I was entranced by the country and its peoples. Chiang Mai, the capital of the north, is a beautiful city; the food there is tasty and cheap and the Buddhist temples and the thousand-year-old buildings are a wonder. Then there are the hill tribes of the region such as the Karen, Lisu, Akha and Hmong who often come into town to sell their wares.

On almost my first day there I wandered into the Wat Ou Sai Kham, a small temple near the guest house I was staying at, just as the saffron-robed monks were carrying in a young man, Thon, who had suffered a motorcycle accident. He was bleeding badly from a deep scalp wound but none of his companions seemed to know what to do. I rushed back to my room at Lek House, grabbed my first aid kit and ran back to the temple. By this time Thon had been moved into the Viran and as soon as I arrived I was taken there by one of the novices. Using cotton wool and applying pressure I managed to stop the bleeding and then cleaned the wound with antiseptic.

Thon had recently been de-robed (he was now a student at the teacher training college) but had come to this temple to seek help after his crash. While I worked on him we talked and I was surprised at how good his English was, for he had no difficulty in responding to my questions about the circumstances of his accident. I was soon to learn first-hand that Thais and motor bikes are a lethal combination.

The incident led on to my making friends with the monks and the Abbot Chaorwat at the Wat, a place which became a second home on my six subsequent visits to Thailand. I spent many days there living with the monks, learning about Buddhism, and in my turn teaching some of them English. As a result I was invited to spend a month lecturing at Wat Chetupon, a large teaching temple nearby.

All that was to be in the future, however, and I was on my way back to my guest house a few nights later, after attending a concert of traditional Thai dancing and music, when Thon caught me up on his motor bike. He stopped and offered me a lift and, as I clambered on to the pillion, I realised for the first time just how small he was as I towered over him. (Compared to Europeans, Thais are small and even someone such as Thon, who was twenty-one years old, looked to me like a teenager.) We roared off up the road on the 500cc Kawasaki as if we were in a Grand Prix, and as he crashed the gears and wobbled around I realised he was having difficulty controlling the beast. Sighting a pretty young lady, he braked so hard that I nearly shot off the bike over the top of him. The Thai girl obviously knew Thon and my chauffeur introduced us, 'This, Mr Dennis, is my young sister. She will drive us to your guest house,' and, without any word of explanation, the young lady clambered on to the bike and took the controls.

I clung on to Thon, who in turn was holding his sister, and I was left wondering if three-up might be against the law as we shot off again in an even more uncontrolled manner. I realised immediately that this small girl who was now responsible for our lives did not know how to handle such a powerful machine. It later emerged that she had only ever driven a moped before this night and, like Thon, had no licence and no insurance!

My guest house was near to the Tha Pae Gate (Chiang Mai is an ancient walled city), and as we roared around the bend into Kotchasarn road our driver leaned the bike over at an impossible angle. She tried to correct this and we shot across the carriageway and crashed. I hit the tarmac with my left shoulder and was dragged along the ground still astride the bike with my two young companions. By good fortune as this is one of the busiest junctions, there were few cars about, although one nearly did run over us as we slithered to a stop.

A posse of policeman in their jeeps were sitting across the road while this was happening and, as we were picking ourselves up to discover that we were bruised but unhurt, an officer came over and started to question my acquaintances about our bona fides. It was then I learned that Thon did not own the Kawasaki and it was borrowed from a friend. He also had no licence or insurance and neither had his sister. Alarmed by these revelations the policeman demanded to know what I, a *farang*, was doing riding on a motor bike so late at night in the company of two young Thais. Though this officer did not speak fluent English, I was impressed by how calm and unworried Thon seemed to be despite our predicament. He talked at length to the police captain and came to an agreement with him about our fate. The authorities would take the motor bike into custody and he and I would go off on the morrow up-country to get the Kawasaki's documents from their owner, who he assured the police also carried insurance for us all. We would return in two days' time to appear before them. No Thais like arguments, even the law, preferring to be *jai yen* (meaning to maintain their cool), so the policeman reluctantly agreed.

The next day Thon and I left Chiang Mai early and journeyed by group taxis to a rice village in the north to find the owner of the bike. When we found him at his parents' Lanna style house he was drunk on rice whisky, although he was only a young man of Thon's age and it was the afternoon. It took us a time to sober him up, forcing him to drink vast amounts of water before he understood who we were and the purpose of our visit. My heart sank to learn that, though the youth did own the motor bike and held the necessary documents to prove this, he also had neither insurance nor licence.

All the way back to Chiang Mai I worried about these omissions, but Thon kept assuring me it would be OK. This was Thailand - the land of the free. Little things like driving licences and insurance certificates should not weigh too heavily with the police, and it was now, in any case, *mai pen rai*. (A Buddhist concept based on the idea of karma and in our case translating, I suppose, as 'no problem'!)

Despite these assurances, when we arrived back at the police headquarters together with Thon's sister we were arrested for the dangerous driving of a motor bike, three-up, without insurance or a licence. At least we were able to prove the ownership of the machine and that Thon had borrowed it with consent, so the charge of stealing the Kawasaki was dropped. After completing the various formalities we were let out on bail, which I had to deposit as my companions had no money to speak of. We were then summoned to appear before the police court the next morning at 10 a.m.

This turned out to be quite an ordeal. When the time came we were marched by two officers into a large room inside the police department. At the end, seated around a table, were several high-ranking officers. The charges were read out in Thai by a clerk, after which we were invited to explain ourselves.

Thon had insisted that he did all the talking on our behalf, and it was obvious he was totally unfazed by our situation. He was smiling as he launched into his defence and, though he was speaking in Thai, I knew that he was quoting from the Buddhist scriptures. He had previously been a monk for several years and he was well versed in his religion. There is tremendous respect in Thailand for Buddhism and their Royal Family and saying anything derogatory about either is extremely dangerous. Thon spoke at great length and when he was finished the chairman of the court invited his sister to speak. She promptly collapsed in a flood of tears and apologised for her behaviour.

I was then asked in English if I had anything to say, but noted Thon shaking his head vigorously, so I simply declared, 'I have nothing to say' and we were dismissed to await sentencing. Sitting anxiously on a teak bench outside the courtroom while they made their decision about our fate, my mind was racing. I could just imagine me in a Thai jail, sleeping on a stone floor, eating only sticky rice for the next ten years - or maybe they would deport me? But Thon was brimming

Thon, Dennis Gray and novice monk, Rungthiva Sawangnam at the Wat Ou Sai Kham, Chiang Mai, Thailand. I taught 'Rung' English, and he is now in his turn a teacher of this subject.   Photo Mr Saki

with confidence and insisted that we would be let off (incredibly as it seemed to me, for we were obviously guilty of all the charges). His sister was not so cheerful and was once again tearful, explaining that if she was fined she would not be able to pay for she had no money, and asked that I do this for her!

Fifteen minutes later we were back in front of the bench. The chairman spoke sternly first to Thon, then to his sister and finally to me, speaking in very broken English. Unbelievably, I heard him say that they had decided to let off my two companions for they were only young and must be given the chance to learn that they had to obey the laws of Thailand, but I was older and should know better. Therefore, they were fining me one thousand baht (£25), and if I appeared before them again I would not get off so lightly! I was about to argue when I noted Thon once again shaking his head vigorously, so I thanked them for their kindness and the way they had dealt with us. Smiles and *wais* all round followed, for the crime had now been dealt with in a manner that everyone was satisfied with, and we were dismissed from their presence.

On the way out of the police station I collected our bail, then paid my fine at the administrator's office, after which I was handed a piece of paper which entitled us to go to the police pound and recover the Kawasaki. Thon and his sister decided to do this immediately, and I stood gobsmacked when they wheeled it out through the security gates, then Thon kicked the machine over, grabbed the controls and both jumped aboard once more. '*Sawat dii*,' they called and were gone, still without any form of licence or insurance. I think it was at that point that I realised Thai thinking is unique.

Later that same week I heard of another illustration of this kind of mindset, for there was a funeral at a nearby Wat of a well-known Muay Thai, a kick-boxer, who had received one blow too many to the head. (The Chiang Mai district is justly famous for this sport.) A grave had been dug -the kick-boxer was to be buried, although normally Buddhists opt for cremation - prayers had been said by the monks and he was just about to be lowered into the ground when his friends remembered that he loved coconuts. All around the graveyard were immense palm trees, so one of his fellow Muay Thai volunteered to climb up and get one to bury with their poor dead comrade.

These coconut-gatherers are brilliant natural climbers. They just shin up the bark of the tree like frogs, with their legs and feet brought up underneath them, gripping the trunk with their hands and feet as they move on up. The fellow in question was a little the worse for wear on Thai whisky, Mekhong, for he had been drowning his sorrows at the loss of his friend. He managed to climb up the tree and grab a coconut, but as he did so he slipped and fell fifteen metres to the hard ground of the graveyard below. Unfortunately, the fall broke his neck and he died instantly. 'Oh dear!' His distraught fellow Muay Thai decided it must be *mai pen rai*, so they picked him up and simply slung him along with the coconut into the grave they had already dug, on top of the other poor dead chap.

The monks continued with their chanting, then covered the two bodies and the coconut with earth. After this they gave each other a few symbolic kicks to remember how hard their dead friend could hit, then set off for an afternoon of Sanuk - another Thai concept which can mean anything from just having a good time and fun with your friends to a wake.

Chiang Mai is geographically close to the Golden Triangle, a centre for drug smuggling, and the jail is full of couriers from all over the world who have been caught by the Thai authorities trying to get the stuff south to Bangkok. It is hard to sympathise with these misguided souls, although the conditions they are kept in could be more humane. Perhaps I am judging too much by European standards, for if you visit the poor of Thailand in areas like Isaan, many of the peasants there are probably as badly off as the prisoners in Thai jails.

On a later visit I was sitting in the garden of Lek House when the French owner of the guest house, Yves, (he had married a Thai), mentioned there was a young British guy being held in the jail on a drug charge, and the police said when they arrested him he had a long rope in his possession. This did not register with me at first, but then I realised it could only mean one thing; he had to be a climber, so I decided to visit him. The jail was an unwelcoming prospect when I arrived there, with massive walls and huge gates. By then I had made many friends in the city and, armed with a note from my friend the Abbot of Wat Ou Sai Kham, the jailers agreed that if I came back the next morning I could see their British prisoner.

When I arrived at the gatehouse at the appointed hour I was strip-searched by the guards, then taken into a large room that was full of men standing around talking in groups. Between them and me was a steel grid with mesh wire across it from floor to ceiling. The female guard called in English, 'Mr Tom, you have a visitor to see you.'

Tom was more than pleased to see me and he jumped to the bars and gasped 'Hello.' I explained who I was and that I was a fellow climber and wanted to help him if I could. First I wanted to know what had led to him being incarcerated in the jail. I listened in silence as he related his story from the other side of the wire mesh.

He was a twenty-five year old climber from Somerset on his way to Australia, but he had taken the opportunity of stopping off en route in Thailand. During his travels down to Krabi and Phii Phii, the main climbing areas, and on his return to Bangkok, everyone had told him to visit Chiang Mai to see the real Thailand. And so, before catching his onward flight to Sydney, he had come north by train intending to stay only a few days for a look around. Within hours of arriving he had run into his present difficulties.

Tom told me he had arrived early one evening at Chiang Mai station. On the journey a Thai who could speak English had befriended him and when they reached their destination this local had summoned a *tuk tuk* and taken him to a guest house near to the University. Having fixed him up with a cheap room, he then offered to return the next morning to show him around the city. As the Thai had been taking his leave he had given Tom a present, carefully wrapped up, which he had told him not to open until he was in his room alone. He had done as he was told and had just opened the gift, which he was astonished to discover contained a large block of cannabis resin, when the room door burst open. It was, of course, the police who arrested him for possession.

Tom insisted it was a set-up, for he had no idea that the Thai who had be-friended him had been a dealer. He had spent the last twelve weeks in jail, lying at night on a stone floor with a single blanket, sharing a small cell with five others in oppressive heat without any fans or coolers. His room mates were three Paki-stanis and two Cubans, all suspected drug couriers. For sustenance he had been eating sticky rice for breakfast and dinner, relying on handouts from Thai prison-ers for other morsels to eat (given from the supplies which they had brought in for them daily by their relatives).

He had now been in jail for three months without seeing a lawyer, or being before a magistrate or even committed. He just did not know what to do and the worst thing was that some of the other prisoners also claimed to have been framed like him, and they had been in jail for years. He'd tried to phone the British Embassy in Bangkok, but was told they did not help persons involved in drug smuggling.

'There must be a consul here in Chiang Mai,' I suggested. 'I'll find out and come back again tomorrow.' I was so sorry for him, for I was sure he was telling the truth. He was in a terrible state physically, with matted fair hair and a tall, emaciated frame. He looked to me like he might be suffering from malaria, which is rife in Northern Thailand. Although I would not normally have much sympathy with someone who had been caught dealing, I did believe him about the circumstances of his arrest.

Most nights a few British expatriates who lived in the city used to meet at a place called Danny's Bar in Chotana Soi, the red light district of Chiang Mai. That very same evening I called in and by good fortune Gordon, part-owner with a Thai of a publishing house catering for the gay sex industry, was there with some of his local friends. In a place like Chiang Mai there are very few UK expatriates, and everybody quickly gets to know each other.

'Gordon, is there a British Consul here in Chiang Mai?' I demanded.

'Yes there sure is, a nice old buffer called Alan Jones. But why do you want him?' I explained about Tom in jail and how, as he was a fellow climber, I felt I had to help him.

'Are you sure he is innocent? Every one of those druggies in the jail will tell you they were set-up! The Thais do not like *farangs* interfering in such cases.' Fortunately, a previous time I had been in Danny's I had been stone cold sober when a fight had broken out between Gordon's Thai boyfriend and a *katoy*. These are known to the Thais as 'lady-boys'; we would call them transvestites. In Thailand both gays and katoys are much in evidence, for there is little stigma attached to being either. In this fight the lady-boy had armed himself with a large glass Coke bottle, which he had smashed and then tried to push the neck into the other man's face. What caused the fight I still do not know, jealousy I would guess, but I will never understand what possessed me, for I jumped up and grabbed the katoy's arm and, holding on to it with all my might, forced him to drop the offensive weapon. At this he simply burst into tears and the incident was quickly over. Normally Thais will be aggressive only if massively provoked, but under the influence of whisky, which is ridiculously cheap, it can be another matter.

I felt Gordon owed me one because of this incident, so I persisted with him and he agreed that he would ring the British Consul for me, as he was an old drinking mate. I am pleased to report he kept his promise - even someone involved in promoting the skin trade is not all bad - and the next time I visited Tom, Alan Jones had been to see him. It took another month to get a barrister up from Bangkok to arrange a court hearing and to get him out of jail. He was finally deported back to Britain and banned from ever visiting Thailand again.

He was taken from Chiang Mai to Don Muang airport in Bangkok in a police car and put on the first available flight back to the UK. He had to pay for all of this, a sum which came to hundreds of pounds. This was despite his pleas of innocence and a wish to be allowed to go on his way to climb in Australia. I was permitted to see him just before he left Chiang Mai and, despite everything, it was obviously a relieved Briton who turned before entering the police car and grabbed me by the hand to thank me.

Thailand - Krabi Peninsula

Climbing was not developed in Thailand until about 1987, but since then it has really taken off. New areas are being discovered all the time, particularly on the islands in the Gulf of Thailand where there are now some fine granite bouldering venues. Most visitors still tend to head for the area on the Andaman sea around the Krabi peninsula in the south of the country, particularly to the islands of Ko phii-phii and Phii-phii lee. There are many other cliffs inland which I have explored in recent years and which have yet to be developed; most are only good for jungle bashes, but a few might provide some excellent routes in the future.

My own first visit to the area in 1991 proved to be an adventure. I set out from Chiang Mai with a young companion, Saki, travelling third class by train. We

away in Bangkok and he was bored out of his skull and wanted to know more about this rock climbing lark. I was about to admonish him for his crazy behaviour but realised that it would be a waste of time, for Thais are the most spontaneous people I have met and Noy just would not understand my strictures. We were all still alive and unharmed so what was I worrying about?

The neighbouring island to Ko phii-phii is Phii-phii lee on which some modern sports climbs have also been developed. This is a much smaller piece of land and is uninhabited, for it is designated as a nature reserve. It is easily reached in about twenty minutes by long-tailed boat from Ton Sai bay.

Saki and I went there for me to do a climb on a cliff called Pile, then we walked north west along the beaches to visit the Viking cave. This is a premier site for the Chao Ley to gather the sea swallows' nests which are used to make the bird's nest soup so highly prized by the Chinese. The price that these items command make them one of the dearest commodities in the world and, though the nesting season was finished during our visit, the grotto was still guarded by some of the gatherers who jealously look after their interests. The Chao Ley are in fact sea gypsies who are not ethnically Thais, and they work around the coasts of Malaysia, Thailand, and Vietnam. They earn their living fishing, diving for pearls and shells and collecting birds' nests; all of which ensure them a good living. They have their own language, red/brown skins and hair, have animistic beliefs and are physically bigger than the average Thai. As I was to find out later that night, they can also be violent.

The Viking cave was impressive when we arrived there; a huge high grotto in which the Chao Ley build tall bamboo structures in order to reach the swallows' nests. I was very interested in all of this, too much so, for it later transpired the guardians became suspicious about my intentions, especially as I had with me a Thai who could speak English and was, by their standards, highly sophisticated.

After a great day out on the island we returned to Ko phii-phii where, after eating our evening meal at the small cafe we frequented, we waded out in the warm and clear water of Ton Sai bay just before sunset to look at the Ao Ling cliff. Saki managed his first climb quite easily wearing my rock boots and being obviously fit and strong. It was a short 6a called 'VD Resort' and he found this very amusing once I had explained the meaning to him. He then swam all the way back to the beach - much to my surprise -while I waded back with the climbing equipment held on my head to keep it out of the salt water. It turned out he had learnt to swim as a boy in a buffalo pool in his village.

Later that night (our last on the island), Saki, who did not drink alcohol, and myself were back on the beach at Ton Sai bay, attending an impromptu party around a bonfire. A group of young Thais had formed a scratch rock band and were entertaining us with popular songs, when five of the Chao Ley we had met on Phii-phii lee suddenly materialised from the darkness surrounding the palm trees. They came over to where I was standing listening to the music and began to act aggressively towards me, gesticulating in the direction of Phii-phii lee and shouting. Although I could not understand what they were saying, it was obvious that they were unhappy with my presence. I had drunk a few Singha beers by this time and, in retrospect, I was too blasé about this threat and did not react with sufficient care to the serious situation I was in.

Saki then intervened and talked to them, trying to calm them down, for it emerged that they suspected me of being a birds-nester, in league with a rival group planning to steal their valuable prizes. When he told me this I simply fell about laughing, which enraged the Chao Ley, and the next thing two of them grabbed hold of each of my arms and held me fast, while the other three jumped around looking menacing. They were all at least as tall as me and, with their angular features, reddish skins and jet-black hair, they reminded me of American Indians. Finally my alcohol- affected brain registered the danger I was in. The locals on Ko phii-phii live in fear of these guys for they often carry and use knives as weapons if they get angry.

'I'm a climber,' I tried to tell them, struggling to break free, but they could not understand English and were now pushing my arms up behind my back and hurting. 'Aagh!' I gasped. 'Let me go.' One of the Chao Ley seemed about to hit me and had drawn back his fist when Saki jumped into their midst. By then I knew him well; his countenance had always been smiling and sanguine when I had been with him, but now he was a different person. He looked menacing, his face a mask without a hint of emotion or fear. He jumped high in the air and gave one or two feints with both his hands and feet at some speed, then he stopped and bowed before them, informing the five Chao Ley that he was from Chiang Mai, and the junior champion of his weight at Muay Thai. If they wished to fight him he would oblige them one after the other, for I was not a birds-nester but his friend. He could assure them I was harmless and if they hurt me he would be most annoyed. It was like something from a Jackie Chan movie, five to one, but Saki looked frightening in the bright moonlight in fighting pose.

The guys who were holding me let go, while the other three Chao Ley stopped moving around and shouting. They looked at Saki in obvious surprise and then they burst out laughing. Suddenly one of them moved towards my Thai friend, presumably hoping to catch him off guard, but Saki reacted at speed, jumping high and just missing the Chao Ley's head with a kick. The Chao Ley jumped backwards in fright.

That seemed to confirm it for them - we were who we had said we were - and the next moment they were all smiles and agreed to join the party with us. I am ashamed to report we got very drunk on Mekhong, but we ended the night the best of friends and the Chao Ley invited us to return the following year to help them with their bird's nesting !

Staggering back along the beach to our bungalow in the early hours of the morning, weaving in and out of the palm trees along the beach and guided by a tropical moon and the ever-patient Saki, I reflected on how lucky I had been that day earlier in the year when I had wandered into the Wat Ou Sai Kham in Chiang Mai. As any Buddhist will tell you, all life is suffering, and the cause of suffering is desire; get rid of that, and you might reach nirvana. Staggering along in the sand behind Saki, I felt I had truly begun my journey towards that won-derful state of enlightenment. Next morning, catching the boat to the mainland as we set out on the first leg of our journey to return to Chiang Mai, I was convinced I was not bound for nirvana, but hell, for my hangover was acute - rice whisky drunk to excess often renders the drinker ill for days.

The Karen

I have many more tales to record from my six visits to Thailand in recent years: climbing solo on outcrops I found north of Bangkok, including one first class crag between the capital and Chiang Mai, travelling on small motorcycles with Thon and his brother-in-law through his tribal homeland near to Chiang Rai to end illegally inside Burma. Other memories include a trip to Khorat (south of which I found an excellent roadside crag), Phimai and into the border region of Cambodia, where there are some impressive Khmer ruins, and sailing down the Mekhong river on a raft with Hmong refugees into Laos, but pride of place must go to my trip in 1992 to visit the Karen in North West Thailand.

The Karen are the largest of the hill tribes and there are around five million of them, mostly in Burma. For over forty years they have been fighting for their own homeland, Kawtulay, in the southern part of that country. They have a proper command structure with an army council, uniforms and generals, and operate as a guerrilla force, the Karen National Liberation Army. Every year in the monsoon they make good territorial gains against the Burmese army, then in the dry season they usually lose this hard-won ground to the superior arms of the opposing forces. This war of attrition is merciless, and many of the Karen fighters have been captured, tortured and killed while their families have been driven out of their villages and live as refugees in camps on the Thai-Burmese border.

In 1992 I decided to go and see this situation for myself and after journeying north to Mae Hong Song from Chiang Mai by bus, I managed a lift in a Karen lorry going south with supplies for one of the refugee camps. Unknown to anyone at this time, the Burmese army were planning a major offensive. After an exhausting journey we had just arrived at the camp, set in a jungle clearing north of Mae Sot, when the whole area was overrun by the opposition troops. Although we were still on the Thai side of the border, I found myself behind the enemies lines!

From there on I guess it was just like being in Vietnam during the war, with Burmese gunship helicopters overhead, firing at anything they felt might be hostile. Within a few days the invaders were thirteen miles into Thailand and I was doing my best to get out again from the war zone and avoid capture. I was the only European in the area, and had no wish to end up a prisoner in Myomar, as the military dictators in Burma now refer to their country.

The refugee camp was terrible; when we had arrived there it had been unseasonably wet, and the poor refugees were wading around their makeshift bamboo dwellings up to their ankles in mud. The Karen are normally such a fine people, clean and colourful in their traditional dress, but in that camp they had been reduced to a terrible plight, relying on hand-outs from the aid agencies. After waiting a few days and unloading and distributing their supplies to the Karen, the drivers of the lorry I had come in on decided they would make a run for it south to the town of Mae Sot. Although still near to the border, they imagined it would be well away from any fighting. I decided to go with them and this turned out to be the most frightening journey of my life.

We started out early in the morning just after first light, but we became stuck and delayed several times by muddy sections on the unmade roads we were travelling. The drivers of the truck were Thai nationals who were being paid to do this work by an aid agency, but they had not reckoned with being in the middle of a battle and, like me, they were keen to escape.

I sat in the back of a lorry full of refugees who had joined us, fearful of their fate at the hands of the Burmese military if they were caught. As usual with the Karen, despite their situation they were still joking and laughing. Suddenly a helicopter appeared out of the sky as we bumped along; the Thai airforce I guessed for we were well inside that country.

The next minute a hail of bullets were whistling around us. The machine turned out to be Burmese and I could see its insignia as it wheeled around overhead to head back towards the border. I didn't wait any longer - I dived off the back of the lorry and ran into the undergrowth at the side of the dirt road we were riding along and took cover. I was soon joined by the drivers, but the Karen just lay huddled together in the back of the truck. By a miracle no one had been hit, but there were several bullet holes in the side of our transport.

I sat in some bushes and wondered if it was safe to get back on board. Being Buddhists, Thais are fatalistic, and the drivers climbed into the cab and prepared to set off once more after checking that the lorry was still drivable. I could not stay where I was in the jungle on my own, so I pulled myself back up into the vehicle to rejoin the Karen refugees, who seemed resigned to their fate.

An hour later we had nearly reached a tarmac road when once again a helicopter appeared out of the sky in the west - another Burmese chopper! This time it came in low overhead and hovered above us as we drove along. I confess, if I had been carrying a rifle I would have taken a pot shot at it, but I then realised this second helicopter was simply checking us out. Realising that we were just a lorry load of mainly women and children, obviously refugees, they let us go on unhindered. The Burmese military don't care how many Karen flee into Thailand; the more the better as far as they are concerned.

We reached Mae Sot without any more alarms, but by then the Thai army was moving in droves and this small town was in the process of becoming a military stronghold. They were bringing reinforcements from the east in with them, together with tanks, guns and lorry loads of supplies, including hundreds of troops, whilst helicopters were landing all over the place.

We learnt that King Bhumibol of Thailand had given the Burmese military seven days to get out of his country or he would declare war. I just could not believe that this was happening around me and for the first time in my life I found myself supporting a proposed military action. By the time I got back to Chiang Mai two days later, the Burmese had retreated back over to their side of the border and apologised for their incursion. If the King of Thailand decides on a course of action, then his people will support him without question. I suspect no other monarch in the world has the kind of standing that Rama IX (his other title) has in his country.

I, too, have nothing but the greatest respect and affection for Thailand and hope to go back there again and again, for it is a special place with very special people.

Hong Kong

Hong Kong could not be more different than Thailand; when you first arrive there the most likely reaction amidst the skyscrapers, neon signs and crowded thoroughfares is one of claustrophobia. It is hard to imagine that there are some unspoilt hills, marine reserves and crags in complete contrast to the downtown area, which is a temple dedicated to money, twenty-four hours a day.

In April 1993 I was invited to the Hong Kong rock climbing championships. These were held on an outdoor, panelled-style climbing wall at the University and, besides the locals, there were climbers attending from the other Chinese-speaking countries. I was surprised at the standard of the routes set for this event and the numbers taking part, for I had no idea how popular climbing had become in that part of the world. The final rounds were impressive, but home advantage helped and local Hong Kong climbers won both the men's and the women's competitions.

After this event I was keen to climb myself, so I persuaded the two ladies who had come first and second in the women's competition to accompany me the next day to a sea cliff called Shek-O. Both were called Miss Lee; you do not use first names in the Orient unless you know a person well. The cliff was situated quite a journey away on the eastern side of Hong Kong island.

We met up outside my boarding house in Kowloon, which is part of the mainland. I was staying in the notorious Chung King Mansions, an ancient rabbit warren of a building containing many businesses, flats and doss houses. Space is at such a premium in this region and I have never stayed in a smaller room in my life. The cost per night was equivalent to staying in a hotel in London, but it was far from luxury.

Setting out from Kowloon, we first caught a ferry to Hong Kong island, then the mass transit railway to Shau Kei Wen. From there we caught the bus to Shek-O village, the terminal of that route. A ten-minute walk brought us to a small staircase facing the sea. We traversed this, crossed over a concrete bridge and up a hill opposite a small path leading down to the left and the top of the cliff. This was followed by an easy descent to the foot of the climbs. I have written this approach down in detail so the reader can understand the difficulties we faced when an accident occurred

Arriving at the base of the crag, I could only gaze in admiration at its location. It was situated on a spur jutting out into the South China Sea and, as we geared up to climb, it was like watching a scene from Lord Jim, with so many junks and lorchas bobbing past on the waves of this typhoon-ridden ocean.

Shek-O is a granite cliff, not very high, but there are some excellent single pitch routes there and the two Miss Lees proceeded to lead me up climb after climb, mainly protected by using nuts and friends. On occasion communication between us proved difficult, for they spoke little English, and I even less Cantonese, but it is surprising how sparse a language one can get by with when climbing. It was obvious from these ascents that they were both highly competent, although I guessed that it was most likely they knew the courses we climbed well and had the cruxes wired.

There were also some fine modern sports routes on the cliff and we had a play around on some of these to finish. After a false start I managed to lead a 6c equivalent route, so I was feeling very satisfied with my day. Just as we were packing up ready to begin our journey back to Kowloon, Mr Chan arrived. I thought he was a tourist, but it soon became obvious that he was a well-known climber by his rapport with my companions. He had come out to the crag for the evening after a day's work in an office and, as night was now drawing in, the new arrival pleaded with my companions to hold his rope while he attempted a repeat of the hardest existing climb on Shek-O.

The climb started almost down at sea level from a rock ridge on the left hand side of the cliff. As the Miss Lees agreed that they would assist Mr Chan, we all clambered down to the start of the route. My role was merely that of a spectator while my Chinese companions made ready. The Miss Lee who had come second in the competitions then set up a belay and, holding the leaders rope through a gri-gri , played this out as Mr Chan started climbing. His route lay up a steep wall seamed with vertical cracks and, as he ascended, Mr Chan placed several camming devices for protection. At about fifteen metres there was a ledge which required a clean mantel to gain and then, above that, a final headwall, the crux of the route.

Mr Chan managed the mantel, after placing a piece of protection nearby, then he started up the last difficult section. From where I was standing at the side of the belayer this looked tough, but our leader was climbing in good style and, just before a final pull-over at the top, he reached a bolt. 'Good,' I thought 'He's safe now.' From his last piece of protection he had climbed about three metres; if he had fallen off before he had made the clip he would have taken a long fall.

The very last move proved to be the hardest on the route and, just as Mr Chan was about to grab a good hold to finish the climb, he shot into space without warning. As he had a bolt just below him this did not appear to be serious, but I watched in dumb horror when he first fell back down the headwall and then continued to plummet down the rest of the climb. The Miss Lee who was holding his rope was screaming, for it was simply running through her hands, burning them as it did so, and she let go. By a miracle Mr Chan hit the sloping rocks below my feet and stayed there, otherwise he would have gone into the sea and getting him out of that would have been hazardous. Unfortunately, his belayer had inadvertently put the rope into her gri-gri the wrong way round and, instead of braking his fall, it had simply allowed the rope to run once it had been loaded.

After we had climbed down and examined his injuries we found that Mr Chan was not too severely damaged, despite the fact he had fallen over fifteen

Mr Chan moments before his fall on Shek-O, Hong Kong.   Photo Dennis Gray

metres. He was talking coherently and had no upper body injuries, but I suspected that both his ankles might be hurt for he could not walk unaided. Our first task was to get him back up to the belay platform, which he managed to do by crawling up on all fours as we yanked on his rope. Having achieved this, we packed up speedily; it was getting dark and we knew we must reach the cliff top while there was still enough daylight left.

During this evacuation my companions turned out to be hardy characters, especially Mr Chan. Despite his injured ankles, he never complained once, although on occasion I heard him gasp when he banged a limb on the rough path as we struggled up the hillside. My initial plan had been to carry him on my back down to Shek-O once we had reached the top of the crag, but by the time we reached that point I realised I could not manage this. I was too exhausted by simply holding on to one of his arms.

After a rest on the summit we set off along the walkway, staggering with fatigue. The Miss Lee who was supporting Mr Chan opposite me began to buckle under the strain. We had needed to make a real effort just to get thus far and we were forced to stop again. While we recovered, the other Miss Lee dashed on ahead to phone for an ambulance.

We had to rest several times en route and by this time it was very dark, but within minutes of our arrival at the road end an ambulance came out of the night with flashing lights and a siren. Mr Chan was bundled aboard and taken off to hospital, where X-rays revealed a fracture in one of his ankles. How he had stood the pain of being supported up that steep path to the top of the crag was a tribute to his fortitude. I subsequently heard that he had made a good recovery and was climbing again but, as a result of his accident, I find myself checking repeatedly that I have put the rope in correctly whenever I use a belay device!

Australia

A country which is without doubt one of the present day crucibles of our sport is Australia. My first memory of anyone travelling 'Down Under' to climb was as a teenager, when some of my friends emigrated there under the government's assisted-passage scheme. For £12 it was possible to begin a new life across the sea; you couldn't come back if you did not like it until two years had elapsed. However, the majority who did go stayed. That was in the early fifties and few of those who did this seemed to know anything before they departed about the climbing potential in their new homeland. Some, like Bill Peascod, discovered an abundance of unclimbed rock on arrival and began pioneering routes almost as soon as they arrived in Oz.

It is perhaps interesting to report now that when John Ewbank from Bradford, historically to become one of the most important of the modern Aussie pioneers, was emigrating at fifteen years of age he wrote to Australia House in London to find out if there was any climbing in that country. They replied they knew nothing about such activities but could recommend lots of beaches. Big John went out to the antipodes believing that the country was one long beach!

In Spring 1993 my chance came to visit Australia, for I was invited to speak at their first ever National Mountaineering Festival, 'Escalade', held in the Blue Mountains of New South Wales, north of Sydney. This took the form of lectures, films and the national rock climbing championships, which were held on a specially constructed tower set in the school grounds of the little town of Mount Victoria.

I liked the Aussies immediately, and one of my old buddies from Leeds, Wilbur King, who lives in the Blues met me in Sydney off my flight from Manchester. I had not seen him for maybe twenty-five years or more, and we sat in the airport lounge catching up on our mutual histories for a couple of hours. Afterwards my friend announced he had arranged for me to stay at a mate's flat in town while I spent a few days looking around and doing a little cragging on the outskirts of the city. The guy who owned the place was away and Wilbur simply handed me the key to the front door, with the address written on a scrap of paper. He then departed pronto back to his home in Hartley Vale, a beautiful valley in the Blue Mountains.

When I found the apartment I thought it surprisingly luxurious for a climber to be renting, situated in a select residential area overlooking the Sydney harbour bridge. Inside the flat I found a note on a table in the front room which read, 'Hi Dennis, sorry not able to be here to meet you, but have stocked up supplies in the fridge. Help yourself, Ian'. I went into the kitchen and discovered an enormous freezer full of a couple of hundred cans of beer! No food, no milk for a brew, no fruit, just amber nectar. What an introduction to the wild colonial boys!

The rock in the Blue Mountains is the nearest to gritstone I have seen anywhere. It is a hard sandstone and seamed with crack lines like our local outcrops in West Yorkshire and the Peak. I really enjoyed the next two weeks; some of the crags are much higher than the edges in the UK - in some cases hundreds of metres high - but it was no wonder that grit-trained climbers like John Ewbank felt at home in the Blues.

I was very pleased to meet up with John Ewbank during Escalade. He now lives in New York and earns his living as a musician, but had flown in especially for the conference. His talk in the theatre at Mount Victoria on the penultimate

Dennis Gray leading a route in the Blues.
Photo Wilbur King

evening, 'Ironmongers of the Dreamtime', was one of the most outstanding lectures I have ever heard. His reception was such that he had to give a repeat performance the next evening to a full house, made up of hundreds of climbers from Australia and New Zealand. It is the only occasion I have ever known a group of activists sit through the same lecture twice!

After the conference and crag climbing in the Blues I said my goodbyes to the locals and set off on my own to explore OZ. It is such a big place - as large as the continental United States - and my first stop was at Cairns and the Great Barrier Reef in Queensland on the north east coast. This is now a major destination for Japanese and the street signs are in their language as well as English. I spent some time snorkelling off one of the islands and even a landlubber could not fail to be impressed by this wonderful world of coral.

I then flew to Alice Springs, which lived up to my expectations, for it was surrounded with red/brown earthy desert, with no other major town for hundreds of kilometres (which is the case in most of the hinterland of Australia). Despite the efforts of the mining corporations, it is still very much a wilderness.

The bars in Alice were just like a scene from Crocodile Dundee and more wild than the Wild West. On my first night there I was sat drinking a beer, minding my own business, when the lady next to me leaned over the table without warning and dealt an upper-cut to the chap opposite. The next moment we were all three ejected outside on to the pavement by two brawny barmen and told to,'Tak yer fucking ook' (they were Geordies!) It made me wary of talking to Sheilas after that - the men in the Outback are pretty tough characters, but the women something else!

It is a pity that you can no longer rock climb on nearby Ayres Rock, but it has been designated a National Monument for it is sacred to the Aborigines. You're now only allowed to follow a tourist route to its summit, but it was worth seeing anyway. I finished by travelling across to Perth in Western Australia and during the journey the barrenness and potential loneliness of the country weighed heavily on my thoughts.

At Albany I'd hoped to climb on the fine sea cliffs but unfortunately my rock contact there, Gordon Brysland, had gone walkabout, so I never managed much in the way of climbing in that area.

My journeys in the Far East have been more about travel and experiencing other lifestyles than climbing for, to be truthful, there is plenty of high-quality cragging to be had near to my home if that was my sole consideration. However, going to a country like Korea, meeting the local climbers, making friends through our sport and experiencing their existence and culture is plenty enough reason for me to pack my gear and travel to such a destination. It more than justifies the expense for me, albeit tykes are famed for being parsimonious!

Chapter Eight

Dancing with Eunuchs

Leeches and Lammergeyers

The Himalaya is variously described as the third pole, a vertical desert or the ultimate in mountaineering on this planet. Superlatives have been used again and again, but success and enjoyment while travelling in these remote regions is perhaps best achieved by adapting to a different lifestyle and by a meeting of minds amidst the inevitable clash of cultures, rather than the emphasis being solely on the trek or climb. Usually reports of expeditions to the world's highest peaks are penned in heroic style or, when disaster strikes, as a tragedy, but rarely as a farce. There was that fictional classic, 'The ascent of Rum Doodle' by W. E. Bowman, but generally it is hard to find something to smile about in the reports of Himalayan mountaineering.

It's a pity, for such endeavours are often made up of eccentrics travelling through lands with a rich kaleidoscope of characters, and anything that can go wrong usually does. An illustration of this was Don Whillans climbing a steep mountain track during a walk-in and meeting a naked Sadhu coming the other way armed only with a begging bowl and an umbrella. It was pouring with rain at the time, for it was the fag-end of the monsoon season. The holy man proffered his bowl towards Don and was delighted when the Villain produced a ten rupee note and dropped it into his pot. He was subsequently bemused when Whillans proceeded to relieve him of his umbrella advising, 'If tha's going to wander round in yer birthday suit yer don't need this mate, yer can't spoil anything. My bloody clothes are getting ruined so I'll buy tha' brolly. Yer can keep the change!'

Incidents like that have happened on most of the eight trips I have made to the Himalaya and in this final chapter I will try to record those I hope provide a balance to the many serious works set amongst 'the abode of snow'.

My first visit to the Himalaya was a memorable mixture of epic and farce. This was in 1961 to Kulu, in the Indian Himalaya. Everyone imagines that such trips will be dominated by team spirit and good humour. This is not the case; what climbers discuss endlessly at 7,000m is not the weather conditions nor the climb, nor even for a moment sex. I quickly found out that food is the leitmotiv on all such trips!

At the time we were the largest group ever to venture into such a low altitude area where the peaks reach a modest 6,600m, but being total novices we had modelled ourselves on the massive K2 and Everest parties of the fifties. At one point we had been offered a one ton generator and had seriously considered shipping it from Liverpool to Bombay and lugging it across India to our base camp.

One item which we took in abundance was Christmas puddings. A company near to Derby manufactured them and donated literally dozens to our endeavour. It is hard enough to make a success of this at home in the festive season but at 6,000m, cooked over a faltering primus stove, it requires the inventiveness of the Galloping Gourmet. After some experimentation we found that puddings fried in butter, which we also had donated to us in tins, made a delicious breakfast, dinner or tea. It was the only trip I have been on where the rations were so simple. All you needed to carry was the brewing tackle, a tin of butter, a frying pan and a pudding or two!

Cooking can be a great problem on Himalayan trips. Again, modern technology has come to the aid of the climber and now most expeditions and trekking groups have the benefit of prepackaged, lightweight butane/propane gas canisters to use at altitude. On my early trips we needed to rely on primuses and had to carry paraffin for fuel. These primuses had to be carefully prepared to use in the Himalaya and needed equipping with high-altitude burners with special nipples; if not fitted they would not function once you reached about 5,000m.

To stay fit at altitude you have to drink pints of liquid every day and melting the snow and ice to do this uses up an enormous amount of energy. On Mukar Beh our Sirdar, Sonam Wangyal, and myself found ourselves at our highest camp equipped with a stove which had a low-altitude burner. Each time we tried to light it our tent filled with choking fumes and on a final attempt it burst into flames. Only the swift action of Wangyal, who drop-kicked it out through the doorway, saved us from a burning. We were then forced to retreat back down the mountain, for without a stove to melt snow we became so dehydrated that we could not climb any higher.

During that first trip we employed six Ladakhi high-altitude porters. This was my first meeting with people of the region and they did not disappoint my expectations. They were Tibetan in origin and spoke an ancient form of that language, and though they were raw recruits to the sport of mountaineering, they proved consummate hill men and formidable load-carriers and eaters!

At the end of the expedition, on a green sward near to our base, we decided to teach these Ladakhis to play cricket. This was by utilising ice axes for wickets, making a bat fashioned from a packing case and a ball from rags tied and wrapped tightly round a suitably sized stone. If you got hit it was worse than a corky! The progress of our novices was amazing, so we felt we were being fair in challenging our porters to a six-a-side test match; England versus Ladakh. I am ashamed to report that they beat us, somewhat deviously because, having feet like iron, they kicked the ball away more times than they hit it and their number of leg-byes gave them a total we failed to equal.

Himalayan expeditions are often a source of legend and in 1961 I thought I saw a yeti near to our base camp – at least I saw something moving at speed along the steepest and narrowest of tracks on the huge cliffs set above us, standing upright and as big as a bear. One of our party actually came face to face with a fully-grown bruin as he retreated down the Malana Nulla, the site of our base, through the wooded part of the valley far below. Fortunately, he was carrying his ice axe and, grasping this and shouting loudly, he lashed out in defence as the animal prepared to attack, just missing its ear. That was enough for the bear who ran off while our team member turned around and sprinted back up the hill.

Playing cricket against the Ladakhis in 1961.
Derrick Burgess wicket keeper and Zangbo
the slogger.   Photo Dennis Gray

On another occasion, Ray Handley fell asleep sun bathing on top of a huge boulder near our camp on the Umroa Thach meadow. He awoke when the sun disappeared and he felt the cold, but it was not clouds which had caused this but two giant lammergeyers who were nesting on nearby crags. They were hovering above his body, possibly deciding on what to devour first. Ray rose up and jumped clean off the top of this high boulder and ran away shouting in terror.

Porters do loom large in Himalayan stories, like the time Whillans fought with some striking Nagars in 1960, or the Creagh Dhu wrestling with their Nepalese in 1953, or the outstanding loyalty of the Sherpas on the prewar Nanga Parbat expeditions. All of us who have been fortunate to visit these regions have similar tales to recount. My own favourite was in 1961 when Ray Handley and I returned to our camp after making the first ascent of one of the Manikaran Spires. We found the two Ladakhis we had with us, Sonam Wangyal and Zangbo, away from the tents, perched on a rock sticking out of the glacier and laughing and singing at the top of their voices. We thought this suspicious high spirits and therefore dug out the bottle of emergency brandy to check it was intact. It was, so we felt guilty about suspecting our faithful, hard-working companions.

The following day we were even more successful and managed the first ascent of the highest of the Manikaran Spires. Returning safely to our tent after a long and difficult climb, we decided to celebrate and uncorked the brandy. How we had looked forward to that moment and the wonderful euphoria that it might bring to our tired bodies, only to find that what was in the bottle was not cognac but cold tea - and Sonam Wangyal and his apprentice Zangbo were nowhere to be found!

In the eastern Himalaya there are two seasons for climbing; either pre- or post-monsoon. They both make equally valid choices, especially with a particular peak in mind. The problem with post-monsoon is that you will be marching at the end of the rainy season, and the rivers may prove difficult obstacles and the leeches will feast on your debilitated body. At times we were covered in leeches walking in to Gauri Sankar post monsoon in 1964. Initially we were most concerned about these and burnt them off with cigarette ends, for if you pull them off the wounds may fester and develop septic sores. After two weeks of marching through the foothills with constant attention from these blood-suckers we became blasé and either let them feed until they had their fill, after which they simply dropped off, or we ripped them away.

By the time we reached our base at a cave in the Rong Shar gorge, Whillans had become infected and had some terrible festering sores on both his calves and thighs. 'Yer'll have ter doctor me Slippery Jim,' he decided. I had never given anybody an injection in my life at that juncture of my medical career, but had been volunteered to be the Doctor Sahib because nobody else in the party was willing.

I was more than a little worried about sticking a needle into the Villain, especially as he warned, 'If tha' bloody hurts me, I'll hurt thee!' Anyhow, lying on his sleeping bag while everybody else was out of the cave, he turned over and bared his bum. I filled a syringe with penicillin, making sure the needle was sterile and that there was no air left in the body of the hypodermic. Then, after picking a spot to aim for, I closed my eyes and stuck the needle in to hear a grunt of pain from the recipient. 'Oh shit!' I thought. However, Whillans just lay there whilst I pumped in Fleming's elixir and when it was over he stood and pulled up his breeches but then cautioned me. 'Slippery Jim, if tha' ever tells anybody tha' had me with me pants down. . . . I'll kill yer!' And I never have, until now that is. By the way, the penicillin did the trick and Don soon recovered sufficiently to take over the lead on the mountain once more.

Before the end of this trip I had an even more embarrassing task to perform. Because we had been threatened with an attack from Khamba bandits based inside Tibet (we were right on the border), a detachment from the Nepalese army armed with ancient rifles came up and stayed for a few days around our base as security. During this time we made good friends with their officer, so when I returned off the hill to find him waiting and pleading with me to descend to Lamobagar, the last village in Nepal, because one of his men had taken ill, I did not hesitate. Unable to understand what was wrong with the patient from the description of his symptoms, we fortunately took with us the whole of the contents of our medicine chest.

After a long and tiring descent we reached the army encampment of just a few tents set before the village, and at the officers behest I moved into the one where the sick soldier lay on his own. He was a young man of about twenty who was crouching on a bed with his knees up, holding himself between the legs and writhing in agony. His superior pulled off the covering blankets to reveal that the man was suffering with a badly infected penis, at the base of which was a huge chancre. Only then did I understand the officer's earlier mime about the poor fellow's condition. I realised that what he had been trying to explain was that this private had caught syphilis, via a lady of easy virtue in one of the villages on the way up to Lamobagar. I had stupidly thought that the Nepalese had been boasting about the size of his own manhood!

One evening a Tibetan, a Khamba tribesman, came to sleep in the cave at our Gauri Sankar base camp. Usually Himalayan peoples are careful where water is concerned and we learned via our Liaison Officer, Hari Das Rai, that he had never had a wash in his life - and he certainly looked as if this was so. He was a huge fellow, carrying an immense load of salt through the Rong Shar gorge to barter for maize in Nepal, which was then one of the most difficult trade routes in the whole Himalaya. He stank of rancid butter, which is added by Tibetans to their salt tea.

I had a lot of sympathy with this dislike of water, as earlier during the march-in I had nearly drowned crossing a tributary of the Bhote Kosi. This had become swollen by the rains and we had rigged a rope from one side to the other in order to get our eighty porters across. The traverser clung to the rope with one hand, supporting himself with a stick in the other hand whilst slowly wading over.

Ian Howell had gone on ahead with the first of our Thamangs and I was at the rear to ensure that there were no stragglers. Such manoeuvres carrying heavy loads are both dangerous and time-consuming, so by the time Ang Namgyal, a young Sherpa, and myself were ready to cross as the last two, the rest of the party had disappeared along the opposite bank. We had all grown fond of my young companion during this march. His good humour and sense of fun had kept us all laughing but now, as he waded out into the middle of the stream, I could see he was petrified. Because of his small stature the water was up to his chest and I guessed that the cold and strength of flow were undermining him.

'Go for it, stop pissing about!' I tried to encourage him, but even as I said this he tripped on a boulder in the stream bed, overbalanced and, his hands numbed by the freezing temperature, he let go of the rope. The next moment he was under the water and being swept away, down towards the main river. I am not a strong swimmer but without thinking I leapt in after him. I am convinced such acts have nothing to do with bravery or courage, because when I hit the water and was also swept downstream by its force I panicked. By luck I was pushed into midstream by the current just as the young Sherpa surfaced, and I managed to grab hold of him. I then tried to float us towards the bank but, unable to swim, Ang Namgyal lashed out wildly and once again we were off on a wild roller coaster. This time I was under the water and drowning as my lungs filled with liquid whilst the Sherpa almost throttled me in his fear by holding on to my neck and shoulders.

By sheer good fortune, just before this tributary entered the main river it widened considerably and thus became much shallower. At one moment I was out of my depth, fighting to survive, the next stood with the water only reaching as far as my waist. Gasping and choking as I went but pulling the Sherpa after me, I managed to wade to safety where I lay on a grass knoll bringing up streams of bile from my lungs and stomach.

Despite his ordeal, Ang Namgyal soon recovered his composure and started laughing out loud at our narrow escape and my discomfort as I spewed out jets of liquid with my clothes soaking wet. As Buddhists the Sherpas are fatalistic and soon seem to recover from such near misses, whether it be from an avalanche or a roaring torrent. For myself, I've never been able to forget that near drowning and at subsequent river crossings in the Himalaya I have only ever gone into the water if there is absolutely no other way round. I would sooner walk many extra miles than try to wade a fast flowing stream.

Miracles and Close Calls

Language and religion are two of the most interesting facets of a visit to the Himalaya; for instance, in the valleys around Nanga Parbat four separate tongues are spoken and no one has yet managed to identify the origins of one of them, Burushaski. There is also much to ponder about in the rituals observed by the locals. In 1968, at the town of Kulu in the valley and mountain range of that name, I attended a ceremony dedicated to the god Siva, when something happened I still cannot explain.

A young man had been chosen to carry an effigy of the god, set inside a model of a palace on a plinth, which fitted over his trunk supported at his waist. Here is the incredible bit, for what held this up were three steel skewers which had been forced right through his body. The subject seemed in some kind of trance to me, and he then had to walk round the bounds of the town carrying this burden, while the faithful followed in his wake chanting and drumming as they went. When this had been completed he was then taken by the officiating Brahmin up on to a dais set on a grass meadow outside the town.

To the beating of drums and much shouting and screaming from the crowd, the skewers were pulled out of his body one after the other by the priest, with great showmanship. Afterwards anyone could go and examine the subject to confirm there was no bleeding, no internal damage, no marks left on his torso. Intrigued, I was among those who did so. Sure enough, there wasn't a mark on him. A trick? An illusion? I am not sure, but I guess there must be some logical explanation for this feat.

Truly, some Brahmins do have impressive abilities. I once met one who had memorised the whole of the New Testament and another, one starlit evening sitting on a balcony in Manali, who knew the name of every star and constellation in the night sky. Many mountaineers have been impressed by the ability of a Sadhu or Yogi to withstand the cold or the heat when they have met up with them climbing in the Indian Himalaya. Kulu is renowned throughout India as the Valley of the Gods and we had a pilgrim come and worship on the Solang glacier, near to our Mukar Beh base camp, wearing only a layer of dhotis. He sat out in the open for hours meditating while we lay in our tents, first to escape the cold, then the heat and glare from the sun. Such feats can be explained by assiduous training, breathing control and an ability to slow down one's metabolic rate, but they are impressive nonetheless. However, nothing yet explains the events I saw that day in Kulu town.

Today's Himalayan mountaineer can undertake climbs that previous generations thought impossible, thanks to an increased spread of knowledge, the development of specialised equipment and improved techniques, although the problems posed by variable weather and oxygen deficiency are not to be underestimated. Altitude continues to pose problems. Though people might be fitter because of arduous training, every year trekkers and climbers are taken ill and die in

The sadhu who came to pray on the Solang Glacier in 1968.

Photo Dennis Gray

the high mountains due to acclimatisation difficulties.

Personally, I've known a companion's judgment to be impaired by such considerations. This was when I was descending off Gauri Sankar with Don Whillans and we had stopped for a rest on a hillside below the moraine, opposite an immense cliff situated over on the other side of the Rong Shar gorge. Suddenly Don remarked; 'Look at those two climbers over there.' Sure enough, looking across this immense reach, I could just make out what appeared to be two figures, resplendent in white crash helmets, climbing together up an impressive corner.

'Don, they must be baboons,' I suggested. 'What would two climbers be doing out here climbing up that bloody thing?'

'They'll be Germans!' Whillans advised. 'They always wear white crash hats. They're everywhere these days.' We then sat and watched with keen interest as the two soloists practically ran up the cliff, hundreds of metres in a few minutes. 'Bloody good climbers, the Krauts,' Whillans was muttering in admiration to himself, just as the leading climber opposite suddenly nose dived ten metres or more back down the cliff, only to grab a tree as he shot past and stop there, hanging one-handed on to a branch.

'There I told you they were baboons!' I shouted out in triumph.

'Naw, they're not,' Don insisted. 'I once saw a German fall off in the Dollies and he caught hold of a sling hanging from a peg to stop himself. Grabbing a tree like that is a piece of duff to any bugger from Munich!'

I gave up after that, for I knew that at sea level no saner climber existed than the Villain. I could only think that the many weeks he had just spent at altitude must have affected his judgment.

The worst thing that can happen due to acclimatisation problems is to develop oedema; though this is a common enough condition, I have only once been with a mountaineer who has suffered in this way. In 1982 I set out to attempt a mountain in the Ganesh Himal of Nepal called the Fang, a fine low-altitude rock peak, together with the Japanese climber Takao Kurosawa, a seasoned mountaineer with a physique like Bruce Lee. He was a master of kendo, but a translator and poet by profession. We had barely time to set up our tent at about 4,700m under this mountain when a storm came racing in. As we lay in our sleeping bags taking shelter, my companion first began to cough, then to make strange gur-

Gaurisankar and Menlungste, Nepal Himalaya.   Photo Dennis Gray

gling noises from his chest as his lungs began to fill with liquid. Fortunately, we had some Diamox tablets with us and, somehow, despite the fact he was almost choking, Takao managed to gulp them down.

A long night passed while it snowed and snowed and my companion's condition became worse. I honestly began to think he might not recover, but he never complained as we both sat up with me supporting him as best I could. By first light it had stopped snowing and we decided we must try to descend to a lower altitude immediately. We guessed that my companion's health would only get worse if we stayed put.

In the freezing morn we packed with the help of a young Sherpa who was with us and set out, with me carrying an immense load, while the porter helped Takao by supporting him as he was so weak. We first had to descend a steep snow gully off the edge of the moraine and I needed to give them both a top rope as they moved down together. To begin with my Japanese friend could hardly stand, but as we dropped altitude he began to recover remarkably, and by the time we had reached the head of the depression below us he was walking and talking normally once more.

We descended 1,000m during that day and then set up a camp at the base of the valley we had walked down. This in an idyllic spot on a grass bank by a stream where we rested for a few days whilst Takao recovered from his ordeal. The surprising thing was that my companion was already fully acclimatised before we had set out from Kathmandu; he had come to Nepal straight from an expedition to the Pamirs where he had climbed Peak Lenin (7,134m). He was a most travelled mountaineer, having climbed at altitude many times without suffering any difficulties before this trip. A further shock to us at the time was that his illness had occurred at such a relatively lowly altitude, which I now understand is often the case.

A few nights later when he was better I asked Takao, 'What was it like? Did you think you were going to die?' There was silence for a long moment and then he replied quietly, 'Yes!' but said in such a manner and with such feeling that I did not pursue the matter any further. Takao recovered totally and, as I write, is still climbing actively. In April 1985, going on alone when his companion had to turn back, he made the first ascent of the North Face of the main summit of Kusum Kanguru (6,369m). A most difficult climb and an impressive achievement.

I have already reported how fearsome the Himalayan rivers can be, but the grand daddy of such streams has to be the Braldu in the Karakoram of Pakistan. Huge boulders go flying down its course when in flood and traversing its gorge on the high road to Concordia, the peaks of the Baltoro and the route to K2 used to be frightening at times. Indeed, when Reinhold Messner first traversed the Braldu gorge he experienced such a gripping passage that he declared he would sooner solo the north wall of the Eiger any day than return through it.

In July 1989 I led a trek to Concordia and the K2 base and when our party arrived at the start of the gorge, appearing like a massive slit in the hillside ahead of us as we approached from the west, it was raining. Coming the other way we met a large Italian party and their porters who had been trying to climb K2 but

The Braldu in spate, frightening to behold!   Photo Dennis Gray

were returning unsuccessful. They had just experienced an epic crossing, for one of their members had slipped down to the waters edge and had only been saved by the swift action of a Balti porter who had clung on to him. Three of their Hunzas had been hit by stones falling off the loose rock walls near the start and had suffered cuts and bruises, while the leader himself had been struck by a rock and was nursing a suspected fractured arm.

The picture he painted of a traverse across almost vertical walls of mud and loose rock was a frightening one; if you slipped the roaring river was waiting beneath your feet. Listening to his account while sheltering under an umbrella I could not decide what to do. It sounded horrendous and I was just about to call a halt to wait for better weather, when our porters took the decision for me.

Without needing to be told the Baltis we had with us, all local hill men, started down into the gorge. On their feet were old sandals or disintegrating boots and on their backs were our 55lb loads, their personal effects and food. Fortunately they were as sure-footed as goats. At first I remained behind with the rest of our group, undecided what to do, but eventually we followed on meekly behind them.

Once into the gorge it was just as the Italians had warned, with huge earth walls which had to be traversed via slippery slopes. In other places it proved necessary to climb to avoid obstacles and these were overcome by way of loose outcrops. Certain passages were only made passable for our heavily laden porters by cutting steps in the mud slopes for them and by giving them a helping hand to descend the more difficult rock steps.

It seemed to take us hours to complete this traverse and to say I breathed a sigh of relief once everyone was safely through is an understatement. It had stopped raining during our crossing and, maybe because of this, I did not see a single stone fall nor did we experience any mishaps like the Italians, but it is still one of most dangerous places I have been.

For the rest of this trek to the base of K2 and back I worried about the need to return through the gorge, but when the time came our return crossing took place on a beautiful sunny day, with the mud slopes dry and stable, while the Braldu river sparkled in the morning light as we scrambled along its banks. Even the rock buttresses we needed to cross seemed firm to the touch. Certainly, this second journey was far from the desperate outing of Messner's description.

When we finally arrived at Concordia after nine days of hard trekking it did not disappoint our expectations. There can be few mountain basins on earth that compare; a 360 degree panorama reveals Broad Peak, the Gasherbrums, Golden Throne, Chogolisa, Mitre Peak, Crystal Peak and, of course, the mountain of mountains - K2.

After our arduous walk-in, for one of our party had been taken ill and we had needed to carry him for many hours to get him to safety, we were sat resting at our camp on the glacier. This was at approximately 4,600m and I was scanning the slopes of Broad Peak set directly in front of us with high powered binoculars. The Peak is one of the fourteen highest summits of the world at 8,046m. Suddenly, I detected a movement low down on the mountain and trained the glasses

On the highway to K2, The Trango Towers.   Photo Dennis Gray

on this area; sure enough I could then see three figures descending the hill. The longer I looked, the more I was convinced they were in some kind of trouble. But what could be wrong? The slopes looked easy, but I became certain that two climbers were carrying a third between them.

I quickly made ready and set off to give a hand with two of our Hunzas, but first we had to negotiate a tricky ice fall to get to the foot of the slopes and reach the stricken trio. It is easy to fail to meet up traversing such a complex area, but fortunately one of my companions had been to this region before with expeditions so he took over the route finding. Three hours of uphill toil brought us within hailing distance of the party in distress. Initially I thought they were Spanish by their response to our shouts and one thing was certain: the voices that replied were female.

Even though I could not understand them I had been right in my assumption that they were in trouble and needed help. When we finally met up on a level patch of ice I was surprised to find this party was made up of two women carrying between them a semi-conscious man. They were all Mexicans, and I was even more taken aback when they pointed to where they had come from; a point far up on the steep slopes above our heads. The sick man had collapsed the previous day at a high camp with pulmonary oedema and these two ladies had carried him back down the mountain. It was one of the most impressive feats I have witnessed and my admiration for these two women and their toughness increased in bounds.

Speed was now of the essence, for we had to get the sick climber down to our camp, so our two Hunzas took over carrying the victim immediately and were later relieved by myself and the biggest of the two Mexican ladies. I am ashamed to report that this woman made my puny efforts at support look weak. We staggered along retreating through the ice fall, carrying our burden by hanging on to his arms over our shoulders. I quickly tired and had to be relieved by Hussain, our Sirdar, while she continued carrying her male friend most of the way back to our tents.

In our party we had an American doctor, Peter Stone, armed with a comprehensive medical chest and while we had been on our way a bed of sleeping bags had been prepared. As soon as we arrived work started on resuscitating the patient, but just the fact of losing so much altitude (the two women had carried the climber down almost 1,600m), had saved his life. By the next morning he was sitting up and taking the hot drinks that we prepared for him. Two days later when we were leaving he had recovered sufficiently to move around ready to begin the walk-out, but he was so weak from his ordeal that he only planned to manage half a stage a day – such a distance on this arduous trek demanding on occasion as much as six hours of effort.

The biggest of the Mexican women, Marguerite, came over just as our party was setting out on the return journey back to Skardu, and announced that they

Walter Bonatti and Julie Tullis.   Photo Terry Tullis

their passengers robbed by armed bandits. These dacoits lived up in mountain strongholds nearby and were active most evenings. The soldiers insisted that we had to stay put until first light, together with the dozens of other vehicles who were arriving at regular intervals on both sides of the barrier. I was dismayed by the news as I had become convinced that if we could only keep going we might yet reach Islamabad in time to catch the flight.

I asked the sergeant who was directing operations if I could see the officer in charge and, during a heated exchange, a young subaltern appeared demanding to know what the problem was. Without waiting to be invited I quickly explained our predicament. I said that my companions' livelihoods depended on our catching a British Airways flight leaving early the next morning and we did not give a fig for the bandits. At this the whole company of our bus joined in with a chorus of approval. Surprisingly, the officer gave way to our demands and agreed to let us proceed provided we would accept an armed guard to travel with us as far as Besham, a further 100kms down the highway. From there he advised we would be out of bandit country and safe from attack, so we readily agreed.

The threat of attack seemed very real once we started motoring again with four soldiers standing in the aisle, rifles at the ready, nervously peering out of the bus windows. This mood of apprehension transferred itself to us and we sat silently in the seats hardly daring to breathe, staring anxiously out of the windscreen ahead. As we rode along it must have been obvious to all how easy it might be to stop a vehicle on this section of road. A lone man armed with a Kalashnikov who knew the ground could hold up a battalion in this wilderness at night, but, nevertheless, we safely reached Besham four hours later. We breathed a collective sigh of relief, dropped off our armed escort near to a local army barracks and were off on our way once more.

All of the time we had been travelling Mohammed the younger had been sleeping like a babe on the back seat of the bus wrapped in a blanket. On the southern outskirts of Besham our senior driver stopped, shouted for his assistant to wake up and come and relieve him. The blanket stirred, its occupant rose to his feet and staggered dreamily down the bus and then, with much yawning, Pakistan's answer to Ayrton Senna took over the wheel while his older companion replaced him on the back seat, under the same tatty cover. Within moments he was in the land of nod.

It turned out Mohammed the older had already driven from Skardu to Gilgit and back the day before he had joined us, and had not been to sleep for more than twenty-four hours. For better or worse we now had to rely on Mohammed the younger to get us to the plane on time. The youth left us in no doubt that he meant to do just that as he crashed the gears, put a foot hard down on the accelerator and set the old bus on course for Manshera, Abbottabad and Rawalpindi/Islamabad. Four hours and 260km to go!

If our former driver had on occasion given us some heart-stopping moments this was nothing once the boy started to motor. We raced around hairpins, nearly hit lorries coming the other way, almost went off the road several times and then I noted that the kid was smoking hashish! He began to cackle loudly as he pushed the bus to its limits, leaving me to seriously worry about the wisdom of this chase. Two of our trekkers became ill as the vehicle swung crazily about the KKH. 'Stop him!' they pleaded in between being sick out of the windows. One even declared he couldn't care less when he reached home, all he wanted to do was get off this f......g crazy bus! The rest of our party sat silently gripping the seat-rest in front of them.

The company I led treks for had a smart agent in Islamabad and he had gone out to the airport to try to get British Airways to delay their departure until we arrived. They had refused but agreed that, if we did make it at the last moment before take-off, our group could go straight on board without waiting for ticketing, baggage-checks or security. Meanwhile Mohammed the younger was driving our bus at high velocity through Abbottabad. At that hour of the morning there was little traffic about, only the odd bullock cart - one of which he managed to clip as we shot past, spread-eagling its owner across the back of his own animal!

I had been as frightened as the rest of our party over this madcap chase, but now my mood changed and Mohammed responded to my cries of *jaldi* with a loud cackle, a puff on his spliff and jammed the accelerator flat onto the boards once more. Forty minutes to go now to take-off, and I became convinced that we were going to make it when we ran into the heaviest traffic of the journey. Despite crazy driving, overtaking on both the outside and inside of other road users, we ended stuck behind several buses. Precious seconds were being lost and we remained blocked from overtaking by a continuous stream of vehicles coming the other way.

Mohammed suddenly decided to act. 'I know special way, Sahib,' he advised and nosed the bus up on to the pavement. Somehow he crept through on the inside then turned down a side street which he drove through at breakneck speed once more. This led us into a heavily populated area with ever narrower avenues but, swinging wildly from side to side, just missing buildings, food stalls, bullock carts and people, we got through. I began to realise that the wee fellow at the wheel knew the vehicle's width to within a centimetre. On several occasions I closed my eyes expecting to hear the rending of metal, but each time I opened them again we had missed the obstacle.

Ten minutes later we turned on to the main road once more, hit a roundabout and there, in front of us, was the airport road mercifully free of traffic. We raced up this as if we had a plane to catch and reached the International Departures terminal with just five minutes to spare. Mohammed drove the old Bedford into the concourse and right up to its front doors, where our agent and the British Airways officials were waiting for us. No time for goodbyes. Everyone sprinted through the building and out across the tarmac to reach the waiting Boeing. The agent, Ali and I stopped at the bottom and watched as our fifteen trekkers mounted the steps leading them into the belly of the aircraft. The door immediately shut once the last one was inside and within minutes the engines had started, take-off formalities were completed and the 747 taxied down the runway.

I stood and watched it go with a lump in my throat. Our party had been together for a month and we had not even managed time to bid each other farewell! Ali and I wandered back through the airport and outside to reach the faded, green, single decker Bedford bus. Mohammed the younger was out to the world when we climbed back on board. I gently woke him and then his older companion to offer them some breakfast as our guests, for between them they had won the race against time.

The road journey from Skardu to Islamabad was the most exciting of my life and I congratulated our two aces on their performance. Their actual driving time was twenty-one hours; this would have been impressive in a four-wheel-drive vehicle, but in a knackered old bus it was simply 'Zindabad!' God knows how long it took them to drive the vehicle back to its base in Skardu, for we never saw them again once they had set out on the return journey.

Rebel Revels

The agent, Ali, was a most interesting man; a double *hadji* for he had twice been on the pilgrimage to Mecca, he was also an Iman at his local mosque who knew the Koran by heart, and a Pathan who had close links with the Mujahedin. Through Ali I was able to travel alone to meet up with the Mujahedin near to Peshawar, the legendary Pakistani frontier town lying at the foot of the Khyber Pass, leading into Afghanistan.

Ali's cousin, Said, met me when I stepped off the bus from Rawalpindi, and with him was a photographer from Paris Match who said he was trying to get some library pictures of the Mujahedin. Said was a huge hard-looking Pathan, dressed in the inevitable shalwar qamiz with an Afghan cap on his head and his beard tinted red. Speaking excellent English, he suggested that we go to meet some of his friends, members of the northern guerrilla army who were camped out in the desert west of Darra Bazaar, a village famous for its arms industry which lies south of Peshawar on the road leading to Kohat.

To get there he bundled the photographer, Thomas, and I into an old black Mercedes which he had parked nearby and threaded a route out through the city. The streets were teeming with men armed to the teeth, like something out of films like 'King of the Khyber Rifles'.

An hour later we arrived at Darra. I could not get over the place as we walked along its main street; every shop, every workplace, every doorway seemed to be taken over by Pathans making or selling arms. You could get anything from a rocket launcher to a facsimile copy of an AK47. The workmanship was first class and to see these apparently unsophisticated tribesman crafting gun barrels was a revelation.

Said seemed to know everybody in town and he led us into the interior of a run down cafe which lay down an alleyway. It was full of Mujahedin dressed like our guide. We were introduced to their leader who made us welcome and invited us to take *khawa* with him at his table. Thomas was asked via our interpreter if he wished to take some photographs, and I was surprised at how reluctant he seemed to be to do this. I would have loved to have taken some pictures of these men myself, but my camera was being repaired back in Pindi.

I could not understand much of what was being said for they were speaking in

Pushto, but Said came and sat with me and explained that these men were Afghans who were members of one of the guerrilla groups. They had only come to Darra to purchase arms and would be returning to their country shortly. They looked a frightening bunch of renegades, each with a bandolier of bullets around his body, grenades in their belts and Kalashnikovs at their sides. I decided that the Russians must have been crazy to get involved fighting such well-armed irregulars. 'Don't they ever have any accidents carrying all these weapons around?' I whispered to Said. '*Kheh,*' he replied enigmatically.

'Come,' Said suddenly motioned to Thomas and I. 'We go now to visit my cousin. Tomorrow he will marry.' Hurried goodbyes and then we were soon back at the car. The heat became ever more oppressive as we headed out west into the desert. This really was Kutcha country with dirt tracks fit only for jeeps, but somehow our driver kept the Mercedes bumping along until up ahead we could glimpse a group of tents around some stunted trees. The largest was where the bridegroom and his friends were currently holding a bachelor party.

On arrival Said's cousin, Mansur, came out to meet us and after introductions we were invited to join in the celebrations. He was a rotund fellow of about forty, and I was surprised to learn he already had two wives and five children. The girl he was marrying on the morrow was fifteen and I was left wondering what life might be like for her in the future. Inside the tent I immediately noted how cool it was, for such shelters are especially constructed with a double skin to absorb the heat.

There were about twenty five men sat in a circle on rugs on the floor and all were Pathans. It was hard to guess their age but most, I think, were contemporary with Mansur. We were greeted with warmth and some hilarity as all were drunk to a man. Within moments of sitting down our host brought a bowl of wine, set it down before us and supplied cups to dip into it. It was rich with cinnamon and very sweet.

It seemed we had arrived just in time for the entertainment which, I was gobsmacked to learn, was to be provided by a troup of eunuchs. Said explained that they always attended at Pathan weddings and that they were 'doctored' when young with the approval of their parents. They could earn a good living as musicians and dancers and some of them were very talented.

The tent door opened and in came six young men, some of whom were carrying stringed musical instruments, wearing bright clothes with tunic tops, baggy trousers and light sequin-covered shoes. The youngest was about sixteen, the oldest maybe twenty-five. I had never heard Pathan music before, nor heard eunuchs sing, but once you picked up on the rhythm and pitch it was interesting to my untrained ear.

The beat increased as the performance progressed and our companions sitting around the circle joined in, chanting and clapping in time to the music. The effect in that enclosed space was electric and the Pathans seemed to be filled with a keen anticipation. Shortly afterwards the eunuchs took up station in the centre of the ring and the audience got to their feet, joined hands and danced, faster and faster, around the six in the middle who continued to play, sing and dance. This went on for such a long time that I thought I would have to stop for a breather, but just as I was about to try to get out of the circle the dance slowed and then halted. Mansur jumped into the centre and, singling out the youngest eunuch, began to dance with him rather like rockers would in the West, but much more suggestively. The youth was coy at first then responded brazenly while the rest of us clapped and shouted encouragement. I must admit the bridegroom moved well for such a podgy fellow.

'Now it is your turn as our guests,' Said said turning to Thomas and I. 'You must dance with the eunuchs to bring good luck to Mansur, for we all must do so at a wedding.' I looked at Thomas and he at me. I think we both realised that to refuse might be seen to be discourteous at least and at worst dangerous – the AK47s were neatly stashed in the tent doorway, awaiting their owners. Who knows what might have happened if we had provoked these Pathans with that much wine inside them?

The Frenchman and I jumped into the circle and he faced the youngest eunuch and I the next, who was about eighteen. He was very handsome with black curly hair, an athletic body and a fine set of teeth. He advanced towards me suggestively as I approached him, and I reacted with embarrassment which the rest of the company enjoyed enormously. Once into the dance it was no different to jumping around at the old Threlkeld bop we used to frequent in the Lakes and, emboldened by drink, I really put my heart into it. The young man opposite me was an artist and he really could move well, unlike my own two left feet. I ended breathless as the song finished and, as we both embraced at the conclusion of the set, I mouthed a *tashakur* (thank you) to my young partner. Just as I had earlier wondered about the morrow's young bride, I could not help wondering about the young eunuch's life and fate.

After we had bade farewell to Mansur, wishing him much happiness with his new bride, and an even more long-winded set of goodbyes to his most friendly mates, Said explained on the way back to Peshawar how eunuchs are adopted into performing troupes when young. They are taught by the older members to sing, play instruments and dance. The entertainers we had met that day were one of the very best outfits in Pakistan.

Arriving back in town in the evening we were taken by Said to a cheap hotel belonging to yet another of his cousins. The Pathans still enjoy very extended family relationships and are spread out over the territories of the old North West frontier, including Afghanistan. Thomas and I agreed to share and so, after bidding Said goodnight, the Frenchman and I settled into a double room.

Once alone, talking freely to him, I found the man from Paris Match fascinating. He seemed to be leading an amazing life for he had learned his job the hard way out in the field. There hardly appeared to be a major conflict or a newsworthy event in the last ten years that he had not covered. He had been everywhere from Ethiopia to Cambodia, South Africa and Afghanistan to the USSR and Central/South America. I demanded to know what he was really doing, for I had found his story about library pictures most unconvincing, guessing that there must already be masses of such material held in archives throughout the world.

He grinned and then began to explain in French as walls have ears in Pathan country. He was out seeking evidence of the Mujahedin's involvement in the heroin trade. He believed they had taken over the means of synthesising the drug from opium grown north of Peshawar, operating from factories on the Afghan and Pakistan border. He felt they were responsible for most of the illegal consignments that were now being smuggled into Europe and they were using the money to buy arms to further equip themselves in the power struggle. 'Bloody hell, Thomas, if they find out what you're up to they'll kill you!' I gasped, frightened by my partner's audacity.

'Le diable est mort,' he laughed back at me.

The next morning I was up and away back to Rawalpindi via Taxila, a Buddhist centre of learning from before the Muslim conquest. I admired Thomas immensely but felt I was an encumbrance to him in his quest and I have to admit he scared me. I wished him good luck and it came as no surprise to learn the following year that his hunch had been right and that he had managed to get a confirmation on his story. Paris Match was one of the first to publish these revelations which caused a political storm. Unfortunately this brave photo-journalist was to die shortly after in Africa, where he was killed in mysterious circumstances whilst covering a tribal conflict.

Solo into Swat Kohistan

I had always wanted to take off on my own travelling in the Himalaya and, after leading several treks in the Karakoram, I decided I would be able to do just that and opted for a visit to Swat Kohistan. This district lies to the west of the Indus valley and east of Chitral, an area with a colourful history. Everyone from Alexander and Akbar to Winston Churchill have been associated with the region, in fact Churchill was involved in reporting the Malakand campaign. Swat was an independent territory ruled by the Wali until 1969, when it became an integral part of Pakistan. The upper reaches of the area, dominated by the superb peak of Falakser (5,918m) remain rarely visited by climbers.

Setting out from Rawalpindi by bus I journeyed over two days, stopping a night in Mingora, to reach Kalam situated at the head of this beautiful valley. En route I had been surprised to see men dressed in something like Greek costume and noted that some of them had fair hair and blue eyes. Conjecture is that their antecedents were members of Alexander's army, but when I arrived in Kalam I quickly realised that this was once again Pathan country. The whole region is dominated by the fearsome Yusufzai clan, who had given our forefathers such a hard time at Ambella and Malakand.

The Swat valley was as beautiful as I had expected, with green hillsides and orchards full of fruit. I stayed the night in Kalam in a cheap doss house and then set off on my own, carrying a heavy rucksack, climbing a steep track leading me upwards into the Ushu valley. As I ascended Falakser came into view and I began to entertain crazy notions of wandering up to its base and doing some climbing.

Ushu, on the Swat river, appeared a restful place when I finally reached there, with many trout in its waters. However, I began to feel uneasy wandering around the village as its denizens did not appear to be too well disposed towards me. I could only surmise from their sullen faces that a lone trekker was not a usual sight in these parts. After a rest I shouldered my pack again and walked on. I spent that night higher up the valley, sleeping in a rough shelter which was obviously used by shepherds. The next morning, after a quick brew made on a wood fire, I was away early to avoid the heat of the day. For a few hours I made good progress, for coming from a recent climb in the Hushe region I found no difficulty with the increasing altitude. I was into rugged terrain by then, climbing an exposed rocky path along the steep sides of a gorge. As I balanced along I noticed two tiny human figures a long way above me, distinctly framed in the clear mountain air. I guessed they were Pathan shepherds, but the closer they descended towards me the more uneasy I became. They were losing altitude so quickly that I realised they could not be with any animals and that they must be chasing after something. I worried it might be me!

As they came closer I was alarmed to notice they were both armed with Kalashnikovs, so even if I dropped my pack and ran away downhill I could not escape them. Though scared stiff, I decided to keep walking towards them and tried to remember some Pushto. When they reached me they were the two most frightening-looking characters I have ever met. Tall and bearded, they were dressed and looked like the Mujahedin I had met on the Afghan border the year before, but they were more ragged, with rips in both their shalwar and qamiz and unwashed.

'*Salaam aleikhum*,' I greeted them as we met head on. Though surprised they wouldn't give way, and I realised I was now their prisoner. 'Hello,' I said in English trying to smile as naturally as I could, but the two men did not seem pleased by this and my mouth froze with fear as one of the Pathans unslung his rifle, slipped its catch and pointed the weapon at me.

'*Ugud*. I'm going up in to the mountains,' I gasped, pointing up to where I thought Falakser must be.' *Ugud* ' I repeated. This brought the most unexpected response, for my two guards began to laugh out loud then one of them cried out, '*Dodai* ! ' I nodded my head, guessing they must think I was a hunter of some kind, but then realised that this is what *they* were. They were not shepherds as I had supposed, but were out after game.

I began to laugh hysterically in relief and this mood carried over to the Pathans, who joined in with ringing shouts of mirth. The rifle that had been pointing at me was lowered and a hand was held out. I have never been so relieved to embrace two other human beings in my life and after sharing some naan we parted in high spirits, they to continue their descent down to the valley, I towards the base of Falakser.

When I had ascended high enough to see its flanks clearly, I realised this was no mountain to try to climb solo, at least not by me. Just before darkness I bivvied out a long cold night in a cave and rose before dawn to see the sun rise on the peak. It was an impressive sight, made all the more acute by being in such a remote spot on my own. After cooking some breakfast on the wood I had carried up with me from the valley, I repacked my sack and then started back down to return to Ushu.

The return journey was accomplished in a fraction of the time taken for the previous day's ascent, and when I reached the hamlet again half the inhabitants of the village turned out to greet me. The headman appeared and he could speak some Urdu, sufficient for me to realise that he wanted me to take *chai* with him. Sitting in his hut I discovered why they had shunned me on the way up - they had thought I was a Russian! They had relations who had fought against that power in Afghanistan and now equated most Caucasians with that country. It seemed I had been very close to being shot by the tribesman's two younger cousins on the path the previous day, for the two men in question had lost brothers in Afghanistan fighting with the Mujahedin, killed by Russian troops. If I had not accidentally confirmed my identity by greeting them in English they might easily have murdered me.

When I returned to Kalam I called in at the police station to say hello and let them know I was OK. On the wall was a large poster which read: 'For their own safety, foreign tourists are advised to contact the local police authorities before proceeding to the valley of Ushu.' After my own experiences there I can only concur with this advice, especially if you're going up there on your own!

The Himalaya is now a feasible destination for everybody adventurous enough to want to go there, and you do not need to be a high standard technical climber to gain a summit. One of my treks guiding in the Karakoram illustrates this point. This was to the Hushe district, which lies to the east of Masherbrum. The trip in to the village by jeep from Skardu was truly memorable, for after a period of heavy rain bridges had been washed away, necessitating many detours, and we

Travelling by jeeps on the route to K2.   Photo Dennis Gray

were forced to stop at Khapalu in the Shyok valley. I think most climbers who visit the Karakoram return with epic stories of the jeep journeys they have made to reach the mountains and after every trip I have made to K2, Nanga Parbat, Hushe *et cetera* I have felt lucky to reach my destination safely.

Like Swat, Khapalu was once a separate entity until it was forced by the Bhutto reforms to join Pakistan, although the Maharajah still lives in his dilapidated palace. We climbed up to this Shangri-la one evening to have a closer look, accompanied by its owner. He had learned we were British via our agent in Islamabad, and had already decided to join our party (which he did, bringing along with him a bearer and cook!) Travelling through an area like Baltistan you welcome such a local dignitary into your ranks for, although the Rajah might have been stripped of his powers, he still carried influence with the locals.

I was to find out why he had wanted to come with us at the end our climb when he told us his story one night sitting around a fire in a campsite at the confluence of the Shyok and Hushe valleys. His father had met his mother, an English nurse, whilst on an official visit to India during the days of the Raj. Falling in love, she had returned to a state wedding in Khapalu, a journey which had taken her many weeks to complete riding on horseback through the Himalaya. On reaching her destination she had never ever left the region again, not even to visit her home or relations in the UK. Thus 'Rajah, as he was known to us, was keen to meet and get to know anyone from his mother's country.

I mentioned this story to Robin Hodgkin who had attempted Masherbrum in 1937 and he sat bolt upright. 'Good Lord!' he exclaimed. 'When we were retreating back down the mountain, badly frostbitten, we met an English woman, a nurse, who helped us. She was on her way to marry the Maharajah of Khapalu. That must have been her!'

The following afternoon on the same trek I had a fortuitous meeting just below Hushe village at about 3,000m, when our jeeps were confronted by another careering down the track through the thick mud, on the edge of control. We had to take action to avert a collision and as it shot past I noticed a huge, fair-haired man, deeply tanned and stripped to the waist, perched on top of a mound of equipment. As he went by he turned around and waved, then I heard him shouting to his driver and somehow a little further down the road they managed to stop.

The immense figure leapt to the ground and came running towards us. He was almost alongside before I recognised him - it was Mark Miller, a larger than life British climber who I had known for many years and with whom in the past I had not always seen eye to eye. Once at a drunken party in Sheffield he had picked me up and thrown me through a door, spread-eagling me into the adjoining room. All this was now forgotten as we shook hands and laughed at our meeting in such a place.

Mark was on his way down from an attempt on a new route on Masherbrum and my party of Himalayan novices looked on in awe whilst this huge, semi-naked fellow told stories of avalanches, rock falls and being pinned down for many days by ferocious storms. Unfortunately, Mark was yet another friend who was to die shortly afterwards, for he was one of the victims of the 1992 PIA Kathmandu air crash on his way to face yet another challenge, an attempt on Makalu II.

I have reported earlier about some of the unusual characters who took part in the groups I led trekking. For the climb of 5,600m Ghondokhoro Peak, an easy mountain in the Hushe area, our cast list was impressive. Amongst others we had, as the doctor for the trip, a burly Oxbridge-educated, former Welsh rugby inter-national while the youngest member of our party was an eighteen-year-old son of a millionaire businessman. We also included in our group of tigers a Knight of the Realm, but the creme de la creme was a formidable middle-aged titled M'Lady, accompanied by her son who had been to school at Eton but was by then study-ing at Oxford.

In the blurb issued by the British tour company who had organised this trek it stated that all those wishing to climb to the summit of the mountain needed to be familiar with the use of ice axes and crampons. On getting into the field I was to discover that few were, but M'Lady decided I could teach them these skills during the walk-in. Each night after a hard day crossing glaciers, route finding and making sure all of our members were safe and into camp I had to hold seminars on the techniques of snow and ice climbing up and down any accessi-ble snow slope and, once we reached our base camp, on some nearby seracs.

The dress adopted by M'Lady whilst trekking was rather like that found in ancient prints such as 'The ascent of Mont Blanc'. She spurned a helmet whilst climbing, preferring a large brimmed hat with a bee-keeper's veil, but I quickly realised she was as tough as old boots. She intended climbing Ghondokhoro Peak; nothing was going to stop her and she was always up with the leading group each day and first into camp in the afternoons. She practised cramponing, cutting steps and front pointing each night until it became too dark to continue. By that time I was usually too cold or tired to hold her rope any longer.

I am proud to report that all these novices climbed the peak and were so thankful for the experience that they bought me a new ice axe when I returned to the UK because mine broke during the ascent. This trek provided new insights into the British upper classes. Each night, despite the cold, they gathered to play bridge in our base tent, bidding for high stakes until midnight or beyond. Our doctor almost covered the cost of the trip from his winnings! When not walking or climbing they read voraciously - not the usual expedition fare, it was the classics they appreciated or modern titles like 'Zen and the Art of Motorcycle Maintenance'. It is not by chance that our aristocrats have survived the ups and downs of the last few hundred years while other nobilities have fallen foul of the march towards egalitarianism.

Nanga Parbat

Nanga Parbat was a name known to me as a boy from the time I read reports about the tragic German attempts on the mountain before the war. Then there was Herman Buhl's autobiography detailing his brilliant first ascent of the peak in 1953. In Kathmandu in 1964 I met Peter Aufschnaiter who had led the Austro/

German attempt in 1939 on the Diamir flank of the peak and was then interned in India at the outbreak of the war. His escape over the Himalaya to Tibet with Heinrich Harrer has become one of the most famous events in modern history. He intimated that we should not take Harrer's book 'Seven Years in Tibet' as gospel, and was critical of the fact that the author had exaggerated his own standing in the adventure. Such interesting titbits aside, when the chance arose to lead a group to the Rakhiot side of Nanga Parbat I signed up immediately.

On our way up the KKH to reach the Rakhiot bridge our own bus full of gear and bodies was overtaken by a small Honda van motoring along at an incredible speed. Ten persons were crammed inside like sardines in a tin. We watched transfixed with horror when it failed to round the sharpest curve at the next set of bends and shot out over the edge to plunge down a rocky bank and into the Indus river. We stopped, as did several other vehicles, and then some of us gingerly climbed down to the wreck lying at the river's edge about a hundred metres below. By the time we managed to reach the stricken vehicle only four bodies were still left inside, the other six had been washed away to eternity by the mighty river.

It took a long time getting the badly injured survivors out and back up the bank to the road, and it was a subdued group of trekkers who finally reached camp at Rakhiot later that same evening.

Several days later, after an easy walk-in, we were camping on the fabled Fairy Meadow, below the huge western ramparts of the mountain. This might be the finest campsite in the whole of the Himalaya with one of the most impressive views, but as a diversion one rainy afternoon I decided to organise a game of soccer in which most of our party took part. The teams were made up of local porters from Tato, two of the Hunzas and some of the members of our trekking group. There was one young boy from the village, fifteen years old, strikingly good-looking and wearing almost rags for clothing, who was ribbed mercilessly by the other porters every time he tried to kick the ball. None of these locals were skilful footie players, but it had also been the same when they had been engaged in carrying loads up from the valley; the youth was again the butt of their jokes.

After the match I enquired of our Sirdar, Hussain, why all the Tato men had picked on this lad. What had he done to deserve so much attention? 'Dennis Sahib,' he laughed. 'He is known as the Widow's Boy. A wealthy woman bought him off his parents. Her first husband was killed by a rock fall in the gorge last year and so she purchased him to keep her warm at night. It is very cold here in winter! He has come as a porter with us to escape from her. She does not know he is with us, she has gone to Gilgit to visit friends for a few days. When she returns she will be furious.' Such is life still in the remote valleys around Nanga Parbat!

A few days on we had set up our base camp under the Great Moraine and one afternoon, returning down its flanks, we could see some other climbers heading up towards our tents from the Fairy Meadow. We were back just in time to greet their leader, Harhai, when he arrived. They were a group of four Hungarians from the Bukk mountains and, incredibly, they had travelled from Budapest with all their equipment across Russia and Kashgar, then down the KKH using ordinary bus services. They were so poor that they had not been able to afford to hire any porters and had carried up immense loads made up of sufficient equipment and food to attempt a new route on the mountain. Their youngest member was only eighteen and was ill with dysentery; he came in to camp a long time after the others.

Looking at these four guys I had to admit that, like the Poles, Czechs, Slovaks and Russians, the Hungarians are made of sterner stuff than we effete West European mountaineers. Here they were several weeks out from home, setting up their tents and making ready to attempt a new route on the Rakhiot flank of the mountain with the minimum of gear and fuss. I was pleased to invite them to a meal in our base that evening and to doctor their sick young friend who, despite his debilitating illness, was still laughing and singing with the rest of us as we got stuck into a bottle of Scotch.

Up above base camp on Nanga Parbat is a cross, a memorial to the German climbers who died before the war on this dangerous and complex Rakhiot face of the mountain. Their names are writ large in climbing history and one in particular was one of my heroes when young: Wilo Welzenbach. His name lives on with his legacy of fine routes in the Alps and the grading system he developed which is still in use to this day, but also because of his example. Caught high on the mountain in a terrible storm in 1934 he might have tried to save himself, but instead gave up some of his own equipment to help a companion, surely one of the most heroic gestures in the history of mountaineering.

After crossing the Julipar Pass and attempting the peak of that name our party was retreating in bad weather down into the shelter of the Patro valley. We had barely descended into that hollow when a motley crowd of locals appeared armed with rifles, stopping us in our tracks. In the valleys around Nanga Parbat such as Diamir, Rupal and Patro some of the inhabitants are very suspicious of strangers. Indeed, at about the same time as we were being threatened Chris Bonington's party, who were filming in the Diamir valley, were faced with a similar situation.

Hussain and myself stood our ground while the leader of this band of brigands made his demands. Fortunately our Sirdar spoke Shina, the same language as this gun-toting headman, and it emerged that they would not allow the men from Tato to come into their valley. There was an ancient feud between them and they demanded that we employ them instead to carry our loads down to Gunnar Farm, two days walk down the valley on the KKH. We either went back the way we had come or sacked our existing porters if we wished to descend via their lands. The weather was abysmal and the thought of our tired trekkers climbing back up over the pass in those conditions was just not on.

The men from Patro had us cornered and jostled and threatened our very frightened group until Hussain and I gave way. Then they became all sweet reason with two days' pay to look forward to. Being unarmed, the Tatos were a much more friendly crowd than the Patro men and passed their loads over to their rivals without protest, resigned to accepting this state of affairs.

After we had paid off the men from Tato, including the two days' pay they would now be losing, the Widow's Boy came to see me. He smiled at me coyly and made some rather suggestive gestures. 'What does he want?' I demanded of Hussain.

'If you will buy him off the widow he will sleep with you every night and keep you warm instead!' our Sirdar laughingly informed me.

'Thank him,' I smiled. 'But I have a special sheet at home which does just that, it's called an electric blanket!' At this news the youth began to giggle, then he ran away off up the hill, waving goodbye while trying to catch up with his companions. The Tato porters had determined to recross the Julipar Pass and reach the Fairy Meadow before nightfall; few Westerners could have kept up with them as they raced up the slopes above us to disappear over the horizon.

As my experiences prove, the Himalaya is becoming ever more accessible, like every other region of the world. If we are not careful we will soon see a single universal McDonald's-type culture spread throughout this planet. We cannot deny the benefits of progress to people like the villagers of Tato, but we must try to conserve wilderness areas. It would be a terrible tragedy if the Shina language was lost to posterity, if the Fairy Meadow was built on or even if a road was laid up the gorge above Tato to the Rakhiot glacier. Geography and natural forces probably ensure that this will never happen, but I hope the district around Nanga Parbat and for that matter the whole of the Himalaya long remains a special place for all the people on this earth.

Epilogue

I think that what enthralled me about climbing as an eleven-year-old was the sense of wonder that surrounded the activity at that time; the rest of society viewed it as an oddball pastime belonging to a small band of eccentrics. Fifty years on, it has become a major sport with designer clothes and equipment and serried ranks of professionals.

It would be so easy to fall back on the old fart syndrome and to wail, 'Things aren't what they used to be!' But like romance, rock climbing and mountaineering are unsullied sports, pristine for each new generation. There may be crowds in the Lake District, Snowdonia or Ben Nevis at weekends and holidays, but wander out to any crag or hill at other times and you will usually still find some space and solitude.

While I have been climbing, each decade has seen a rich trawl of characters and their activities have spawned many legends but, because of the large numbers now taking part, it is not as easy for such figures to be identified. If Al Harris was to reappear in Llanberis today would he be as much an icon as he once was? Would iconoclasts like Don Whillans, Al Rouse or Johnny Cunningham, who were all in their day Vice Presidents, still be elected to high office in the BMC? Will we ever again experience a writer and lyricist such as Tom Patey, who so debunked mountaineers and mountaineering in essay and song?

I take heart from reading Paul Pritchard's recent book, *Deep Play*, which reaffirms so many of my own feelings about climbing. I was visiting the Lancashire area regularly when he started to climb and there was a good scene at Ian Lonsdale's pub 'the Black Dog'. I am certain Paul was influenced by the figures around in those days who were active at such unfashionable climbing grounds as Hoghton, Wilton and Anglezarke before he moved on to live in Llanberis.

When he arrived there during the slate climbing boom of the 1980s he joined up with a rare cast of personalities, both climbers and locals, and from this rich seam he went to achieve success in Scotland, Patagonia and the Himalaya. His book drawing on those experiences ranks alongside the best literary works in the history of our sport.

It is interesting to consider the continuity that this reveals. If you were to draw a climbing family tree of all those involved in *Deep Play* it would, I am sure, yield many surprising points of contact. Paul freely admits the influence that the writings of Menlove Edwards, that outstanding rock climber of the thirties, had upon him. He also shared some of his most important ascents with one of his contemporaries, Johnny Dawes, who I had several madcap adventures with when he was young. They included the time outside Buxton, when only his miraculous reflexes saved us from certain death crashing into the back of a bus at high speed. He had to take a split-second decision and we shot through on the inside, overtaking with all four wheels of his car riding up on the pavement. He was subsequently banned from driving for his efforts!

To cut many long stories short, I would like to finish with the time I introduced Johnny to Don Whillans. This was near to the end of the Villain's life and,
inevitably, took place in a pub late one night at a party in Hayfield.

Don was by then overweight, very unfit and drinking heavily, but he had lost
none of his sharp wit or sense of his worth. Inevitably, when egos like those two
were involved there had to be a clash, even on a friendly basis. It was like the old
lion confronting the grown cub and we spectators sat back expecting fireworks.
We were not to be disappointed, for Johnny was soon ruffling Whillans' feathers
and, as of old, he was not prepared to back down from such a challenge. After
various bits of sparring they started an arm wrestling contest over the bar which
quickly took off around the room and became more like Crabtree than Stallone.

We onlookers held our breath, for the competition was getting out of hand
and tables were being knocked over and pints spilled. It looked like old age was
getting at Don when suddenly he put in a supreme effort and forced Johnny's
arm to the floor, making him submit or he might have been injured. After that
the two combatants got on like a house on fire, although after sharing about six
rounds of the local brew with him, Dawes decided he was not keen to try to out-
drink Whillans pint for pint.

For some reason we subsequently decided to drive back to Johnny's flat in the
early hours of Sunday morning. As we drove through the wet deserted streets of
Stockport at about four in the morning, Dawes turned to me absolutely seriously and confessed, 'You know, I let Don Whillans beat me at arm wrestling. I
took pity on him as he was old and past it!'

'Did you Johnny?' I laughed, but he did not convince me. Don was still a bar
fighter right to his end while Johnny is a master of balance climbing!

Thus the torch has been handed down from generation to generation of climbers. No one knows where the next scene or hot spot will be in Britain, let alone
abroad and usually by the time such a happening is widely recognised (like
Llanberis in the eighties) the action has moved elsewhere, with new personae
acting independently. Pioneering is carried out by only a small number of activists, but the challenge of a cliff face or mountain flank remains no matter how
often a route is repeated.

Such activity will always throw up its share of unusual personalities, for by its
very nature climbing will always provide a rich vein of humour and legend.
When I was young I met the Creagh Dhu climbers from the working class
districts of Glasgow and they were a great source of folk tales in that era. Another
group of Scottish climbers, though not so well documented, were almost an
equal provider of such stories; namely the members of the Rannoch Club. Their
leader was Jock Nimlin who led the first ascent of Raven's Gully on the Buachaille
Etive Mor. I met him as a boy in Cameron's barn in Glencoe and later read his
seminal article 'May the Fire be Always Lit' in the the Scottish Mountaineering
Club Journal.

This expresses the sentiments I wish to finish with. Nowadays it may not be
possible to enjoy the camaraderie that climbers like the Scots enjoyed in Glen-

coe and on Nevis in the thirties, but as our sport continues to evolve I do hope it will always provide a vehicle for friendship and fun. Without these it would be a much poorer entity and lose much of its power to inspire the continuing flow of myth and legend on which climbing and climbers have always thrived.